PERSPECTIVES ON BRITISH SIGN LANGUAGE AND DEAFNESS

PERSPECTIVES ON BRITISH SIGN LANGUAGE AND DEAFNESS

Edited by

B. WOLL, J. KYLE and M. DEUCHAR

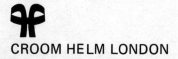

CROOM HELM LONDON

© 1981 B. Woll, J. Kyle and M. Deuchar
Croom Helm Ltd, 2-10 St John's Road, London SW11

British Library Cataloguing in Publication Data

Perspectives on British sign language and deafness.
1. Deaf – Means of communication
2. Sign languages   3. Psycholinguistics
I. Woll, B.   II. Kyle, J.   III. Deuchar, M.
419   HV2474

ISBN 0-7099-2703-7

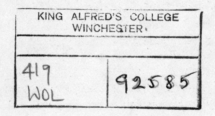
Printed and bound in Great Britain
by Billing and Sons Limited
Guildford, London, Oxford, Worcester

CONTENTS

Contents

FOREWORD AND ACKNOWLEDGEMENTS

This book originated with a symposium on British Sign Language held at Lancaster University in April 1980. It brought together a wide range of interests in both audience and speakers, and represented the first meeting of its type devoted solely to issues of BSL and deafness. Modified versions of the papers presented there form the basis of this book, with chapters grouped under the three headings of Psychological, Linguistic and Communicative Aspects. This division, while separating the chapters into theme areas, does not represent any clear-cut divisions; indeed, research on BSL has been characterised by close cross-disciplinary contact. The introductions to each section will, however, provide an overview of the background and approach to each chapter.

Acknowledgments are due to too many people to mention, but thanks must go to the Royal National Institute for the Deaf, whose generous support enabled deaf people to attend the Symposium; the members of the British Sign Language Workshop, especially Gloria Pullen, Lorna Allsop, and Maggie Carter, who is largely responsible for the appendix on the notation of BSL; Jenny Mill-Roberts and Liz Young, to whom many thanks for their patient handling of the manuscript; David Kitson and Martin Connell for the artwork; and most particularly, the deaf community of Great Britain.

PART ONE: PSYCHOLOGICAL ASPECTS

INTRODUCTION

James Kyle

The rising star of Cognitive Psychology has within a very short space of time altered the perspective and role of psychologists in every applied setting. The elaborate proliferation of theory based on information processing and language development approaches has produced a search for suitable applied problems to examine its effectiveness. The resurgence of psychological interest in the reading process is a particular example of where this psychological approach has come to rest. Applied psychologists have followed trends through learning theories, skills analysis and mental testing and currently have begun to add the notions of process, conceptual development and cognition to their picture of the developing individual.

Inevitably Cognitive Psychology has many focal points, not a single theory, and it is through the examination of special cases or issues that its ideas can be evaluated. Since education is nearly always the first to feel the weight of psychological interest, so the developing child is a target for theoreticians. While reading has been used to examine the psycholinguistic features of processing theories, it has been found essential to investigate the developing representational system which will carry the structures necessary for speech and communication. Although memory research has begun to focus on children's strategies, a traditional target beginning to be explored is the 'non-language' group of deaf people.

William James in 1901 was one of the first to attempt to examine this control group through a deaf and dumb man whom he knew. He confidently wrote of the man's visual and tactile images which carried his thought processes. This constituted the extension of the basic philosophical theories of ideas and images as representation in memory and thinking, to the control group whose images cannot be auditory and are unlikely to be related to speech. Stout (1899) considered the psycholinguistic perspective with deaf people not as alinguistic but rather as users of an imprecise visual gestural language which would be the only suitable vehicle for their thought process. At that stage the nature of deaf people's processing could have been

the foundation of the psychological representational theories which
are currently acceptable today. Unfortunately the mental test movement changed that.

By using average and normative performance as the criterion on
reasoning tasks the early psychometricians were able to classify the
subnormal and deviant groups within the population. Unfortunately,
deaf people fell into this category. Pintner and Patterson's (1921)
discoveries of weaker intelligence performance by deaf children des-
troyed their value as a control group since if their intellect was affected
by lack of speech and hearing, then they could no longer be balanced
against normal hearing children in evaluating language and cognitive
development. Only gradually did the research studies establish that
deaf people's intelligence was similar (Vernon, 1967) and their slight
discrepancy in IQ was most likely due to culture and language bias in
even non-verbal intelligence tests (Kyle, 1980c). So it is once again
possible to consider the problems of the developing language skills of
deaf children as indicators of the type of strategies which are most
effective in hearing children. Nevertheless the warnings of Blank (1965)
and Dawson (1979b) on the dangers of treating deaf children as non-
linguistic on the one hand or as a homogeneous group on the other
must not be ignored.

So how might work with deaf people cast light on the theories of
Psychology? If one postulates the developing child as functioning in
a world where communication is of prime importance and where its
overt basis gradually becomes an inner base for cognition, then the
characteristics of deaf children where the level of communication
skill may be more accurately measured, will throw considerable light
on the cues and strategies used by the hearing child to support his
communication. In the same way, comparison of the nature of storage
and retrieval will cast light on the representation necessary for memory
and language.

Conrad in Chapter 1 considers the whole range of these issues. His
concern here is with Education but he sets the questions for Psychology.
His theme is a very clear one: the poor language development and
reading development of deaf children. In presenting this he touches
the core of problems faced in Cognitive Psychology and in placing
them in the educational context sets the challenge for both psychologists and educationalists. If development through speech is seriously
affected by lack of hearing how might we produce the strategies for
language development and, most practically, the skills which are a
priority, those of reading ability? The answer is not simple; it does

not rest solely on introducing signing into the classroom, but will depend on the use made of their signing skills by teachers and those concerned with deaf children.

Wood's work in Chapter 2 represents one of the first answers to Conrad's questions. By comparing teacher-pupil interaction in young children, he can highlight the differences in communicative strategy employed. His two reported lines of research concern the child and teacher talking (the informal) and the child learning to read (formal). He shows very clearly that there are marked differences in teaching style in these settings. By comparing with hearing children he can point to the over-emphasis of control and repair in the conversation of teachers of the deaf, and thereby an inability for language extension through conversation. The child who is asked closed questions never progresses in conversation. Equally, reading shows the greater incidence of control by the teacher. What is critically important is that David Wood suggests that these teaching styles can be altered to produce significant gains at least in the short term.

Both Dawson (Chapter 3) and Kyle (Chapter 4) follow a similar approach which differs from the general language development model examined by David Wood. Their questions revolve around the noticeable differences in deaf people's reading and remembering and they try to discuss the generality of the psychological models of human functioning for these settings.

Dawson tackles this in older deaf school children where traditionally problems in dealing with syntax in English has been seen as 'deafisms' and a sign of educational failure. Her research suggests, through a controlled study of recognition and recall, that forms of English most closely related to Sign Language syntax are most easily recalled and recognised by deaf children. Her concern is that these reflect features of deaf children's approach to the learning setting. They indicate again that our traditional views of spoken language processing and deaf children's use of their 'language' may be compatible.

Kyle takes more traditional short-term memory tasks to deaf adults and discusses the comparative recall of signs and words when reinforced by 'Sign Codes' or 'Speech Codes'. The issue here is a central one to Psychology since it has firmly placed memory processing in the hands of a code which is speech. In theoretical terms, however, the code is simply a device for access and storage and could just as easily be replaced by another type of code. If deaf people use a different code, as seems likely, then their processing need not theroetically be different. In effect, deaf people do not all demonstrate the use of sign language codes and again we must reconsider how simple our hypotheses have been in the past.

Finally, Llewellyn-Jones in Chapter 5 considers the language problems where bilingualism is involved. In this context, his concern is with the interpreter who needs to have two language codes available to him. The effectiveness of interpreters is dependent on the level of their processing of both the source and target languages. Using contemporary models he reports some research on the processing involved in transferring from speech to sign language and evaluates the effectiveness of conceptual framework that Psychology has provided.

In these chapters we can see the emergence of a more constructive view of deaf people and sign language. Psychologists no longer concern themselves with discovering retardation, but have begun to focus on the positive issues of central importance to the cognitive development of deaf children.

1 SIGN LANGUAGE IN EDUCATION: SOME CONSEQUENT PROBLEMS

R. Conrad

We are now at last – or perhaps once again – at a point of history in Britain when it is reasonably safe to discuss the use of sign language with most educators. Even the generation who will shortly retire, and who, a decade ago vehemently dismissed the use of 'that stuff', now recognise that a tide is flowing which is hard to fight. Certainly there remain a few diehards – and some still in high places in the world of education. But the tide is rushing past them now. My point is that we no longer need to argue the case for sign language in education. Sign language is here and it will stay – for quite a while.

We are right at the very beginning of this though. The RNID's formal commitment to signing in education is still very recent. The National Deaf Children's Society has made no such commitment. The British Association of Teachers of the Deaf remains cool – and some would say obstructive. It is still very difficult for teachers to get a thorough training in sign language. Training in sign language is possible – and in one college at least it is mandatory. But many of the schools which have welcomed sign language as a principal medium of instruction are therefore suffering from the inadequacies of teachers' sign language knowledge.

So although the tide has turned, it is not running very fast. It is tempting to compare with the United States, but unfair. There, signing has always been strong in many schools and the presence of Gallaudet College has ensured a steady flow of fluent signers into the educational system. Just the same, on a recent visit, I was fascinated to see a class of profoundly deaf 10-year-olds grasping the meaning of idioms such as: 'straight from the horse's mouth'. I am sure this could not have been done by speech alone. It is worth noting in this connection that a study by Jensema and Trybus (1978) shows that children prefer to shift into a sign mode when hearing loss is as low as 70 dB. Nearer home though, in Sweden for example, teachers can now easily get 120 hours of sign language instruction during their basic training. The effect of this in class is dramatic in terms of the communication interchange between teacher and pupil, and between pupils.

13

Here is Britain, then, certainly not a world leader in the use of signing in education but ahead of Italy, for instance, which is actually closing down schools for the deaf and forcing all deaf children into an exclusive oral mode: a reverberating echo of the 1880 Milan Congress I suppose. But by and large, it is hard to see now though what will prevent this sign language tide from gathering strength. My concern is that we will tend simply to tumble with it when it is crucial that we should be in control of it. So for this reason I have chosen the role of devil's advocate. I want to look critically at certain assumptions which have come to underpin the pedagogy that has been called — I think tendentiously — Total Communication.

Before doing this, it is worth reminding ourselves of the nature of the pressures which drive some of us to seek radical change in educational methods. In fact it is rather more than this. What we are discussing here is a broader social and cultural revolution; leading towards a society where deaf people are encouraged to use sign language, instead of being punished for it. But some 90 per cent of deaf children are in hearing families. Sign language is not their native tongue. So the tools for the revolution must be forged in the earliest years.

Attention then has necessarily focused on what happens in school. If in fact deaf children left school now, with the same level of achievement as hearing children — with good, easily understood, speech — with a joy in reading good books — with a facility for understanding speech just like anyone else — then there would be no need for revolution. So it is worth taking a few minutes to draw attention to the reality.

We start with a typically misleading average. The average child in our schools for the deaf leaves for the big harsh vocational world with a reading age of about nine years. That makes all tabloid newspapers too difficult, and all instructional manuals, governmental forms, operating procedures for machinery, safety regulations, and so on, all beyond comprehension. But if the child has a hearing loss of about 90 dB or more, when in most cases a hearing aid is not going to help much, then his reading level is not nine years, but about that of an eight-year-old hearing child (Conrad, 1979). Alas for TTY and Ceefax and captioned TV news. This young deaf person cannot read enough to profit from them. But it is even tougher than that. Fifty per cent of children are below that nine-year average. And these 50 per cent are real children. They sit at desks, they look at the blackboard, they try to understand what teacher is saying — and many of these real children cannot read at all when they leave school — in fact 35 per cent of the entire school population are unable to begin a test of prose comprehension, even at the seven-year level.

Now let us discuss the other 50 per cent — those above the nine-year level. What reading ability do you need to get useful information, without too much struggle, from, let's say, the mass circulation newspapers? Let's be generous. Maybe the reading level of an 11-year-old will be sufficient. Well, regardless of degree of deafness, 75 per cent of our deaf school-leavers don't make it. And if they are profoundly deaf then 85 per cent can save their newspaper pennies, unless they just want to look at the pictures (Conrad, 1979). 85 per cent of profoundly deaf children do not reach an 11-year-old level.

Perhaps these children can survive without reading; though I don't know who could accept that. But speech is a different matter. Here are all the pleasures of witty conversation, the swift exchange of scintillating ideas. Furthermore the ability to achieve clear intelligible speech lies at the heart of oral education. This is really what it's all about. The news here is not too good either. Here also forget about whether strangers can understand the speech of deaf children: the shop assistants, the bus conductors, the man on the next lathe, the man you want to sell your old car to. What about teachers themselves? The ones doing all the speech training? In fact, if the children are very deaf, beyond 90 dB, then their own teachers find it at least very hard to understand three quarters of them (Conrad, 1979).

So when understandable speech cannot be achieved by most deaf people, and reading is outside the experience of most deaf people, and lip-reading so difficult that even highly educated deafened adults require sign or print to help out, then clearly it is time for change.

The trouble is, that the concept of oral communication for the deaf, who are living in a speaking society, is highly alluring. So we have, ever present, this challenging goal for parents and teachers who themselves can hear and speak perfectly well. There is this compulsion to sustain the concept — though in fact it can only be sustained through a structure essentially of delusion.

Oral success is a bit like bending spoons. We've all seen, with our own eyes, spoons being bent on TV. We've all met one or two deaf people whom we would agree were successes orally. But the fact that spoon bending or oral success occurs is of trivial interest until we know how it occurs. In both cases, what is crucial is that the outcome must demonstrably depend on the alleged cause.

In the case of oral success this cause-effect demonstration has not been made either. Without doubt there are some profoundly deaf people who are as oral as I am. There are some, not many, but a few. But it should be pointed out that we have no genuine knowledge of why they are so successful. Most relevantly, when we start to try to identify specific characteristics that these people share, in no case do we find anything which could have been due to particular educational procedures. We find characteristics which belong by nature to the person, such as the development of his deafness or the level of his intelligence. Or we may find characteristics which have permitted him to derive unusual benefit from a variety of fortunate circumstances. We may find an unusually lucky match between the specific nature of a person's deafness and the physical characteristics of a particular hearing aid — at the right time. Or exceptionally favourable medical and nutritional conditions at birth and in early infancy. And of course there must be many more.

There are two problems here. First we do not know just which are the really important factors: which contribute much — which contribute little. So we do not know which to aim for. But then we also do not know just how these external factors might interact with the deaf person's own biological make-up. In much more simple terms, we simply do not know how to make oral successes. That, perhaps, is why there are so very few of them. What is quite certain is that it is not the result of any single particular type of educational procedure. If we think of the basic communication skills, there is no school in Britain which, at this time, is taking in a truly representative sample of deaf children and sending out, ten years later, a population of children who are significantly more oral than any other representative sample (Conrad, 1979).

Yet teachers have tried. For a hundred years most teachers have really worked hard at the prescribed oral method. But then, medical advances have made things increasingly easy for them. Engineering came up with the transistorised hearing-aid, social services supported families most in need of extra help. If there are more oral deaf people now than there were 50 years ago it has had very little to do with the nature of their education.

So we come now to the crux. Oralism seems to have failed deaf children in two major ways. It has failed in its crucial function of providing children with any effective mother tongue. This is not something which ordinary schools expect to have to do for hearing children. But oral education has elected to do this for deaf children, and it has failed. It was therefore bound to fail in its second role of providing the rudiments of essential knowledge which are the accepted tools for survival and development in a highly technological society; and which are basic rights.

Now many people have argued that if deaf children can be provided with a mother tongue, not necessarily oral — and we mean sign — then the second role is much more likely to succeed. It is this logic that I now want to evaluate.

Language is not just for learning things in school. We all know that. We also all know that children can easily acquire sign language. I have taken the view that any language is better than no language, so I see the case for the use of sign language from the very earliest years as overwhelming.

Much of this book discusses questions which relate to the use of sign language as a language mode in its own right — both social and linguistic. I want to address myself to the other aspect. That is the implicit assumption that sign language is suitable for teaching, what I'll loosely call the basic school subjects. In fact, in the context of the term Total Communication, this assumption is explicit. I want to look at aspects of that assumption which lead us to expect — not merely hope — expect that by using sign language in school, deaf children will end up significantly better educated than they are at present.

So far as I know, there is not yet published evidence that educational programmes principally using sign language, or using Total Communication methods, are resulting in higher educational standards. This statement should not be taken as criticism. In the first place it takes time to collect reliable information based on standardised tests. It also takes time to publish it. Secondly, it is only in the USA that there has been a sufficiently strong signing base for this kind of evaluation to be worthwhile. Even there, we are only now entering an era when a sufficiently large population of children will have spent their entire school lives in such programmes (Jordan *et al.*, 1979). And I mean as creative and formal policy, rather than as rejects from oral programmes. Thirdly, one would expect a large variation in the fluency with which hearing teachers can instruct in sign language; many would have had no more than a relatively short course. So it will inevitably be some time before this necessary information becomes available in any meaningful way. In the meantime we continue to place our hopes on indirect evidence; that is, our hopes that signed instruction is beneficial.

The significant advance in acceptance of sign language as the natural language for deaf people has largely a social basis. This we must applaud. But we act as if there is a case for using it in education as well as teaching it. A great deal of the impetus for this has depended on studies which examined school performance of children who were native signers, when compared with those who were not. A number of such studies have been made in the last 20 years (e.g. Meadow, 1968; Stuckless and Birch, 1966a, 1966b; Vernon and Koh, 1971). As a result of them, we have tended to accept as a valid assumption that fluency in sign language is advantageous in learning certain school subjects. This is an assumption which has held an important place in the argument for Total Communication in schools.

Now it is perfectly true that there are all kinds of extenuating circumstances which need to be taken into account when we examine the results of these studies. But the actual performance data that are available to us ought to make us regard the assumption of the value of signing with great caution in this particular case.

Let me take just a little time to look at these studies in a little detail. The earlier ones undoubtedly lacked certain essential controls which were then designed into later experiments. The most recent one – the Brasel and Quigley (1977) study – has no such defects. There is a general point which should be made, and that is that inevitably all of the studies used a relatively restricted sample of children. Even when the entire population of any one school is tested – or even several schools – all kinds of sampling bias *may* be present which would affect the value of any generalisation. That is a risk which is inherent in studies of deafness. The total available population is just too small. Most schools will not have a truly representative population of pupils. On the other hand, if more than half a dozen independent studies all consistently showed an advantage for early signing, then this criticism would be greatly weakened.

In fact we have tended to assume that there is such consistency, when unfortunately there is not. Most of these studies examined speech intelligibility, lip-reading and reading prose. Being a native signer in fact gave no advantage at all with respect to speech quality or lip-reading. This is really the only conclusion that can reasonably be made when all of the reports are considered. But the ability to understand printed English does seem to be helped by knowing sign language. This disposition of results seems logical. It is hard to think of a theoretical formulation which could imply that knowing sign language would greatly improve speech sounds. I would think the same would be true for lip-reading as well. The results for reading though are more plausible. The signal – the printed word – is clear, unlike the lip-read word. The opportunity for some direct translation –

print to sign — is obvious. What bothers me is, first, that the recorded advantage for the signers is quite small. It is around about one year of reading age — though varying from study to study. Second, my impression is that the larger advantages show only in those studies where important controls are missing. For example, in one study showing a two-year advantage, there is (in my mind), some doubt that the groups were of the same intelligence level. The Brasel and Quigley study shows a reading-age advantage for the signers of about a year and a half. I'm a little worried about this too. Both groups had very high intelligence — around an IQ of 120 — and I'm not sure whether a difference of one and a half years would generalise to more ordinary children. Our own study in Britain showed no differences at all when children were matched for intelligence and hearing loss. Having deaf parents and signing at home neither helped nor hindered (Conrad, 1979).

Taken together, there are two features of these data that are relevant here. First we need to be most cautious about any claims we make that knowing sign language bestows specific benefits in school. But second, and on the other hand, in none of these studies is it evident that classroom instruction of the signing children was in sign. In other words, whatever benefit the signers had from their language it was probably in spite of what teachers were trying to do. We might guess — but only guess — that were teachers and pupils both efficiently using the same language, then considerably greater advantages would be seen. But at present we do not know.

Then there is another assumption that is beginning to find favour in support of the proposition that deaf children should learn sign language as their mother tongue. It has been reported that early signing is associated with high IQ or advanced cognitive function, however one sees it. The facts are sparse but intriguing. It has long been recognised that children whose deafness is hereditary have higher nonverbal intelligence than those whose deafness is acquired through disease or mishap at some time before, during or after birth. The most popular and plausible explanation is that deafness itself is irrelevant for nonverbal cognitive function, but that accident or disease is often damaging. This of course is true whether or not deafness is present. The best estimates suggest that genetically deaf children have an average IQ of around 100-102 — that is, average — whilst the IQ of those with acquired deafness is about 95, and those with clear additional handicaps are down to about 85 (Ries and Voneiff, 1974). None of this has much to do with early signing because the vast majority of children whose deafness is hereditary have hearing parents who do not sign.

But in 1969, Brill published a little-noticed account in a rather obscure magazine (Brill, 1969). This reported that children at his school with two deaf parents, and who signed at home, had significantly higher IQ than a control group of deaf children with hearing parents who did not sign. The actual value of IQ reported was in fact 113, but this has little significance because it was in no way based on a random sample. It was though much higher than for the non-signing group.

The next important statement was reported to a scientific meeting, and it used material drawn from a survey by the Office of Demographic Studies (Karchmer, Trybus and Paquin, 1978). This used a representative sample of 5,663 deaf children in the USA. The average IQ of the children with two hearing parents was 97 — but this would have included multiply handicapped children as well. Of interest here though, the IQ for the children with two deaf parents was 108. This figure is based on more than 300 cases — and so a very important result.

The only other data I know come from our own study in the UK (Conrad, 1979). Our results are in agreement with the other two. Children with both parents deaf have significantly higher scores on Raven's Matrices than do genetically deaf children whose parents are hearing.

So given these concordant data, it begins to seem highly attractive to regard this superior intelligence that has been found, as a glorious spin-off from early signing. Were the facts absolutely beyond dispute we would have additional gilt-edged support for the importance of sign language as a mother tongue for deaf children. And it may all be true.

On this evidence, all children, hearing as well, ought to be raised on sign language! So before we get too euphoric it seems that a good deal more evidence is needed. Neither Brill, nor Karchmer *et al.* have a direct comparison with genetically deaf children of hearing parents. We do, but we've had difficulty transforming Raven scores into more conventional IQs (Kyle, 1977). We have a difference, but I'm not yet certain that our signing children are significantly above the hearing average.

But even if there were complete confirmation, we must question whether it would represent a boost for signing. In a sense we are back to spoon-bending. We may have a fact, an unusual one, a fortunate one, but unless we know the *why* of it, we use it in argument at our peril.

Three broad speculations to account for the known data are in circulation at present. The least attractive is that deaf parents best understand the problems of being deaf. This is supposed to give them an edge over hearing parents with deaf children. One might see, in an obscure way, that this might be a factor. But hearing parents presumably understand the problems of hearing children, and they end up with an average of just 100 – not more. Then there would be a problem with respect to hearing children of deaf parents. They should be well below average. There is not the slightest evidence for this. So I don't think that explanation is helpful.

Then it has been suggested that this might be a genetic factor. That is, that the genes which carried deafness also carried high IQ. If one allows some genetic contribution to intelligence, this has something to commend it. But our study did partly control for this; and we found lower IQ when deafness was genetic but signing not used in the home. So we come to the most attractive of the currently available explanations, and the one most likely to tempt us here.

This is that the high IQ of these children is directly due to their early language development when compared with non-signing children. The difficulty is that hearing children also have early language development; and they do not have an IQ of 108, but 100. But signing children, so it is said, develop sign language earlier than hearing children develop spoken language. There is evidence: from Brown (1977), from Ahlgren (1977), from McIntire (1976), at least. We must ask what kind of evidence this is. In the first place these are isolated studies of a few carefully chosen children. They may or may not be typical; it would be foolhardy to assume that they were. Certainly we can think of reasons why it might be easier for a child to get into sign earlier than speech. It's easier to see, easier to make – if you're 18 months old – and almost certainly at that infant level, more natural. But how much earlier does it need to be, if later on it will reflect in significantly higher IQ? There isn't all that much time between birth and 18 months, and much of it is not very useful. This explanation seems immensely attractive and distinctly implausible. Perhaps we have a fact, but I don't think we have an explanation. We must still be very wary of associating early signing with superior cognitive function.

I referred earlier to the school performance of children educated in oral programmes. We might glance now at what we would expect – or hope for – from a well-established use of sign language in schools. I do not want to talk about the great benefits in interpersonal communication between deaf people. We can take that for granted. I would rather consider certain effects of the improved communication there would be between deaf children and their hearing teachers when it was in sign, in particular what this will buy in terms of formal education. To narrow the discussion to what is surely one of the more important areas, I want to take time to look at the prospects for literacy, and to look at some of the attendant problems.

I do not think I need to justify this choice. I have already referred to the dismally low standards at present achieved. But there is also the point that reading is the communication skill that seems least dependent on speech. What kinds of problems are involved then, and what levels of performance might be expected when children are taught to read English using sign language — with or without speech as well?

The first thing to reflect on is that most (more than 90 per cent perhaps) deaf children will reach school age with very little language at all. Nothing remotely comparable to that of five-year-old or even three-year-old hearing children. Since there is widespread agreement that no child is ready to begin learning to read until he has reached some level of language knowledge, this knowledge has to come first. The language of course will not be the English language which is what he will learn to read, but sign language into which he will translate. There are important questions concerning the linguistic level at which translation will take place: whether at word level or concept level or what. Or whether translation might prove to be as difficult as learning to read Chinese when you only know English, or as simple as learning to read the written English of Jane Austen when you only know the English of urban slums. Ignoring these, more basically we are going to need to know how much school time will have to be spent simply on teaching sign language, *before* it will be worth while bothering with English print. I don't believe we have any idea of how to define reading readiness in this case. But it seems highly likely to me that deaf children will not profitably start to learn to read until long after hearing children are off the ground. In other words, do not expect similar rates of progress and do not expect similar levels of attainment.

Now as soon as we begin to consider the most basic steps in learning to read we hit on a problem which some people have considered to be soluble only by using oral methods. This is the problem of the role of phonics. How important is it for a child to learn the rules which permit him to decode printed symbols into speech sounds? In the present context, the question arises in a somewhat distorted way. No one is thinking of using sign language alone in the classroom, but always together with speech. So if in fact phonic rules are crucial, the teacher is in a double bind. In the first place she cannot sign phonic rules, but if she does use speech for them most of her pupils will derive very little benefit. If there *is* good evidence that a child who fails to understand the rules of grapheme-phoneme translation must remain a very backward reader, then we have an adequate explanation for the poor reading ability of deaf children, and there would be no hope that instruction in sign would help. This seems too simplistic.

The question of the importance of phonic rules in early reading has rattled around in the world of education for a long time, and the fashionable answer has changed all too frequently. There are two broad issues. First, is it essential to know these rules? Then is this knowledge necessary throughout all stages of learning to read, or perhaps only during the very first steps?

It is easiest to answer the second question. Most of us are reading silently at 200-300 words a minute. Our eyes move from one fixation to another so fast, that we do not clearly see each word, let alone each phoneme as such. The visual strategy used by most adults reading ordinary prose, simply rules out the possibility of decoding graphemes, in the form of letters or groups of letters, into phonemes or sounds of speech. Even at the word level, we do not silently say each word to ourselves as we read. We may say some, but probably not even most. Clearly our understanding of what we read depends on some kind of synthesis which is well above the level of the rules of grapheme-phoneme correspondence. It has to be at least at the word level. But then, at the word level, we can just as easily recode into signs as into speech. And if the level of synthesis is higher than words, so that we absorb off the page complete phrases or sentences as chunks of meaningful language, then again sign is at no disadvantage. But all this comes later — after we have learned to read. So now we come back to the first of the two broad issues. In order to read that well, must we first master and use the simple rules of English phonics — together with all of the exceptions and irregularities?

The facts must surely be against this as an imperative. According to one authoritative source (Chall, 1967), up to about 1965 in the USA, emphasis in teaching reading centred on learning to identify a basic 50-100 words by sight. Only later was the nature of the alphabetic code introduced. But Americans learned to read. Of course it is easy to see how phonic rules can help. But consider the very first Ladybird Book of Key Words. The first word is *apple* and the plural adds *s*. The very next word is *baby*, and the plural already breaks the rule. There are, of course, many many more cases like that, where the rules do not help.

The value of phonic rules, insofar as they exist and are usable, is to permit a child to reach the sound of the word — its spoken form — which he already knows. This value is limited largely to those words which do follow the rules. Whilst the deaf child who is precluded from using phonic rules may lose out on the words which follow the rules, at the earliest reading stages he may actually gain by being forced into a word-sign translation mode, when words sound alike but look different: the *wait* for a train and the *weight* of a ton of bricks. There is no sign confusion here.

In other words, there does not seem to be an overriding need to exploit grapheme-phoneme rules in order to learn to read English words. What I doubt, though, is whether there is even the beginnings of a body of knowledge which would guide a signing teacher through these initial steps. In fact it is probably true that few hearing children are taught to read by any single pure method. But they have the immense advantage that pupil and teacher are in the same language. Few hearing teachers of deaf pupils will be able to shake off the burden of oral manipulation of printed words. Whenever they fail, they will lose their deaf pupils. We have got to have an intensive examination of just how signing can best be used, not only just in isolation, but when speech is also being used.

We can begin to see some of the outlines though. We need not be too overwhelmed by the fact that print can be analytically decoded into speech. It can be, but it doesn't have to be. English print is a moderately regular symbolic representation of speech sounds. But there are many languages where this is not the case. Without going into Chinese or Kanji Japanese, here is a nine-word sentence that few people will have any difficulty understanding; few eight-year-olds would. $4 + 5 = 18 \div 2$? There are no graphemic features in those nine symbols which give any clue to their spoken form. If one had not met those symbols, it would be as hard to translate that sentence into speech as into sign. It is a sentence with zero grapheme-phoneme correspondence.

It seems clear, not only from that numerical sentence, but from the evidence of many languages, that grapheme-phoneme correspondence rules are not a prerequisite for reading the printed form of the language. But the way children are taught to decode such printed words and sentences must be based on a different concept of the relationship between print and speech, or print and sign, than is usually the case with, say, English.

Essentially we have to be deeply concerned with the theoretical and pedagogic problems of teaching a large number of names of objects.

In this case, the objects are pictures — printed words, or groups of words. For the case where no extraneous phonic aids are built in, we have little idea of what is involved in terms of time, and child-capacity. But it is encouraging to remember that long before a child starts to learn to read, he has learned the names of a large number of objects and descriptors and activities. There is nothing in the appearance of a ball which gives a clue to the pronunciation of its name; there is nothing in the appearance of a boy and a toy which would help him to remember that their names sound similar. Almost all of our spoken vocabulary is learned, or acquired, this way. But it did take time. Do we really have to spend three years or so waiting for a deaf child to acquire a few hundred print-sign correspondences? We have a set of unsolved problems here: not insoluble, but unsolved.

Although the importance of phonics in teaching reading has been minimised here, in practice it is unlikely that phonics are ever rigidly banished. With English this feature is just too useful. But it is simply not available in sign. I suspect that we have a lot of signing classroom experience to go through before we begin to discover what a loss this is, and how to make it up.

Basically it is appropriate to be cautiously optimistic that acceptable levels of reading English can be taught in sign language; cautious principally for the reasons given. There are few, if any, research projects concerned with elucidating the cognitive operations involved in learning to read English through sign. There are plenty of reading programmes, especially in the USA, but they seem to be concerned with classroom tactics rather than with learning theory.

The necessity for concurrent speech in the classroom is likely to impose a harsh discipline on the hearing teacher. One sees all too commonly a so-called Total Communication class where the teacher is orally patiently explaining the phonetic difference between two words to a bewildered small deaf child. Whatever her hands were then doing, they were certainly not signing the same information. We are going to have to find ways to exploit the limits of look-sign learning. Conventional early reading material which is geared to the sequential nature of spoken English will have to be modified. We are going to need a thorough examination of the structure of sign language in order to see how its features can be utilised in preparing written text which is still English, because reading English is the end product.

There is reason for optimism because we can identify most of the major problems. Then, reading readiness is crucial. Perhaps we must delay reading for a couple of years until the child can really communicate naturally in sign. Teacher readiness is equally crucial. Here we are more or less in political priorities. How far can teacher training programmes be obliged to take seriously enough, teacher training in sign language?

Finally, a challenge. There are many people who are more comfortable communicating and thinking in sign than in speech. They are the people who should be addressing the problem of how to begin teaching a deaf child to read. It is quite likely that the really significant insights, and not only with respect to reading, will come from that source and not from psychologists or teachers who are as trapped in their oral language as they are in their skins.

2 SOME DEVELOPMENTAL ASPECTS OF PRELINGUAL DEAFNESS*

David Wood

Introduction

A major reason for the current interest in sign languages and their place in the education of deaf children arises out of the generally depressing picture that has emerged over recent years from studies of the linguistic abilities of pre-lingually, severely/profoundly deaf children. Throughout the world, where detailed statistics have been gathered, the same, generally gloomy picture has been drawn. We now know that the majority of deaf children leaving our own schools and units, for example, achieve reading ages of around 8-9 years of age (Conrad, 1977b) and that other language abilities — intelligible speech, lip-reading skills and writing ability — all show similar substantial deficits. The move towards sign in classrooms is seen by many as the brightest new hope for achieving better rehabilitation and mental health amongst our deaf population.

In this chapter I shall be reporting the results and implications of some of my own work and that of a group of eleven colleagues in the Department of Psychology at Nottingham. Our researches cover a wide area. One of our concerns lies with the impact of deafness on mother-infant interaction. This is the work of Dr Gregory and her immediate colleagues and is reported in Chapter 14. We are also working on the linguistic and information processing abilities of deaf adolescents and adults (e.g. Beggs and Foreman, 1980; Beggs and Breslaw, 1980). However, the work I shall be concerned with in this chapter is focused on interactions between pre-lingually deaf children and their teachers in classrooms. This research is designed to 'go below' the general statistics describing the achievements of deaf children to discover the daily, recurrent problems that face both the child and his teachers; problems that explain why, given a tremendous investment of human and financial resources, many deaf children still fail to achieve functional linguistic competence.

* The research reported in this chapter was supported by Grant No. G975/548 from the Medical Research Council.

The work I shall be describing is guided by a number of questions relating to the impact of early deafness on the social and interpersonal processes that underly normal development in hearing children. We now know from a great many empirical investigations, that the mature person brings a whole range of 'untaught' skills to bear on the task of child rearing. In particular, studies of early language development have shown how parents and other adults are continually adjusting both their speech and their general patterns of behaviour to fit the capacities of the young. Our language to young children, for example, is quite different to that addressed to other mature language users. Indeed, it shows gradual changes in form and function as the child talked to grows and develops. We modify our phonology and syntax together with what we talk about and how we talk about it to fit the child's level of language and mental ability (e.g. Snow and Ferguson, 1977). No one yet knows exactly how important these adjustments in adult behaviour towards the young are in facilitating normal growth. We do not know, for example, how far a child who is not exposed to such tailor-made language would be able to develop his own powers of speech. But the ubiquity of 'motherese' — the term given to adult language towards children — its systematic quality and its spontaneity in the reactions of adults to children, all point to a central role for it in the process of human growth.

Intuitively, one might well expect that any handicap in the child is likely to threaten this repertoire of basically natural skills. A child who looks older than he acts and thinks or one who thinks with a degree of sophistication beyond his language ability, is surely likely to engender behaviour from the mature person that fails to match with his own capacities. Deafness, we feel, is one of the handicaps most likely to induce such chronic disruptions in the socialising and facilitating behaviour of parents and teachers. The deaf child's normal or near normal intelligence and mental abilities progressively outstrip his powers of linguistic comprehension and production. As he grows older he tries to grasp and express ideas of ever-increasing sophistication in a language progressively less up to the task. What effect does this ever-increasing tearing apart of cognition and language have on those who try to rear and educate the child and how, if at all, can different methods of education help overcome the problems to which it leads? More fundamentally, what is the *nature* of those problems? This is the general set of questions addressed in this chapter.

Another, related, concern of the research I shall be discussing centres on individual differences in the abilities of deaf children with similar levels of intelligence and hearing loss. Although the depressing picture relating to achievements in the deaf that I have referred to holds over most children studied, it is also true that a number of children violate the general pattern and develop linguistic abilities well in advance of their peers. How far such important differences are due to some fortuitous factors located 'in' the child, and how far they are due to different patterns of socialisation and education, is our major question. By looking at some of the common problems engendered by deafness and at the different techniques that parents and educators bring to the task of solving these, we hope to gain some insights into how far changes in human response to deafness in the child may overcome what we see as the secondary, social consequences of the handicap. In this light, new work on signing in schools is clearly important. How far does the use of sign – particularly with children from non-signing homes – ameliorate the social and educational consequences of the handicap? However, I must admit at the start that we have yet to undertake any systematic work in signing classrooms and have only been concerned to date with different oral approaches to the task of educating the deaf. This weakness in our studies is not due to a conscious desire to exclude signing from our research, but is a reflection of the fact that signing is not yet well established in our schools. Conrad may be right in his sense that the tide of opinion has changed in favour of signing but, if so, the watershed it has released is, as yet, only lapping at the gates of some of our schools.

The two investigations discussed in this chapter are, then, concerned entirely with interactions between children and teachers who adopt an oral approach to education. Our aim is to uncover some of the problems the child faces in his attempts to learn what language is all about and to try to discover aspects of teaching styles that influence the difficulty of his task and the value of his efforts.

Conversations with the Young Deaf Child

During the first year of our classroom-based research, we spent a good deal of time observing lessons in a number of schools in an informal way to get the general feel of what the educational experiences of deaf children are like. We talked to teachers and even tried out some lessons ourselves. By the end of this time, we had come to know a number of teachers and children extremely well and also identified a number of commonplace classroom activities that we felt were worth detailed study. The selection of these activities was guided by our initial hypotheses about the 'secondary' consequences of deafness that I referred to above. We had expected that the deaf child would meet considerable problems in his attempts to understand and develop language, not only because of his poor reception of speech, but also because the nature of his handicap would tend to dislocate the natural abilities of the mature person to respond to his communications in a way that would help him to discover more about the nature of language.

Our initial observations left us with a strong impression of marked variations in teaching styles with deaf children that needed detailed study. These differences in teaching approach were often associated with well-articulated differences in teacher goals and philosophy. Some teachers, for example, see an important part of their job as language *teaching*. Feeling that the deaf child is cut off from a natural access to knowledge of language, they consider that they have to provide additional information to him about the quality of his voice and the well-formedness of his utterances. They thus see their role as helping the child to learn about language in a special and often highly structured way. Other teachers, however, feel that a conscious attempt to instruct the child in the rules and sounds of speech before he has developed 'naturally' an expressive ability of his own, can only serve to further disrupt his language development. They thus try to maintain normal patterns of language use and avoid any emphasis on rules and structures in speech. Such differences were often made quite apparent in the course of conversations between different teachers and their children. Consider the following brief, condensed excerpts from our recordings of classroom conversations, for example. They took place in 'news sessions' where teacher and children are involved in talk about what happened over the weekend, out of school.

1. *Mother's Day*

Teacher   What did you do at the weekend?
Child   Mummy . . . flowers.
T   Oh, you gave mummy some flowers. What, for mother's day? Yesterday was mother's day, wasn't it? Say 'Yesterday was mother's day'.
C   Yes . . . mo . . . da . . .
T   Say 'Yesterday was mother's day'.
C   Yes . . . day
T   Yesterday was mother's day.
C   Yes'day . . . mother . . . day.

T   Oh, and you gave mummy some flowers.
C   Mummy . . . grandma . . . flowers.
T   You mean, you gave mummy *and* grandma some flowers. Say 'I gave mummy and grandma some flowers'.
C   I mo . . . mum . . . grandma . . . flowers . . .
T   Oh, you gave mummy and grandma some flowers?
C   No.

2. Weekend Entertainment

T   What did you do at the weekend?
C   Mummy . . . TV.
T   Oh, I haven't got a TV.
C   Mummy TV . . . Coffee 'foof' . . . TV . . . 'foof'.
T   On the TV? It went foof?
C   Coffee . . . drop on TV . . . foof.
T   Oh dear.
C   Me . . . Jason football . . . me Forest 3 . . . West Brom 2 . . . West Brom . . . Rubbish!
T   Who do you support?
C   Forest . . . you support?
T   I don't like football.
C   You . . . not football?
T   No.
C   You . . . No TV?
T   No.
C   You . . . do weekend?

These brief transcripts illustrate some of the problems that teachers face. These children, although producing mainly two- or three-word utterances, are eight years of age. The hearing child's two- or three-word utterances, which emerge at around eighteen months to two years of age, are almost exclusively concerned with the here and now — with what has just happened, is happening or about to happen in the immediate environment. The two-year-old's mental capacities are not developed enough to enable him systematically to recall and relive the past nor to plan far into the future. Consequently, his listener can usually work out what he is talking about by paying attention not only to his speech but also to his gestures, actions and general demeanour. Consequently while his speech is ambiguous, his *meanings* are usually clear to a sensitive and attentive listener. But the eight-year-old deaf child using two or three words *can* remember, plan and reason. So his nonverbal behaviour and his ongoing actions are often an insufficient guide to what he is meaning, and the ambiguity in his two or three words cannot be fathomed easily. The teacher in the first transcript offers a number of hypotheses to the child about what he means in an attempt to clear up her uncertainty and having satisfied herself that she has fathomed his meaning, she offers him instruction as to how to express himself more clearly and unambiguously. But she runs the danger in so doing of further confusing the child and of robbing the conversation of any real interest.

The second teacher is much more relaxed. She seems willing to let ambiguities pass *or* to assume that she understands and to continue the idalogue on that assumption. She does not 'repair' the child's speech nor try to solicit better formed utterances from him. Here, perhaps, a danger is that the exchange will not provide the child with any new insights into how he might express himself more intelligibly in the future. Does he *need* more articulated feedback about his voice and his grammar if he is to make progress as a language user?

We have analysed and evaluated such differences in the conversational styles of teachers in two main ways. A common goal that teachers pursue with deaf children is to encourage them to speak and to *use* what language they have as fully and readily as possible. The appropriate (and telling) metaphor that one often hears from teachers is that of 'getting language out of the child'. We have examined in most detail the conversations between 20 children and their four (very different) teachers, in order to determine how far variations in teaching style are associated with different patterns of language use from the children; and to see if some facilitate more conversation from the child.

Our evaluation rests on two different analyses of 'moves' in teacher and child speech. The first concerns the *control* of the conversation and the second the major *functions* performed by different utterances. First, we briefly consider control.

Control of Conversation

Imagine you are listening in to a conversation between teacher and child, and have just heard the teacher speak. We recognise seven major categories of utterance that can occur, which are listed and illustrated in Table 2.1.

The first three move types in Table 2.1 exert a measure of direct control over the child's next move. After an enforced repetition, a compliant child will attempt to repeat what has already been said. After a closed, forced-choice question, his answer should include one of the two words specified in the question, after an open one, he should produce an utterance centred on the semantic category specified in the question — 'Who?' 'What?' 'Where?' and so forth.

Table 2.1: Outline Coding of Conversational Moves

	Move type	Example
1	Enforced repetition	Say 'bye-bye' for me
2	Closed question	Was it Mummy or Daddy?
3	Open question	When did you go?
4	Contribution	I don't like tea
5	Phatic	Oh, lovely
4/2	Tag contribution	I'm always happy, aren't I?
5/2	Tag phatic	That's lovely, isn't it?

The remaining categories do not exert such direct control. After a contribution, the child might continue with his own line of conversation; he could simply react to the teacher's utterance or take over control himself by asking a question. After a 'phatic' move, the child might also continue along his own theme, or start to draw the topic of conversation to a close, perhaps, with a similar move of his own.

These are obviously highly simplified options, and the full coding system includes a number of sub-categories that I have not the space to discuss here (Wood, McMahon and Cranstoun, 1980; Wood, Wood, Griffiths, Howarth and Howarth, 1980). It is possible in some circumstances to follow a question with a question, for example ('Did you go to town on Saturday? Why do you want to know?'), and it is also possible to take multiple turns in which a question is answered, say, and then followed up by a contribution or a further question. However, in our analyses of both conversations between adults and three-to-five-year-old hearing children and that of talk between teachers and their deaf children, we have found that while adults often display such complex options, children (generally speaking) do not. They almost never follow a teacher's question with one of their own, and only occasionally do they take multiple turns. In fact, both the hearing preschoolers and our deaf primary school children responded very systematically and rather similarly to different moves in adult speech. For example, they usually answered questions and then stopped talking. After a teacher's contribution they usually continued with their own line of talk or asked the teacher a question, and after a phatic move from the adult they also continued the theme with a contribution of their own.

This systematic quality of deaf children's responses to teacher talk is important for two major reasons. In the first place, it shows that the deaf child *is* quite capable of reading the major force of his teacher's utterances. He seldom confuses closed questions with open ones, for example, and almost never treats questions as contributions. In spite of the children's relatively poor command of grammar they are not unskilled at this more basic level of communication. Perhaps, as in Woll's studies reported in Chapter 7, the children are exploiting subtle aspects of nonverbal behaviour to determine what sort of utterance and demand is being made on them.

The second implication is that it is *not* necessary to continually question the children to keep them talking. They will continue to take turns in the conversation after contributions and phatics from their teacher and, hence, need not be continually driven by questions.

Another result of this initial analysis was the finding that different types of moves from teachers are correlated with the loquacity of the child being addressed. In general, the teachers who exerted a lot of control by frequently asking questions and demanding repetitions met with much shorter utterances and fewer multiple turns from their children than those who asked fewer questions and made more personal contributions and phatics. This result also parallels our findings with pre-school hearing children. They too say less, ask fewer questions and generally make no spontaneous comments to those adults who ask a lot of questions. Even when we take account of the deaf child's degree of hearing loss and his mental age, these same relationships hold between teaching style and his linguistic activity.

This result suggests that the dialogic framework established by the teacher, measured by the degree of control she exerts over the children, plays a part in determining how competent and talkative the deaf child appears in conversation with her. Although his hearing loss clearly constrains his ability to talk, there is scope within these constraints for the teacher to facilitate or depress his language use. And since, in general, teacher questions and control were high in conversations with the children (as they tend to be in hearing classrooms too, e.g. French and MacLure, 1979) this implies that teachers often produce a dialogic framework within which children are actually inhibited from their most free-flowing talk.

Functions in Teacher Speech

The second analysis of the teacher-child conversations concerned the main *functions* underlying teacher speech. We differentiated three main types of function:

(a) *Repair* – in which the teacher goes back over what a child has said to clarify his meaning, improve his phonology or correct his syntax.

(b) *Substantive moves* – in which she carries the topic of conversation forward perhaps by asking a question designed to solicit fresh information or by making a contribution of her own about the topic at hand.

(c) *Moves of continuity* – which let the child know that he is being attended to or keep turn-taking moving along smoothly. Each of these different functions can be realised in a number of ways – as open and closed questions, phatics or contributions.

This analysis also yielded one useful finding. In the first place, the incidence of *repair* in teacher speech was far more pronounced in conversations with the deaf than with the younger hearing children. One of our four teachers spent almost 70 per cent of her time in repair. For each conversational move that the child made – answering a question or making a contribution – she dedicated, on average, two moves designed to clarify, idealise and improve that move. The other teachers were less committed to repair – the least repairing making some 13 per cent of her moves of this type. Overall, however, there was a significant correlation across teachers in the frequency of repair and the child's degree of deafness – the deafer children were repaired more.

This result underlines another basic problem facing the deafer children. They not only have to work out what type of utterance the teacher is making – a question or whatever, but are also continually faced with the problem of deciding whether the move refers back to what they have already said, or on into new conversational territory. The high incidence of repair in fact makes their task as a conversationalist more difficult. Rather than easing the child's difficulties in dialogue, teachers high in repair added to his problems. As in the first transcript above, continual attempts to clarify and improve the child's language simply led teacher and child deeper into mutual uncertainty and misunderstanding.

In general, then, our analysis of conversations reveals a number of unusual and abnormal features of conversations with the deaf child that varied in frequency across the classrooms studied. The high incidence of control in teacher speech actually seems to depress the child's attempts to converse, while frequent repair leads him into additional problems, further increasing his dependency upon the teacher for regulating the discourse. Arguably, then, the abnormal features of conversations are also pathological and counter-productive — at least, counter-productive in getting the child playing an active role as a conversationalist.

In a follow-up to these studies, we have worked with a number of teachers and helped them to modify their conversational styles systematically. We have mounted joint experiments in the classroom in which the teachers adopt a number of different strategies — some high in closed questions, others in open questions, contributions and phatics. These experiments have shown both that teachers can change style and also that when they do so, their children also change and become more or less active in conversation. Where the teacher makes more contributions and relaxes her control to give the children more of her own responses and reactions to the topic of conversation, the children take longer turns, say more and generally play a more controlling role in the interaction. Thus, whilst increasing control and repair may be a frequent response to the child's deafness, they are *not* inevitable and, once relaxed, conversations flow more freely and develop more normally, with each participant playing a more equal role in controlling the course of talk.

Reading Lessons

One of the most well documented aspects of the deaf child's linguistic abilities concerns his performance in reading. As Conrad (Chapter 1) and others have shown, deaf children with severe losses — particularly those with mean losses in excess of 85 dB in the better ear — are unlikely to have developed reading ages beyond the 8-9-year-old level on leaving school. We have recently undertaken a comparative study of deaf and hearing children with similar age levels on formal reading tests which shows also that this level of achievement in the deaf child is often *not* equivalent to a normal reading age. Deaf children tend to achieve their test scores in a quite different manner to hearing children and in a way that suggests that they are often not reading like a younger hearing child but are in fact capitalising on rather special strategies for handling the test which demand little knowledge of grammatical devices in language. We have also studied eye movements during reading by deaf and hearing children (Beggs, Breslaw and Wilkinson, 1980) which show that many mature deaf readers display abnormal eye movements as they 'read' texts, further casting doubt on the conclusion that they learn to read even like normal 8-year-olds.

In spite of such generally poor levels of achievement considerable time and effort are put into the teaching of reading in our schools. Children and teachers work long and hard at reading lessons and some teachers try to use reading from the very early stages of schooling as a primary route to language development. Why, given all this investment, are reading standards generally so poor?

On theoretical grounds, given what we know about the reading process (e.g. Smith, 1978) we have every reason to doubt that language can be acquired through the printed word. Where the child does not possess 'inner speech' (Conrad, 1979), and hence cannot phonologically represent printed words, and where he lacks the syntactic devices that help to specify the meaning carried by strings of words, the task of decoding and making sense of printed language would seem to be an immensely difficult, if not impossible, task. In addition to these structural features of language, there are deeper and more basic differences between speech and print that cast doubt on the value of written language as a primary vehicle for language teaching. During the hearing child's language development, the language that he hears is often related directly to his perceptions, feelings and actions — it is continually integrated with his immediate experiences (Snow and Ferguson, 1977; Edwards, 1978). Ample opportunities are provided for language to be brought alive. The task of relating reality and speech is greatly simplified because those who already know and can talk bring their speech into correspondence with the child's ongoing nonverbal experience. But print lacks this immediate correspondence with reality. The child in reading has to set up mentally that which is being talked about and, hence, arguably needs to *possess* the language which he is expected to read first.

Although there are a number of strong theoretical reasons like these that cast doubt on the value of print as a primary vehicle for language learning, human ingenuity being what it is, it may be that teachers of the deaf have discovered special techniques for exploiting print that essentially bypass or overcome these theoretical difficulties — though levels of achievement cast serious doubt on this possibility. To try to understand more fully the relationships between the deaf child's experiences in learning to read and his ultimate performances as a reader, we have undertaken a comparative study of reading lessons of deaf and hearing children (Howarth, Wood, Griffiths and Howarth, 1980). This sheds some light onto the problems of both teacher and child and gives some insights into the reasons why all the time given over to reading often bears little fruit.

Our method was basically a simple if laborious one. First, we made video-recordings of 16 deaf children being taught to read in the classroom from their reading primers in a normal lesson. We then searched our local hearing schools for teachers using the same books and recorded a (usually much younger) hearing child being taught to read from the same pages. In this way, we matched 16 deaf and hearing children.

The lessons were dramatically different. We looked first at the number of times teacher or child stopped during the course of reading the text. Deaf children stopped far more themselves and were stopped more frequently by their teachers. Indeed, in general, hearing children seemed loathe to stop reading — they would usually have a go at reading an unfamiliar word, often making a mistake in the process that was picked up by the teacher. Deaf children seldom tried to guess or get over difficulty — they would stop and look to teacher, signalling their greater dependence. More important, however, were the reasons for stops. As in the analysis of conversations just discussed, many teachers of the deaf used their lessons to pursue multiple goals — they were not only involved in helping the child learn the correspondence between sound and print, but also using the lesson for teaching vocabulary, syntax and speech itself. Deaf children's stops were often given over to long periods of language teaching. Little drawings, cartoons, dramas acted out with dolls were used in an attempt to teach vocabulary. At other times, the lesson became an exercise in speech training as the teacher attempted to improve the child's phonology.

The main upshot of these frequent stops was an extremely slow rate of reading. Many of the deaf children were reading well below 40 words or so per minute — some as slow as 11 words per minute. It seems highly unlikely that going through print at this rate — even if the child can grasp the syntax involved — could possibly lead to an understanding of the text. All this suggests that what is going on in the reading lesson for many deaf children has little to do with developing a normal reading process. At best, one suspects that they acquire a few more words of printed vocabulary — usually concrete words at that — with no progress towards mastering larger sections of print, connected speech the eye movements needed to scan lines of text.

These results relate back to the studies mentioned earlier of reading test performance and eye movements. In looking at text, most deaf readers work one word at a time — some show highly abnormal scanning patterns as they search out individual words that they recognise. In reading tests, they also tend to pick out odd words that are known and then make a guess at the story or description in which they are embedded — usually achieving no real comprehension of what is written.

This admittedly small-scale study thus generally reinforces the theoretical arguments put forward earlier. The reading lesson is ill-equipped for teaching language *de nouveau*, and where language ability is poor, reading itself cannot be established. The multiplicity of goals embedded in the reading lessons of many children leads to a disjointed, complex activity that seems to preclude the development of some of the most basic skills upon which reading rests. Thus the experiences of at least some deaf children in the reading lesson are abnormal and on the basis of our observations to date, seem of little value in developing either linguistic or literary competence.

'Teaching' Language

The two studies just reported, together with work that has examined other teaching situations (e.g. Wood and Wood, 1980), show that the deaf child is not only handicapped as a learner by poor reception of speech, but also by the generation of a range of other learning problems engendered by his handicap. But are these secondary problems inevitable?

Our small-scale intervention study, in which teachers modified their conversational styles, did show both that change is possible and that it can exert short-term effects on the child's language. More generally and informally, in our work in the many different schools we have visited, we have found groups of children who are performing much better than the general pattern I have just outlined. They converse relatively freely with each other and their teachers, control conversations and read faster than other children of similar intelligence and hearing loss, occasionally performing as well as hearing matches. It is not possible at present to say with any confidence why such children perform so well, but in general they are in educational settings where teachers show a minimum incidence of high control and repair; where the teaching of reading is left relatively late on the grounds that it cannot be established prior to the development of expressive language ability; and where, in general, children are geared to a normal school curriculum with little or no emphasis on 'teaching' language as a separate discipline.

We simply do not have the quality of evidence yet, however, to be confident that these features of teaching philosophy are causally related to higher standards of performance in children. It is equally possible on the basis of our present piecemeal evidence that children who, for some unknown reason, do particularly well, enable teachers themselves to teach more normally. However, in looking at the results of our study of conversation and reading, I am struck by the fact that in both situations, at least some of the child's problems stem from the teacher's attempts to 'teach' him his language. In conversations, increased control and frequent repair, inspired by a desire to make what the child says clearer and less ambiguous, increases the difficulty of his task and render many of his utterances functionless. Solicited speech engenders no more shared knowledge, passes no new information, makes nothing happen. It serves no purpose other than pleasing teacher. Constant backtracking, going over the same ground, robs the child of initiative, and magnifies the problems of deciding what talk is all about. The child's dependency is increased, because the criterion that measures the effectiveness of his communications is not whether people act or react as he intends, hopes or expects; rather, it resides entirely in the approval of his listeners, an approval based in their knowledge of the language that the child himself lacks and does not understand.

In reading, too, the multiplicity of goals set up by some teachers makes the child's task more complex, obscures any true purpose in reading, disrupts meaning and increases his dependency. 'Teaching' language, then, not only changes the nature of the communications to which the child is exposed but also strikes at the basis of his relationships with others. None of us doubt that the deaf child is handicapped by how *much* he fails to hear. But such dislocations to normal patterns of linguistic function also change the nature of *what* it is that he receives and communicates. Thus not only the content but also the form of his language experiences is threatened.

Although our current evidence does not enable us to say with confidence that particular teaching styles do exert a major effect on the deaf child's achievmenets, these results and the implications that we have drawn from them, inspire some confidence that future work may well establish such a conclusion.

I have no doubt that many educators will feel that sign language, as the 'mother tongue' of the deaf, will naturally lead teacher and child to circumvent the sorts of problems I have been discussing. I have already said that we ourselves have not yet examined signing in the classroom, and clearly the sorts of analyses we have been discussing need to be extended to the study of manual communication. However, research emerging from the United States already indicates, as Conrad anticipates in his chapter, that signing will not prove a ready-made solution to all the problems of deaf children and in particular those children who have not been raised in signing homes. In one study, for example, Craig and Collins (1970) used Flanders' system for analysing classroom interactions to compare lessons in oral and Total Communication classrooms. They found that the pattern of teacher control in the two sorts of classrooms was similar. As in our study of conversation, teacher control through questions was high. Extending our findings to this work, we would hypothesise that using signing does not of itself lead teachers to provide a more optimum dialogic framework for their children to work in. In another study Dalgleish and Mohay (1979) found that teachers who set out deliberately to *teach* sign, much as some teachers in our studies try formally to teach speech, lead their children to develop linguistic structures that are abnormal when measured against the linguistic productions of children raised in signing homes.

These are small-scale studies and cannot be used as a basis for firm conclusions but they do suggest that the nature of teacher behaviour itself and the attempt to teach language formally continue to exert a tremendous influence on the deaf child's knowledge of language, over and above the medium of communication being employed. In a third study, Marmor and Petitto (1979) have found that teachers who are not native signers produce signs in lessons which are not compatible either with the structure of Ameslan or English. Again, the study is small scale, but it too suggests that the sorts of problems I have been discussing — particularly in the development of the basis for literacy — are *not* going to meet ready-made solutions from the combination of sign and speech.

In conclusion, it seems to me that a central question which transcends all the arguments about the best medium of communication with the deaf child, asks how far it is possible to 'teach' the child his language in schools. Given what we know about normal language development and our emerging awareness of the problems faced by the deaf child in his interactions with others, we must seriously doubt the value of any approach to education that treats language in sign or speech as a 'system' to be learned formally as an object of knowledge. I believe that the value of any linguistic environment for the child will be measured not by the frequency with which a teacher talks, signs or both, but by the extent to which what she says and does relates to and extends the child's own perceptions, intentions and feelings — in the *process* of communication and not the modality in which it is couched.

We can only hope that an improvement in the deaf child's lot *can* be obtained by changes in the social basis of his education. For my part, I hope that the many controversies that surround the issue of the medium of communication with the deaf will not prevent us from looking beyond the structure of language systems themselves to study how different languages are used in the home and school. If they do inhibit us from so doing it is my view that they will obscure that which we are all searching for in our attempts to help deaf children achieve their true potential.

3 PSYCHOLINGUISTIC PROCESSES IN PRELINGUALLY DEAF ADOLESCENTS

Elisabeth Dawson

The relationship between prelingual deafness and language processing ability is an area of interest to Educational and Cognitive Psychology. Recent interest in child language, first language learning and generative grammars generally is reflected in an increased concern with the language abilities of the prelingually deaf. This has led to the development of research in two directions: 1) studies of deaf people's proficiency in English; and 2) studies of sign language as the 'natural' language of deaf people. Many of the studies reported in this volume fall into the latter category, in particular the work of Brennan, Deuchar, Lawson and Woll.

The study described in this chapter was carried out in the context of a much broader investigation of the thought processes of a group of profoundly and severely prelingually deaf adolescents attending the Northern Counties School for the Deaf (NCSD), Newcastle upon Tyne (Dawson, 1979). In both this chapter and Chapter 4 the concern is with the use of sign language as a mediator in memory. In the case of my own research the present study grew out of an earlier finding that word recognition appeared to be mediated by sign language; a facilitatory effect of sign mediation was found in a lexical-decision task. The deaf children responded faster and more accurately than the hearing controls to pairs of words which had sign equivalents compared with words which did not (e.g. country, week, mile). Before embarking upon a detailed description of the effect of three types of language (standard English, 'deaf English', and sign language using English glosses) on the deaf children's ability to remember simple sentences, a brief review of the relevant literature will be presented, beginning with studies of the written language of deaf children, followed by some studies of deaf children's understanding of, and memory for, written language.

Many researchers have studied the verbal behaviour of deaf people, but since the oral language of most prelingually deaf individuals is relatively unintelligible and therefore difficult to transcribe, only a few researchers have been concerned with the language element in their speech (e.g. Brannon, 1968; Gemmill and John, 1977; Pressnell, 1973). Most of the studies have, therefore, concentrated on written language. Techniques that have been developed and used to study the syntactic structure of young children with normal hearing and their emerging grammars (e.g. McNeill, 1970; Menyuk, 1971) have also been applied to study the written language of deaf children.

Experimental Studies of the Written Language of Deaf People

The overall picture emerging from experimental studies of the language of deaf children is rather confusing and somewhat contradictory. At one extreme there are those who suggest that there is no difference between the language of deaf and hearing children. For example, Heider and Heider (1940, p. 42) wrote: 'It is often quite impossible to say of a single composition whether it is written by a deaf or by a hearing child.' At the other extreme Howarth and Wood (1977) state:

> There is now some evidence that, however language is taught to deaf children, whether manually, orally or by 'total communication', the deaf are not only linguistically retarded but also linguistically different. Studies of both language production and language comprehension suggest that the underlying organisation of knowledge and experience is somewhat different for the deaf. (pp. 6-7)

Many comparisons have been made between the language of deaf and hearing children, looking at the productivity, complexity, the distribution of different parts of speech and the correctness of language used, beginning with the early work of Thompson (1936) and the classic study of Heider and Heider (1940). In an attempt to understand these studies they will be divided into three main groups according to the conclusions drawn concerning the language of the deaf.

A few examples will be given to characterise each of these three main groups beginning with those studies which are based on the supposition that the language systems of deaf and hearing people are the same, although possibly with some retardation in linguistic development and a greater number of grammatical errors made by the deaf. Heider and Heider (1940) studied the sentence structure of deaf and hearing children and expressed the differences in quantitative terms, as a degree of retardation. They concluded that 'Generally deaf children resemble younger or less mature hearing children' (p. 73). However, they did also observe differences in sentence structure, including more simple sentences and the use of a 'relatively large number of sentences which are shorter both in number or words and in number of clauses than those of the hearing'. They go on to state: 'The whole picture indicates a simpler style, involving relatively rigid, unrelated language units which follow each other with little overlapping of structure or meaning' (p. 98).

Simmons (1962) also investigated the flexibility/rigidity of word usage using pictures to stimulate written composition. She measured the type-token ratio (TTR), i.e. the ratio of the number of different words used to the total number of words in the language sample, and found that the deaf children had a lower TTR than the hearing children, indicating less diversity of vocabulary.

MacGinitie (1964) used sentence completion tests to study ability to use different word classes in context, rather than their frequency of occurrence in free composition. Deaf and hearing subjects were required to complete each sentence by filling in the omitted word. MacGinitie found no striking differences in the pattern of difficulty of usage of different word classes for the deaf and hearing children. A similar technique, the Cloze procedure, was used by Moores (1970) who reported that, in addition to poorly developed grammatical abilities, the deaf children exhibited restricted, stereotyped modes of expression and limited vocabulary.

More recently Davison (1977) analysed the errors in written language produced by a group of prelingually deaf children and found them to be '. . . both deviant and delayed'. She states that 'a continuum of language development was seen, from systems which varied to a greater or lesser extent from standard English through to complete acquisition' (unpublished abstract). Davison concludes that the existence of such a continuum suggests that deaf children are developing English rather than an idiosyncratic 'deaf language', even though the pattern of linguistic development is not exactly the same as for hearing children. All these studies are essentially alike in their assumptions that the language systems of deaf and hearing are similar.

Secondly, there are those who have attempted to study the language of deaf people as a system in its own right, rather than as a deviant form of standard English. Myklebust (1964) described the grammatical errors made by the deaf as 'deafisms' but did not attempt to study the linguistic system responsible for generating such errors. Perry (1968) analysed all the written compositions produced by his deaf and hearing samples quantitatively in terms of the number of mistakes and the number of sentences, and qualitatively, analysing the type of error. As a result, he also concluded that deaf children produce characteristic errors — so-called 'deafisms' — and found, like Myklebust no evidence for a decline in the number of mistakes made by the deaf children with increasing age. He found that expert sorters could 'correctly classify sentences written by deaf and hearing children' (p. 153), evidence which suggests that there must be some characteristic, distinctive features for such a classification to be possible.

Ivimey (1976) attempted to discover the syntactic structure of the language of the deaf. He analysed in detail the written language of one profoundly deaf 10½-year-old girl, using Chomsky's 1957 model of syntactic structures. On the basis of such an in-depth analysis he concluded that 'The language of at least one deaf child is not a loose concatenation of English words. It is rule based and the syntax is not congruent with that of normal English', and that 'The differences are so great that it seems more appropriate to categorise this corpus of data as a system of language "sui-generis" ' (p. 112).

Finally, the third approach assumes that deaf people lack a linguistic system, that they have no system of rules to generate language. This final group comes nearest to the assumption that deaf people may be treated as 'alinguistic controls'. Fusfeld (1955, p. 70) described the written language of the deaf as a '. . . tangled web type of expression in which words occur in profusion but do not align themselves in an orderly array'. Furth (1971, p. 68) goes on to further elaborate this point:

> Most deaf persons in our society know some English words or phrases; but admittedly the most vital aspect of the living language is not single words but the structure of the language into which single words are fitted to form meaningful sentences . . . It is precisely this general structure that hearing children assimilate with relative ease and the vast majority of deaf children fail to attain with an adequate degree of competence.

To those unfamiliar with deaf children, the above categories of findings may appear contradictory. However, they are probably less puzzling to those who have gained experience of the deaf within *different* deaf schools, with their various selection procedures, communication methods and educational techniques. It is perhaps even to be expected that studies of the written language of different samples of deaf children drawn from different educational establishments, such as those previously discussed, would produce contradictory findings.

An extreme case of the differences that exist between deaf schools is exemplified by a comparison of the Northern Counties School for the Deaf (the school used in the present study) with the Mary Hare School, from which Davison (1977) selected her sample. The latter, being the only deaf grammar school in Britain and consequently highly selective (for intelligence, ability to lip-read and to benefit from an 'oral' education), is attended by the most 'verbal' deaf individuals in the country. The NCSD, on the other hand, is a non-selective school, and is one of the most 'manually' oriented deaf schools in the country. The differences between these two samples of deaf children are such that it is highly probable that any conclusion drawn from analyses of the structure of written language of the pupils in these two schools will differ markedly.

Observation outside the classroom in the NCSD showed that the deaf children were able to communicate information fluently and efficiently between themselves using sign language. Yet, when required to relate some incident using written language, they were unable to do so at the same level of sophistication, and were reduced to a fairly basic level of communication. However, as we shall see from the 24 written sentences selected for use in the present study, the meaning of their written language is not totally obscured by the deviant grammatical structures, although the frequent and regular departures from standard English are striking.

Since verbal language must be formally taught to deaf children, it is also quite possible that language production may be directly related to the particular type of instruction received, and to the methods, including the form of communication, used. Therefore, the language of deaf children may have to be regarded, in part at least, as a product of schooling. Walter (1955, 1959) considered this problem, first studying a group of children from a single school in Australia, and then following this up with a further study of 58 deaf children taken from three Australian and four English schools for the deaf. She found some similarities but also many variations. The similarities serve to remind us of the common problems shared by most profoundly or severely prelingually deaf children in learning verbal language, and the variations indicate the differences due to circumstances.

Deaf language, whether written or spoken, shows infrequent use of tense, and omission of various 'grammatical' features associated with English. Examples such as 'I want go', 'There lost the dog', and 'Your lives nearly shops' should all be quite familiar to, and easily recognised by, many teachers of the deaf, parents of deaf children and the few psychologists, linguists and psycholinguists who are interested in the language production of deaf children. All the above examples were produced by prelingually deaf adolescents of average or above-average nonverbal intelligence. Similar examples have been reported in the French publication *Communiquer* (June, 1973, p. 49), e.g. 'La petit garçon peur la souris', and 'La voiture va achète avec tout neuf'. Other examples are also to be found in the literature, for example Fusfeld (1958, p. 255) quoted a note written by a 19½-year-old deaf boy, who, after 13 years of schooling in the United States, wrote: 'Tell mother I wants she come here at 1.00 between 1.30 because I have some dirty sweaters and shirts and she can take them and wash and need money'.

A report on the work of the Schools Council Project on the language development of deaf pupils (Wollman and Hickmott, 1976), includes a short passage of free composition, written by a 9-year-old deaf child:

All about me.
I am 9 year old. I am boy. I have live in Farm. Live Mummy, Daddy with Elaine. I am baby calf. I am have house. I am sheep. I am have small house. I am cow. I am have new cars. I am cat. I am have garden. I am baby chicken. I am have barn. I am have cock. I am have gate. I am have geese. I am have flowers. I am have yes tractor. I am have bales. I am have yes trailer. I am have blackberries. I am have blackcurrants. (p. 6).

The use of stereotyped repetitions or 'carrier phrases', such as 'I am have' creates a relatively rigid style and may well reflect confusion between set language patterns that have been taught and learned by heart, and which are reproduced at a given signal. Heider and Heider (1940, p. 75) also noted that the deaf used '. . . more fixed phrases that could be learned and used as units'.

All the evidence presented so far would seem to indicate that there are some very important differences between the written language of deaf and hearing people. In most of these studies, however, the principal concern has been the categorisation of errors and the description of written language, whereas in the present study the central issue is the effect of different language structures on memory recognition and recall, and goes beyond the descriptive level.

Odom and Blanton (1967) compared the learning of 4-word segments of written English by deaf and hearing children using:

(i) English phrases of the form Verb + Article + Adjective + Noun (e.g. 'paid the tall lady');

(ii) the same words in non-phrases of the form Noun + Verb + Article + Adjective (e.g. 'lady paid the tall');

(iii) the same four words in a scrambled order (e.g. 'lady tall the paid').

The hearing subjects recalled the English phrases well but the other two forms interfered with their ability to recall the phrases correctly. The deaf children, on the other hand, showed no differential recall as a function of phrase structure, i.e. there was no facilitation for recall of English phrases. Odom and Blanton concluded that the deaf do not possess the same perceptual or memory processes with regard to English as hearing children, but went on to observe: 'This is not to say that they may not possess these characteristics with regard to Sign. It might be possible to conduct an experiment similar to the present one, but defining the segments according to the structure of Sign' (p. 605). If deaf subjects were using a Sign code, the experimental variable, English structure, would be irrelevant to them. This was one of the ideas that was followed up and tested by the present author and which Odom and Blanton (1970) themselves examined. They used three types of reading material:

(i) A standard version of a paragraph comprehension test.

(ii) A series of sentences representing the same information but designed to approximate the syntax of ASL.

(iii) The same sentences with scrambled word order.

They found that the deaf subjects were able to understand the sentences written in ASL better than those written in English, whilst the hearing subjects were better able to understand the English sentences than those written in sign language. Both groups experienced the greatest difficulty with the scrambled word order. Compared with the hearing subjects, the deaf experienced greater difficulty with the standard English paragraph.

Sarachan-Deily and Love (1974) investigated the underlying grammatical rule structure in the deaf. They tested two groups of deaf students (aged 15 to 19 years), one group had been taught using simultaneous fingerspelling and speech (the Rochester method), the other by a purely 'oral' approach, and a group of hearing controls. Each subject had to remember 12 standard English sentences presented individually. A sentence was scored as correct if it was recalled as an exact copy of the original. The errors were classified as 'agrammatical-sentence errors', 'grammatical-sentence errors', and 'sentence deletions'. They found that errors made by the hearing subjects rarely violated English sentence structure, whilst the recalled sentences of the deaf subjects frequently included '. . . a gross violation of English sentence structure' (p. 696). These results also suggest that the deaf students had a limited syntactical competence for the basic rules of English syntax.

Even more recently, Charrow (1975) investigated the idea that there might be enough commonality among deaf adolescents' errors in written English to justify the use of the term 'deaf English' and its recognition as a non-standard dialect. Her aim was to discover whether the deaf children would find 'deaf English' (DE) easier to process than standard English (SE), and whether hearing controls would make more errors on the DE. Her results showed that the deaf subjects did find the DE sentences easier to remember and repeat back than the hearing subjects, but that they did not find the DE sentences any easier to recall and repeat correctly than the SE sentences.

An Experimental Study of the Effect of Language Forms on Memory

In the light of these earlier studies, the present study was designed to compare the effect on subsequent memory of three language forms:

(i)   standard English (SE) as investigated by Odom and Blanton (1967, 1970);

(ii)   sign language (SL) as studied by Odom and Blanton (1970):

(iii) 'deaf English' (DE) as studied by Charrow (1975).

The latter language form was included in the investigation in an attempt to determine whether there was sufficient similarity between the ungrammatical errors in the written language produced by deaf adolescents (the 'deafisms') for DE to be considered as a non-standard dialect of English, perhaps of a similar standing to Black English Vernacular (Labov, 1972a). It was suggested, therefore, that if this were the case, one would expect deaf people to find DE easier to process than SE.

The samples of DE used in the present experiment were collected from the unaided, free composition of deaf adolescents from the same classes as those who were tested. Since written language may well be affected by the educational and communication methods used with the deaf children, as suggested by Walter (1959), it was felt to be important that the language samples should be generated by deaf people of the same age, who had been taught by the same teachers using the same methods as the experimental group, since language teaching methods and communication methods are likely to influence language production and the type of errors made.

All the deaf adolescents tested in the present study were familiar with SL and fingerspelling and chose to communicate manually whenever they were free to do so, indicating a definite preference. In the classroom, however, English was taught and used as the basic means of communicating all taught subject matter. The effect of such a situation on their ability to process language was therefore under investigation.

Learning, one must assume, involves understanding. Children would probably find it more difficult to memorise language which they did not understand, or which was not part of their linguistic competence. If a person is to memorise sentences and reproduce them accurately, then he or she must have access to a system of internal linguistic rules similar to those used to generate the sentences. In so far as language is rule-based it must reflect some deep-lying competence; a fundamental assumption underlying this investigation was that if a deaf child repeatedly produced or reproduced certain syntactic forms, grammatically correct or otherwise, then it may be inferred that a system of rules is being used to generate these features.

If the language form of a sentence is not the same as that normally used during cognition, it is likely that the preferred language mode will mediate, or even interfere with, subsequent recall or recognition, though probably less so in the latter case owing to the nature of the cues that are given. The structure of a sentence generated during recall should provide a useful indicator of the structure of language used cognitively. The critical distinction that is being made here concerns the difference between psittacism and language used for basic understanding and cognitive functioning.

The following experiment was designed to test two hypotheses:

(i) that deaf children should find it easiest to memorise sentences written according to the syntax of SL because of their obvious preference for, and ability to communicate fluently in, sign language.

(ii)   that deaf children should find it easier to remember DE sentences than SE sentences if the 'deafisms' found in 'deaf English' are characteristic of a deaf dialect and are generated by a linguistic system rather than random occurrences.

Method

Subjects 48 deaf children from the Upper School of the NCSD were selected − 6 at random from each of 8 classes. All the children were either severely or profoundly prelingually deaf − hearing losses ranged from 65 − 120 dB in the better ear. Their ages ranged from 13.2 to 16.5 years and their reading ages ranged from 6.9 to 8.7 years as measured by the Young's group reading test. There were 24 boys and 24 girls in the sample.

Materials Single sentences were typed on to each of 72 cards for visual presentation. In addition a further 24 cards were prepared with four alternative forms (SE, DE, SL and a distractor item) of the same sentence, each written on a single line, one under another, for use with the memory recognition group. Duplicated copies of a page of mental arithmetic problems were used during the 30-second intervals between sentence presentation and subsequent recognition/recall. These intervals were timed with a stopwatch.

Design and Procedure 24 short sentences, written by deaf children in the same classes as those children who were to be tested, were selected. Each sentence contained typical 'deafisms', such as the incorrect substitution of the preposition 'to' and the use of the present instead of the past tense of the verb in the sentence: 'We arrive to London late' instead of 'We arrived late in London'. The sentences were collected from samples of unaided, creative, free composition. Each of the 24 sentences was subsequently translated into a written form of sign language using English glosses using the guidelines suggested by Hoffmeister, Moores and Ellenberger (1975). Each sign was translated into its closest English equivalent and the same English gloss was used for all occurrences of any given sign. It should be noted that the English gloss is merely a symbol for the sign and is usually neither syntactically nor semantically equivalent to its English gloss. At the conclusion, every SL sentence was considered to be natural, grammatical and semantically interpretable by native signers from the Newcastle deaf community. The original 24 sentences were also 'translated' into standard English using the closest, most common English equivalent.

A written form of sign language looks very different and rather strange — a problem that Dr Conrad refers to in Chapter 1 when he mentions that sign languages cannot easily (if at all) be represented in print. Whilst a written version of SL is very strange, and the author would not want to advocate its use in the classroom, for the purposes of the present study it did allow for language structure to be controlled for, without confounding presentation medium (written versus manual), in order to discover whether language form alone affected the deaf children's ability to process and remember the sentences. Consequently a great deal of time and care was taken in the translation and compilation of the collection of sentences used. Four experienced teachers of the deaf were consulted throughout the procedure, including a bilingual individual whose parents are deaf and had been pupils at the NCSD. Four ex-pupils of the school were also used to judge the acceptability of the translated sentences. Only after extensive discussion with all 8 local 'experts' were those sentence constructions, which they felt to be typical and correct, according to the 'rules' of British Sign Language, included. (The full set of sentences is shown in the Appendix to this chapter.)

The 48 deaf adolescents were divided into two groups by allocating three individuals from each class to one group and the remaining three to the other group, matching the two groups for reading ability. Each person was tested individually and read 24 sentences presented one at a time — 8 sentences were written in SE, 8 in DE, and 8 in SL. The order of presentation of the sentence was random with regard to language form. Each stimulus card with a single sentence written upon it was viewed for 20 seconds, followed immediately afterwards by a period of 30 seconds of unrelated mental activity — straightforward addition sums (e.g. $33 + 18 = ?$). When the 30-second interval had ended, one group was required to attempt a verbatim recall of the sentence, whilst the other group was required to recognise which of four alternatives they had previously been shown — a multiple-choice task. The four alternatives consisted of the SE, SL and DE forms of the sentence (one of which had been presented), and the fourth alternative was a distractor item, which somehow differed in meaning and was obviously wrong (e.g. the 'opposite' or 'negative' meaning was conveyed). This distractor item did however include approximately the same words as the other three choices, and was included to test whether the deaf adolescents had understood the meaning of the sentences they had read, or whether they were merely guessing — one would expect 25 per cent to be correct by chance alone.

The recognition and recall groups were scored independently. For each individual, and for each group, the total number of correct answers was recorded by language form. This scoring was 'blind' and was undertaken by an ex-pupil of the school.

Results

Preliminary analyses revealed no significant sex differences and thus boys and girls were combined in all subsequent analyses.

Table 3.1: Mean Recognition and Recall Scores as a Function of
Language Form

	Language form		
	SE	DE	SL
Recognition group[a]			
Mean score:	6.1	6.0	7.3
Recall group[a]			
Mean score:	2.8	2.9	5.3

Notes: Maximum score = 8
[a] There were 24 subjects in each group

Group Data Reference to Table 3.1 shows a marked difference in the mean scores of the memory recognition and recall groups: recognition performance was consistently better than recall performance over all three language forms, but the difference was reduced for sentences written and presented in SL. The mean scores for both recall and recognition of sentences presented in SE and DE were very similar, and were lower than for sentences presented in SL. The distribution of the recognition and recall scores for the sentences written in SE, DE and SL is clearly shown in Figure 3.1.

A randomised blocks analysis of variance was performed on the transformed scores (an arc sine transformation was used) of the recognition and recall groups separately. No significant difference between subjects was found in either the recognition or the recall group. Performance of both groups did, however, differ significantly according to language form ($F(2,46) = 10.7$, $p < .001$ for recognition; $F(2,46) = 14.5$, $p < .001$ for recall). Orthogonal comparisons of the SL and SE/DE treatments showed a significant difference in favour of SL for both recognition $F(1,46) = 21.28$, $p < .001$) and recall groups

Figure 3.1: Recognition and Recall Scores as a Function of Language Form

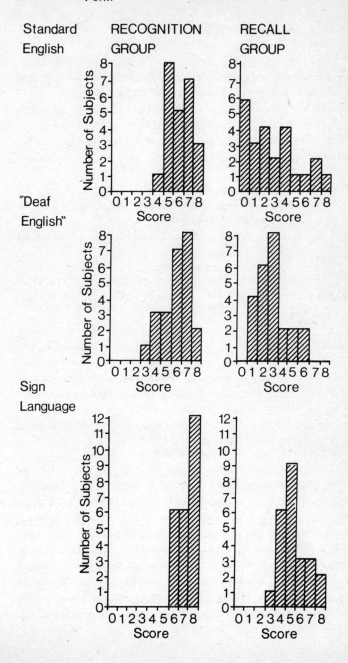

$(F(1,46) = 27.51, p < .001)$. Neither group, however, showed any difference between the SE and DE treatments.

Individual Data A detailed study of the memory performance of individual subjects showed that in the *recognition group*, 12 (that is half the group) recognised all the SL sentences correctly; 3 recognised all the SE sentences correctly; 2 recognised all the DE sentences correctly. In the recall group, 2 recalled all the SL sentences correctly and no one scored less than 3; 1 person recalled all the SE sentences correctly; 6 were unable to recall any of the SE sentences correctly; and 3 were only able to recall one SE sentence correctly. No one recalled all the DE sentences correctly.

Table 3.2:   The Changes of Language Form, between Sentence
             Presentation and Subsequent Recognition of the 99
             Sentences Incorrectly Recognised

		Language form of presented sentence			
		SE	DE	SL	TOTALS
	SE	-	29	7	36 sentences were 'corrected' to SE
Language form of sentence subsequently 'recognised'	DE	22	-	11	33 sentences were 'corrected' to DE
	SL	12	18	-	30 sentences were 'corrected' to SL

Sentences which were incorrectly recognised or recalled (by the criterion that the sentence produced from memory did not match the sentence input into memory) were of particular interest. In the recognition group a total of 99 sentences (17 per cent) were incorrectly recognised (see Table 3.2). Out of a total of 576 recognition responses, the distractor item was chosen only on 12 occasions (11 after presentation of SE sentences and 1 after a DE sentence). These results from the recognition group were not very illuminating since the alternative language forms were actually presented for the subjects to choose between. When the original form of the sentence was not correctly recognised by the deaf subjects, they showed no preference for selecting either of the alternative forms (Sign test (Siegel, 1956) x = 12,

$z = 1.55$, $p < .05$ when the original sentence had been presented in SE; $x = 18$, $z = 1.46$, $p < .05$ when DE; and $x = 7$, $z = 0.7$, $p < .05$, when SL).

The recall group recalled 313 of the 576 sentences (54 per cent) incorrectly, and of these, 71 were recalled in the exact words of one of the other language forms, not previously seen by the subjects (see Table 3.3). It is interesting to note that all of the 10 sentences corrected to SE could be attributed to just three individuals from the group of 24. The 15 sentences which were 'corrected' to DE provide further evidence of the generation of typical 'deafisms'. The vast majority of the sentences (65 per cent) were 'corrected' to SL in spite of instructions, that were clearly understood, to recall the *exact* form of each sentence presented. When either SE or DE sentences were forgotten, significantly more subjects recalled the exact SL form than the alternative form (Sign test: $x = 14$, $z = 2.0$, $p = .04$ when the original sentence had been presented in SE, and $x = 7$, $p < .05$ when presented in DE).

Table 3.3: The Changes in Language Form, between Sentence Presentation and Subsequent Recall, of the 77 'Corrected' Sentences of the Recall Group

		Language form of Presented sentence			
		SE	DE	SL	TOTALS
Language form of sentence recalled	SE	-	7[a]	3[a]	10 sentences were 'corrected' to SE[a]
	DE	14	-	1	15 sentences were 'corrected' to DE
	SL	28	18	-	46 sentences were 'corrected' to SL

Note: [a] Only 3 individuals from the group of 24 adolescents contributed to this score.

The grammatical errors made in the written recall of the 126 SE sentences which were not correctly recalled (out of the total of 192 SE sentences presented), were classified according to type. By far the most frequent error made by these deaf adolescents was the incorrect use of verb tense which occurred in 55 of the 126 sentences; the infinitive or present tense was most frequently substituted for the actual verb tense of the original sentence. In 24 sentences, a preposition was omitted, and in a further 14, an incorrect preposition was substituted. The indirect article was omitted on 24 occasions, and the direct article on a further 13. In 24 of the sentences a noun was used in the singular instead of the plural. Other errors, such as the use of the incorrect possessive, the omission of possessives and word order reversal were also recorded, but occurred less freuqnetly.

Discussion

The deaf adolescents predictably found it more difficult to recall the sentences, rather than merely recognise which sentence they had previously been shown, as has previously been found with hearing subjects (McDougall, 1904; Postman and Rau, 1957; Bruce and Cofer, 1965). The results from the recall task were more interesting than those from the recognition task, since the deaf subjects had actually produced the form of each response sentence themselves, and if these responses were more than rote memory of meaningless strings of words, then they should reflect an internal system of generative linguistic rules.

The results clearly showed that the deaf adolescents' ability to recall the SE sentences was very poor, with fewer than 35 per cent correctly recalled. One might, therefore, be tempted to conclude from this result that these individuals need to use English syntax more effectively as an aid to recall. An alternative and more likely conclusion would be that these results reflect a greater and more basic problem associated with inability of this particular group of deaf adolescents to use and process SE adequately. Even after reading a short sentence written in English, the majority were unable to remember the simplest of grammatical constructions. Compare this, however, with 66 per cent correct recall of sentences written in SL. A similar pattern of results also emerged for the recognition group, although more sentences were correctly recognised than correctly recalled. SL sentences were both significantly better recognised and recalled than either the SE or the DE sentences, which suggests that SL was being processed more efficiently by these deaf adolescents than either DE or SE.

Length of sentence, however, was a confounding variable. Since SL is less redundant, the SL sentences were generally shorter than the other sentences, an average of 4.5 words per sentence written in SL,

3. *Psycholinguistic Processes in the Prelingually Deaf*

compared to 6.0 and 6.1 for the DE and SE sentences, respectively. A memory span factor may, therefore, have been operating, which could explain the similar performance scores for the DE and SE sentences, and the better performance for SL, on the basis of sentence length alone. The number of words in a single sentence ranged from 3 to 9, but a close examination of the results showed that the deaf subjects had been able to remember SL sentences which were up to 8 words long, and yet had failed to remember short sentences of 4 words written in SE and DE. Number of words in the sentence (when all the sentences were relatively short) did not, therefore, appear to be as important as differences in language form, in determining relative ease of subsequent recall or recognition.

To the extent that recall and recognition reflect ability to process English, these deaf adolescents did not appear to be as much at home in SE as in SL. The experimenter certainly observed many of them, during test administration, using signs, and also fingerspelling the occasional word. Presumably, therefore, a deaf person who uses SL brings to the acquisition of English many skills and grammatical structures which may well influence cognitive processing. The recall of the SE sentences may, therefore, have been mediated by SL. The differential recall as a function of language form, in favour of SL, supports the suggestion, made by Odom and Blanton (1967), that deaf children might be able to process SL in memory, since they did not seem able to process and recall English as well as hearing children; and also corroborates their experimental findings (Odom and Blanton, 1970).

The overall group results showed that the deaf adolescents were better able to recall the SL sentences than those written in DE and SE. Whilst this was true for the majority of the group, there were three individuals whose performance was in the opposite direction. They were better able to recall SE sentences than those written in SL; these three individuals were responding more like the hearing controls studied by Odom and Blanton (1967, 1970). They also 'corrected' 10 sentences to SE when they had been presented with sentences written in DE or SL. These individuals, at least, were sufficiently familiar with simple grammatical constructions in English to be able to transform the original input into correct, grammatical English, although not specifically requested to do so. It would have been interesting to discover whether, in fact, they had consciously switched to SE, or whether the correction had been unconsciously made during processing. Unfortunately, it is not easy to get a deaf child to introspect usefully on his/her activities, and it was not, therefore, possible to discover this information. One clear fact that did emerge, however, was that these corrections were not the result of a basic lack of understanding of the instructions on the part of the subjects concerned, and they were seemingly unaware of their 'mistakes'.

There was nothing that was obviously different in the background, the hearing losses or the linguistic competence of these few deaf individuals to explain why, or how, the differences might have arisen, but it is clear that it is exceptional cases such as these who should be studied in detail in the future, in an attempt to discover the developmental factors contributing to their success. For it is the goal of everyone who is involved in teaching language to deaf children to improve their competence in English — spoken and written — and their ability to read. When such 'successes' occur, they should not be dismissed as surprising exceptions, instead teachers need to be aware of, and understand, the reasons for both the apparent successes and, conversely, possible causes of failure to develop verbal language.

'Deaf English'

The results clearly showed that neither group was able to remember the DE sentences better than those written in SE, as was hypothesised. In fact both the recognition and the recall scores for the DE and the SE sentences were very close and significantly lower than those for the recognition and recall of SL. There was no apparent difference in the deaf adolescents' ability to process the DE and SE sentences. This finding corroborates that of Charrow (1975) who also reported that DE was not processed very efficiently by deaf children, and no more effectively than SE. Thus the 'deafisms' which seemed to be typical, did not appear to be a non-standard English dialect common to a group of deaf people, even within a single school. The ungrammatical errors that were repeatedly generated by the deaf adolescents were not subsequently reproduced accurately in memory. It would perhaps be interesting to repeat the above experiment on a more individualised basis, to discover whether individuals would always recall the non-standard grammatical features which they persistently generate.

It is interesting to speculate about the origin of 'deaf English' and to consider why these recurrent non-standard features, that are so resistant to correction, and which remain even after years of being taught English in school, should arise in written English. How does 'deaf English' originate? One is still, I believe, justified in using the term, if only to identify and describe the forms of non-standard English generated by deaf people. There have been a few recent attempts to explain why deaf children make the errors they do.

The nature and occurrence of these errors suggest two possibilities:
1. Linguistic interference from sign language; as Ivimey (1977, p. 93) writes, the major difficulty in perceiving language is '. . . not so much in the sensory modality involved in communication as in the structure of the cognitive model they bring to the communicative act'. Certainly most of the mistakes analysed in the sample of 'deaf English' collected for this study, and most of the grammatical errors made by the group of deaf children in the recall of the SE sentences, involved verb tense, omission or incorrect use of prepositions, and the omission of both definite and indefinite articles. The same types of error have been reported by other investigators (for example Ivimey, 1976; Quigley, Montanelli and Wilbur, 1976; Wilbur, 1977) and yet would be rarely observed in the written language of hearing adolescents of average or above-average intellectual ability. Verb tenses are not conveyed in the same way in sign language as in English (see Brennan in this volume), and prepositions and articles are used less frequently. The source of many of the errors may, therefore, be traced back to sign language, suggesting some kind of linguistic interference from the children's knowledge of sign language.
2. Lack of sufficient experience of the correct form; Moores (1974) suggested that deaf English may be attributed to lack of adequate instruction in English, and does not accept the possibility of interference from signs.

The first of these two possibilities might warrant the use of the term 'deafisms' as suggested by Myklebust (1964); and the second, the term 'learningisms'. This latter term was suggested by Ivimey (1977) who reports that young children such as Adam and Eve (Brown and Bellugi, 1964) and immigrant children, as well as deaf children, all make similar mistakes, and futhermore that they all share a common lack of exposure to English. He writes: 'Thus we may conclude that instead of regarding the mistakes made by the deaf as "deafisms", arising from their specific handicap, or through the medium of communication used in their education, it would be more appropriate to see them as "learningisms" ' (p. 98). Ivimey, unfortunately, does not extend this idea further as an explanation, and whilst it is probably not a complete explanation of the kind of mistakes that are found in deaf children's written language, the concept of 'learningisms' should help us to understand why, after innumerable corrections, many deaf children continue to make the same mistake repeatedly. An example from McNeill (1966, p. 69) will elaborate this point — it is an exchange between a mother and her child.

C   'Nobody don't like me'
M   'No, say "nobody likes me" '
C   'Nobody don't like me'
        "
        "
eight repetitions of this dialogue
M   'No, now listen carefully, say "nobody likes me" '
C   'Oh! Nobody don't likes me'

This dialogue is a good illustration of the relative impenetrability of a child's grammar to the adult's grammar, in spite of numerous repetitions. Even when the mother emphasised the distinction saying 'No, now listen carefully, say "nobody likes me" ', the child was still unable to imitate this sequence of three words. When the grammatical transformation is beyond the child's linguistic competence, imitation and repetition appear to be of limited value. Normal hearing children gradually develop and achieve adult grammatical competence in English, i.e. they are able to generate an infinite number of grammatically correct sentences. This, then, is where the similarity must surely end, for the deaf child rarely arrives at the point of linguistic competence where grammatical English is easily produced. We can, however, draw from present knowledge and understanding of linguistics and language development, to help understand further the situation regarding the learning of verbal language by deaf children. The bizarre sentence constructions of many deaf people may reflect the underlying linguistic rules used to generate them. This being the case, no amount of correction, or drilling of surface structure, therefore, will improve the deaf child's ability to generate grammatical English (as shown in the example quoted by McNeill, 1966) when the linguistic rules governing the transformation from deep to surface structure are responsible for language output. It is at the transformational level that one should perhaps seek for, and find, differences between deaf and hearing children.

If correct English syntax is not achieved after ten or more years of special education under the present system, it is unlikely ever to be so. It would seem inconceivable that many of the simpler rules of English grammar are not assimilated, despite access to correct written English and repeated correction, unless one accepts that the errors are more than 'learningisms'. Moores (1974), and possibly Ivimey (1977), too, seem to be denying the deaf children's fluent knowledge of sign language, and ignoring, or underestimating, their intrinsic linguistic abilities. When a hearing person is learning a foreign language, for example French, it may be frequently observed that native knowledge of one's own language initially interferes with one's written or spoken production of the foreign language. Similarly, it is likely that native knowledge of sign language would also interfere in an equivalent manner. Knowledge of sign language, including the structural features of sign language, could influence cognitive functioning and be responsible for the linguistic rules and the transformational grammar that generates non-standard English. Those who deny that sign language may ever constitute a child's first and primary language clearly cannot contemplate the possibility of such a source of interference.

Brasel and Quigley (1977) have also recently studied the influence of certain language and communication environments in early childhood on the development of language in deaf individuals. They recognise that early language input influences the child's developing language ability, and found that when the language was ASL this interfered with the children's ability to learn the grammatical rules of SE. The main difference between their study and the present one is that Brasel and Quigley refer specifically to ASL and in the present investigation the language was a dialect of British Sign Language. It would appear that deaf children draw on their knowledge of sign language when their environment includes models of this language and that this can subsequently affect verbal language development. Similarly, Tervoort (1975) has also suggested that knowledge of SL might be a possible source of interference. Using the example of a deaf child signing: 'Mad you me not', in which the signs for all four words are simultaneously present, Tervoort comments that correct English word order has little, or no, reality for the particular child concerned. It is, however, the contention of the present author that early acquisition of SL need not of necessity interfere with subsequent verbal language development, and that the cause of the observed interference from SL might be found in current language teaching practices. This idea will be further developed in the following section.

At the present time, then, researchers appear to be more or less agreed on the nature of the language problems of many deaf children, and the type or errors that are repeatedly generated, but are still at a speculative level regarding the origin of 'deaf English'. The hypothesis has been put forward here that the errors in deaf written language are both the result of 'learningisms' and 'deafisms', and not either one, or the other, as previously suggested by Ivimey (1977). Both would appear to be inextricably linked in the language development of deaf children. This idea must, however, remain a possibility until further more detailed data are available concerning the syntax of British Sign Language.

Language Teaching Methods

The present findings suggested that SE appeared to be like a foreign language to many of the deaf adolescents who were tested. The majority seemed to be more at home using, and processing, SL. Teachers of the deaf can no longer afford to ignore the evidence that many deaf children use SL to mediate between the world of the classroom, where verbal language skills are taught and emphasised, and their own internal thought processes. It is still the case, however, that few teachers acknowledge, or make use of, competence in SL. English is largely taught to the deaf using English as the teaching medium, as if it were their first and native language, when, for most individuals in a residential school setting, it obviously is not. It has to be remembered that many deaf children begin school at the age of two or three. At this early age the basic need to communicate is such, that the young deaf children often quickly acquire sign language from the few deaf children who have deaf parents, and who have been surrounded by sign language communication, at home, since birth. In a residential community, therefore, the difference in communication abilities between the deaf children of deaf parents and those of hearing parents is rapidly and considerably reduced. By the time such children reach their teens they are all fluent users of SL, whatever their home background. This knowledge of sign language, in some cases native, and in all cases fluent, may be a further possible factor contributing to the deaf children's inability to acquire the level of competence in verbal language that one might hope for from the amount of classroom teaching, in terms of both hours and years, that has been aimed at developing this language competence. The efforts are sadly not reflected in the majority of the deaf children's knowledge and use of English, as Conrad's (1979) findings have also shown. Some deaf adolescents appear to remain better able to use and process SL than SE.

It may be then that the underlying principles of language teaching methods used in deaf education are at fault, and that failure of the majority of deaf children to develop proficiency in verbal language may primarily be due to shortcomings in instruction, and not due to inherent learning or linguistic difficulties of the deaf. In fact, Brennan (1976) published a significant paper in which she examines some of the linguistic assumptions on which these methods are based. She argues that 'Many of the principles underlying the methods of deaf education are totally unrelated to linguistic facts and are frequently at variance with present insights into the processes of language acquisition and the nature of language' (p. 11). A linguistic evaluation of the situation together with the experimental evidence presented both here and elsewhere (e.g. Conrad, 1979) are surely sufficient to warrant a reappraisal of the language teaching methodology. No teacher in Britain would teach a foreign language to a hearing child ignoring the child's knowledge of English; the foreign language (L2) is taught using English (L1) as the teaching medium. Perhaps then English could be more effectively taught to deaf children on the same principles, as an L2, drawing on the theory of foreign language teaching, and using SL as a language base, the L1, to teach English. Such an approach would be similar to teaching SL to hearing people, (only in reverse) where SL is taught as a foreign language, and as Ingram (1977) observes, sign language instructors have been forced to look 'to the heritage of second language teaching for more effective methods and materials' (p. 3).

In fact, as long ago as 1958, Fusfeld suggested that 'The task of acquiring language in the case of the deaf child is very much like our attempting to learn a foreign language' (Fusfeld, 1958, p. 258). This idea that English is like a foreign language to deaf children has subsequently been endorsed by Charrow and Fletcher (1974), who found that deaf children of deaf parents who used ASL at home, scored higher on the 'Test of English as a Foreign Language' than deaf children of hearing parents.

Perhaps the time has come for deaf educators to consider seriously some of the practical suggestions that are being made both in the US by Stokoe (1975), and, more recently in this country, by Brennan (1977), who are advocating that teachers should teach English via sign language. Clearly there are a number of deaf children who could benefit considerably from such an approach. It is clear that educators of the deaf cannot afford to be unaware of the advances of knowledge in linguistics, particularly in the field of language learning, which corresponds so directly to their particular problems and needs.

Throughout the present investigation emphasis was placed on the effect of language form on ability to process and either recognise or recall simple written language. It is likely, however, that the effect of modality is far greater. SL, by its very nature, is very different from written English. It would be interesting therefore to repeat the study presenting SL sentences manually and require the sentences to be recalled in SL. The facilitative effect of SL on memory processing is likely to be even greater under these conditions. And, as research into the syntax of BSL progresses (see Woll and Brennan in this volume), it should become possible to undertake a further, detailed linguistic analysis of the written language of deaf individuals and relate this to our increased understanding of the structure of SL.

The requirement of exact recognition or recall of sentences from memory in the present study was a necessary prerequisite for an investigation of the possible sources of linguistic interference during cognitive processing. In everyday life, however, it is normally quite sufficient to recall the content of a message without necessarily retaining its original, formal linguistic structure. The experimental requirement of exact recall may, therefore, have placed excessive and unnatural demands on the deaf adolescents; could they understand more verbal language than they were able to reproduce? It is generally accepted amongst teachers of foreign language that receptive skills make fewer demands than productive skills (e.g. Brooks, 1964; Pit Corder, 1973). This possibility was investigated in a subsequent study in which comprehension of short stories written in SE and SL was assessed. The same deaf adolescents were tested and it was found that they understood stories written in SL significantly better, as judged by the number of comprehension questions correctly answered, compared with matched stories written in SE. Hearing control subjects on the other hand performed consistently better on the SE stories than those written in SL (Dawson, 1979). The results of these two experiments taken together clearly demonstrate that at least for one particular sample of deaf adolescents the structure of SL, even when presented in an unnatural written form, facilitated both memory processing and comprehension of simple language. Such a finding must lead the psychologist to ask the question of educationalists: Does the fact that nearly all linguistic input in the classroom is SE affect the amount of information, in particular general knowledge, that is learned by deaf children whilst at school? This question clearly needs further urgent consideration by both psychologists and educationalists alike.

Acknowledgements

The author would like to acknowledge her gratitude to the Headmaster, staff and pupils of the Northern Counties School for the Deaf, Newcastle upon Tyne. This research was supported by the Social Science Research Council.

APPENDIX: The Different Language Forms of the 24 Sentences used in the Study

Note: The italic sentences are the distractor sentences that were used in the recognition task.

		Language Form:
1	a. The boy kick the dog.	DE
	b. *The dog kicked the boy*.	
	c. Boy kick dog.	SL
	d. The boy kicked the dog.	SE
2	a. We late, London.	SL
	b. We arrived late in London.	SE
	c. *We left London late*.	
	d. We arrive to London late.	DE
3	a. *How much does it cost?*	
	b. How much money you got?	DE
	c. Money you got, how much?	SL
	d. How much money have you got?	SE
4	a. We walked two miles yesterday.	SE
	b. Yesterday we two miles walk.	SL
	c. Yesterday we walking two miles.	DE
	d. *Tomorrow we will walk two miles*.	
5	a. Last night I see monster on T.V.	DE
	b. *Last night I saw T.V. on the monster*.	
	c. See monster, last night, T.V.	SL
	d. Last night I saw a monster on the T.V.	SE

		Language Form:
6	a. I have enjoy self.	DE
	b. I have enjoyed myself.	SE
	c. *I have not enjoyed myself.*	
	d. I enjoy self a lot.	SL
7	a. *Where is your school?*	
	b. Where you live?	SL
	c. Where you lived?	DE
	d. Where do you live?	SE
8	a. I want to go to the library to read.	SE
	b. I want go library read book.	SL
	c. *I want to read the library in the book.*	
	d. I wanting go to library, read book.	DE
9	a. I am fed-up to obey you.	DE
	b. I am fed-up of obeying you.	SE
	c. *You must obey me.*	
	d. I fed-up obey you.	SL
10	a. My little brother, home, hate.	SL
	b. *My little brother hates home.*	
	c. I hate my little brother at home.	SE
	d. I am hate with little brother at home.	DE
11	a. My father and uncle have same face like twins.	DE
	b. *My father and uncle are twins.*	
	c. My father and uncle look like twins.	SE
	d. My father, my uncle look like same.	SL
12	a. I watched a bad film.	SE
	b. I watch bad film.	SL
	c. *I watched an awful film.*	
	d. I watched bad films.	DE
13	a. It is my birthday today.	SE
	b. *Is it my birthday today?*	
	c. My birthday, today	SL
	d. I am birthday today.	DE

Language
Form:

14 a. I like visit in his school.   DE
   b. *He likes to visit my school.*
   c. I like to visit his school.   SE
   d. I like see his school.   SL

15 a. *I went home in a ship.*
   b. I go over water, in ship.   SL
   c. I went abroad in a ship.   SE
   d. I went to abroad in ship.   DE

16 a. I can swim as well as you can.   SE
   b. I can swim same as you.   DE
   c. *I cannot swim as well as you can.*
   d. I swim, same you.   SL

17 a. Mother puts cake in oven to cooking.   DE
   b. Mother put cake in oven, cook.   SL
   c. *Mother puts a pie in the oven to cook.*
   d. Mother puts a cake in the oven to cook.   SE

18 a. *Her favourite lesson was sewing.*
   b. Her favourite lesson is sewing.   SE
   c. Her favourite, sewing.   SL
   d. She likes best lesson is sewing.   DE

19 a. He has two cats, one big, one small.   SL
   b. *He used to have a cat and a kitten.*
   c. He has a cat and a kitten.   SE
   d. He has one cat, one kitten.   DE

20 a. I sometimes wearing a short dress.   DE
   b. I sometimes wear a short dress.   SE
   c. I sometimes wear short dress.   SL
   d. *I sometimes wear a long dress.*

21 a. I have been take my friend to park.   DE
   b. *I took my boy-friend to the park.*
   c. I took my friend to the park.   SE
   d. I take friend, go park.   SL

		Language Form:
22	a. The child likes to play with sand.	SE
	b. Child like play sand.	SL
	c. The child likes play with sand.	DE
	d. *The children like to play with sand.*	
23	a. *It was raining hard so we went home.*	
	b. Little rain, we went home.	SL
	c. It was little rain so we went home.	DE
	d. It was raining a little so we went home.	SE
24	a. I paid 8 pence for the chips.	SE
	b. I pay 8 pence, chips.	SL
	c. *I did not pay for the chips.*	
	d. I pay 8 pence to the chips.	DE

4 SIGNS AND MEMORY: THE SEARCH FOR THE CODE*

James Kyle

While a large part of the reports in this book concern language, a very large area of language use still remains to be investigated. It is a part of this area which I wish to consider.

> In speaking of Language, we must remember that what primarily concerns the psychologist is not any special system of external signs such as gestures, articulate sounds or written characters, but a certain psychical function — a peculiar mode of mental activity. (p. 459)

This was written by G.F. Stout and is drawn from a discussion on the sign language of deaf people. What is remarkable is that it was written in 1899. He accurately discriminates gestures in isolation, from the language of sign since it is only in the language that concepts may be analysed. He draws on an earlier account by a deaf man, Kruse, of the importance of sign language:

> What strikes [the deaf man] most or what makes a distinction to him between one thing and another [is that] such distinctive signs of objects (i.e. gestures) are at once signs by which he knows these objects and knows them again — they become tokens of things. And while he elaborates the signs he has found for single objects, that is, while he describes their forms for himself in the air, or imitates them in thought with hands, fingers and gestures, he develops for himself suitable signs to represent ideas which serve him as a means of fixing ideas of different kinds in his mind, and recalling them to his memory. And thus he makes himself a language . . . a way for thought is already broken and with his thought as it now opens out, the language cultivates and forms itself further and further. (quoted Tylor, 1878, pp. 19-20)

* Research has been supported by Department of Health and Social Security Grant: 'Sign Language Learning and Use', 1978-81.

71

This account was originally written before 1865 and it quite clearly describes the development of a *sign code*, a *way of thinking in sign*. Klima and Bellugi in 1979 are just as adamant about deaf people's ideas of sign use:

> Deaf parents tell us that their children sign to themselves in their sleep — we have observed deaf toddlers signing to themselves, and their toy animals before bedtime, when they thought they were alone. . . . We have seen deaf people repeating a grocery list in sign, and signing to make clear to themselves something read in English. Deaf people tell us they dream in signs, plan conversations in signs . . . (p. 89)

and they asked the question which is the concern of this section:

> Is this inner 'voice' in the hands related to the way deaf people process the symbols of their language? (p. 89)

Is this a code similar to the code of hearing people in their inner speech? If it is then all we need to do is substitute signs for speech. The importance of the question lies in the link between inner speech and reading in the developing hearing child — how could a sign code based on the different structure of sign language fit into the sequential pattern of written English?

Despite Vernon's (1967) claims for the equality of deaf people in thinking, early researchers chose to equate language use with intelligence and consequently classified deaf people as of low ability with only concrete thought.

The whole question of how language, whether in speech or sign, is related to thinking is a very complex one and psychologists have only recently begun to reconsider it in relation to the notion of representation. It is suggested that language forms a very important basis for storage of real life events. The nature of this storage and its organisation has become a focus in attempts to examine how thinking and memory work. If deaf people's storage and organisation is different then there is some likelihood that their thinking will somehow be different. But if the organisation or representation of meaning can be shown to be similar then one expects their intellectual and cognitive capacities to be equivalent to that of hearing people. The differences may then be seen only in expression in sign language.

Research which bears on this question may be examined under three headings: (a) Representation and Organisation in Semantic Memory; (b) Neurophysiological Evidence; and (c) Short-term Memory.

Representation and Organisation in Semantic Memory

Myklebust (1964) has suggested that there exists an 'organismic shift' which arises due to deaf people's different experience of the world. This suggests that deaf people in looking at the world see and organise it in a different way; they extract features which emphasise the patterns of movement and use these as a way of classifying. Meadow (1976) claims that deaf people are more likely to request specific examples in explanation rather than vague references (although this must be contributed to by hearing people's poor use of sign language), and show characteristics of different perceptual organisation. Green and Shepherd (1975) using a technique called the Semantic Differential (which tries to examine the system we use for meaning, by obtaining ratings of a range of concepts) found some differences between deaf and hearing children. Two major factors were in common (Evaluation and Potency), but the presence of an organisational system based on sensory judgement with respect to vision and touch in deaf children, differed from that found in hearing children. A factor concerning abstract shades of meaning was found in hearing but not in deaf children. However, at least some of the differences may be attributed to the study's reliance on written tests for these profoundly deaf children.

Hans Furth (1966) takes up this theme in his work claiming that deaf people's performance on standard tests is different because of their lack of experience of the concepts which have been primarily learned through speech. His particular concern is that deaf people's performance can only be accurately examined when spoken language variables are reduced and under these conditions deaf people perform as well as hearing people. Oleron (1977), while producing a number of studies showing deaf children poorer at problem-solving tasks, acknowledges the role of spoken language experience. The nature of this evidence suggests that deaf people's performance is at a disadvantage, but this is primarily, due to the difference in language experience.

However, this difference does not mean that features of representation similar to hearing people are not seen. Green and Shepherd (1975) did find many features in common. Both the major dimensions of Evaluation and Potency were found in their deaf children. Moulton and Beasley (1975) in a learning task showed an effect of the semantic associations between words, a feature also of the performance of hearing people.

Work specifically using sign language, paradoxically, tends to reinforce the similarities between deaf and hearing people's organisation when considered at the highest category levels; that is, we all use concepts similarly though we express them in a different way. Newport and Bellugi (1978), in looking at category membership in ASL, show this very clearly. Rosch, Mervis, Gray, Johnson and Boyes-Braem (1976) had previously suggested there may be major differences in categorical structure. While there are no single signs for categories such as 'parents' or 'tool' or 'furniture', compound signs made up of individual examples carry the meaning of the category:

CLASS	SIGN COMPOUND
PARENTS	MOTHER, FATHER
TOOL	HAMMER, SCREWDRIVER
PEOPLE	MAN, WOMAN
FURNITURE	TABLE, CHAIR

The compounds when signed, are slightly shorter in execution than the individual signs would be and can be shown to vary in movement. On initial examination it seems that this is also true in BSL, so that although the way of expressing categories is different, compounds equivalent to the category name are still used, and may perform a similar role in organisation.

Siple, Fischer and Bellugi (1977), in a direct study of recognition memory based on longer term storage, suggest that signs from ASL are encoded and stored in memory like lexical items from any other language. This means reliance on closeness in meaning as a way of storing information permanently and this is exactly what spoken language seem to do. Items sharing meaning are stored closely together and are often substituted for one another. The major point is, however, that the access to the representation appears to be primarily in sign.

A final aspect which reflects organisation in longer-term memory is the production and reception of language and this has been studied in relation to the reading and writing of deaf people. Quigley (1979) reviews some of the work in this field which highlights the weakness of deaf children in English grammar. In a series of studies he showed that awareness of syntactic rules is considerably less well developed in deaf children. In both reading and writing deaf children have difficulty attributing the actions to the agent, and appear to use simple linear rules based on key words. Extracts of writing reflect the problem:

> One day a boy help boy, boy ran fast. Man came barn boy. Man help boy a water. Man hold boy. Boy is happy. (p. 291)

A translation into sign language would aid understanding of this. Savage (1978), too, emphasises these points in a study of handwriting. In a brief examination of two deaf adults' written comments on research on deafness, I noted that 58 per cent of the errors were due to the use of an incorrect verb form, e.g. '. . . that they have *pick* up but when *ask* the meaning of . . .'; 28 per cent were due to an incorrect article, 'a', or 'the'; while only 7 per cent were due to incorrect spelling. This tends to support the notion that BSL syntax is being used to present the idea, even when it is to be written with English words. It is then apparent that the different form of tense marking for verbs and the absence of articles in sign are reflected in the writing.

Sorensen and Hansen (1976) have noted the looser structure of Danish Sign Language and have found syntax to follow 'object-subject-verb' order rather than 'subject-verb-object' as in spoken Danish. The type of writing produced by deaf children could be claimed to be explicable in terms of a direct transfer of one language code into the other's vocabulary. This is particularly likely where knowledge of the use of the second language is limited.

However, Quigley *et al.* (1976a) suggest that it is often deaf children's attempts to use an inappropriate sentence frame which creates the problem. 'Subject-verb-object' is a rule built up through long school practice and represents an aspect of our overlaying of the child's natural language to try to build the rules of the second language, English. This would contrast with a system which tried to reinforce the concepts of the first language, but show how they can be differently used in the second language of written English.

Ulijn (1977) has done some experimental work on reading in a second language. Dutch students had to read instructions in French which were written to be similar to (cf. BSL), or to contrast with (cf. Signed English), Dutch sentence structure. There was no consistent effect of the syntax on the comprehension of the text. Ulijn concludes that syntax *per se* is not a determining feature in comprehension in the second language. In the UK our attitudes towards bilingualism have always been loaded with concern, while other nations have had to accept the problems of second language learning and use. Our knowledge of bilingualism and how to teach children with a different cultural background and experience is relatively new. It largely derives from the greater numbers of immigrants into the UK. We often find their language skills are much weaker when faced with English texts and problems, and that some allowances must be made in their education. Equally, we have spent very little time examining the native language competence and capacity of deaf children while spending a great deal of time exploring their deficiency in what will inevitably be their second language.

The study of organisation in memory and the little we know of sign language use, reinforces the idea of difference between deaf people and hearing people in the way their system is used, but a similarity at the core in terms of categorisation and the use of meaning. Although syntax is different it is not disordered and the development of a second language competence is not disallowed by the structure of his first language. Related to the question of whether there is a difference in the type of processing, is whether this is an inevitable consequence of hearing loss, or whether it is due to our inability to establish the English language in deaf children through education as Bench (1979) claims. A growing amount of neurophysiological work is relevant to this question.

Neurophysiological Evidence

Kyle (1978, 1980a) has considered some of the available evidence on auditory deprivation from birth. It has been known for some time that visual deprivation over a period of time from birth, produces deterioration of the capability for higher-level processing of visual information (Zubeck, 1969). When cats are reared in dark environments their subsequent ability to use their visual sense is seriously impaired, even though they are exposed to normal lighting conditions for a long period of time. Gregory and Wallace (1963) indicate the likelihood of the same problem in humans in a well-quoted study of a man who was given his sight later in life. He never really began to organise his visual world as a sighted person would. This idea is particularly relevant as it most closely parallels the situation where born-deaf children are later provided with a hearing aid which boosts their residual hearing capacity. The issue is whether auditory processing suffers from the same deterioration as vision when deprived of sound stimulation at a very early age.

A series of studies of animals deprived of sound at birth, by rearing them in sound-proofed surroundings, indicates that there are problems of perceiving sound at a later date, even when the animal is restored to normal hearing surroundings (Batkin *et al.*, 1970). Stein and Schuckman (1973) indicated that direct stimulation of the cortex after deprivation produced much poorer responses in the auditory cortex of animals deprived of sound. They claim that the difficulty arises at the cortical level where, it could be proposed, the processes of organisation and identification of complex sound takes place.

In a comprehensive review of a wider range of literature, Ruben and Rapin (1980), offer strong evidence on the importance of early sound stimulation in creating the necessary processing in the central nervous system. Their investigation covers anatomical, electrophysiological and behavioural evidence which argues that the development of the auditory system is centripetal. It develops from the inner ear to the auditory cortex so that the hearing environment determines cortical maturation for complex auditory function. Deprivation of this sound at an early age is effective in upsetting this normal growth in animals and according to Ruben and Rapin, '. . . one would be surprised if the same were not true for man, since his central nervous system continues to develop after birth'. The degree of this loss need not be total. Eisen (1962) describes the examination of a normally hearing seven-year-old who had middle-ear infections up to the age of three. His sound and speech discrimination was disturbed, and he appeared to have problems expressing his thoughts in words. Because of the start of sound processing at a very early age in the infant, any disturbances may have important effects. Skinner (1978) has indicated that at two weeks the infant can recognise the overall rhythmic patterns of speech and discrimination of intonation patterns is evident by eight months. Although these may be arguments for early diagnosis, Ruben and Rapin point out that even with a hearing aid a child's acoustic environment is abnormal. The implications are far reaching in that auditory-based skills such as those we use in teaching reading may be unavailable to deaf people and more consideration should be given to other language processing features available.

Ruben and Rapin do consider the cases of Victor (Lane, 1977) and Genie (Curtiss, 1977) where severe language deprivation produced serious problems of later spoken language learning. In Genie's case, even though her hearing was normal, there is evidence which suggests her language function became based in the right hemisphere of the brain rather than the left as it is with normal hearing people (Curtiss,

1977). It is very tempting to predict that deaf people relying primarily on visual/spatial information develop their language function in the right hemisphere, which is the locus of visual/spatial processing in the human being. It would certainly fit in with the difficulties in complex auditory/spoken language functions experienced by deaf people and be reinforced by the apparent ease with which most profoundly deaf people acquire sign language.

The research in this field is still in its infancy, but there are a number of relevant studies. The main approach has been to show linguistic and non-linguistic stimuli to either the right visual field (RVF) or to the left visual field (LVF), for very brief intervals of time. This is done by splitting an image into two components presented to different sides of the retina in the eye. The image projected to the RVF has direct access to the left hemisphere of the brain. The most common result has been of a weak superiority effect of language processing decision for deaf people, but very strong effects for hearing people where the left hemisphere is much quicker. In a task requesting people to judge whether a word flashed briefly corresponded to a sign (Ross *et al.*, 1979), deaf subjects performed better when presentation was to the right hemisphere, while hearing people performed better when presentation was to the left. Poizner *et al.* (1979) present further evidence that deaf sign language users tend to localise function in the right hemisphere rather than the left.

This neurophysiological evidence lends support to the idea that deaf people's processing of language has changed because of early auditory deprivation. The sign language then occupies the language function, but possibly in a different part of the brain from the temporal-sequential processing of speech, and it is reflected in a different language code. In turn this fits with our psychological findings of clear differences in the expression of the language code although similarities in its basic function of dealing with meaning.

A particularly popular way for psychologists to study these differences in expression of the cognitive code has been in the paradigms of short-term memory tasks. Much of this work has been done by asking people to watch or listen to simple stimuli, usually verbal, in sequence and then immediatley to recall the items. The vast literature on Short-Term Memory (or Primary Memory or Working Memory) has been criticised for its artificiality in terms of language use and memory use. However, the very strong links of the process of reading to coding in Short-Term Memory have been highlighted by the work of Baddeley (1979) for hearing children and Conrad (1979) for deaf children.

Short-term Memory

Differences in Coding

When people remember verbal stimuli over a short period of time, they tend to do so by translating the information into a code for ease of retrieval. This code is usually a 'speech' one for hearing people. In remembering a telephone number, it is common to repeat the number in sequence, silently, to preserve it in memory. The same is true in remembering letters (Conrad, 1964) and also in remembering words (Baddeley, 1966). Dyslexic children appear not to use this speech code (Bakker, 1972; Baddeley, 1979) and often show speech perception problems (Jorm, 1979; Valtin, 1979). Not surprisingly deaf children have difficulties in using a speech code and this effect is greatest when hearing loss is greater than 85 dB (Conrad, 1979).

The evidence for this difference in processing by deaf children in their short-term recall is reviewed at length by Conrad (1979) and this will not be repeated here. However, it is important to point out that while it can be established that a difference exists, it seems that profoundly deaf children are not easily classified as to what they do use when speech coding is not available. O'Connor and Hermelin (1973) suggest that a visual store can be used for sequences of nonverbal information and Dornic *et al.* (1973) suggest that visual, dactylic and category coding take place. Dodd and Hermelin (1977) report that a phonological code is possible, based on visual information from lip-reading. Given the inability of deaf children to use speech satisfactorily, and the relative infrequency of deaf children who have acquired sign language at an early age, then it seems likely that many children will develop idiosyncratic methods of recall which will prove resistant to experimental method. This is the most common finding.

Sign Coding

A small number of studies have examined the recall of signs among deaf adults and it is there that the first positive indications of the existence of a sign code can be seen. Bellugi, Klima and Siple (1974) asked deaf people to remember lists of signs and recall them immediately. Their results indicated firstly, that recall curves (proportion of items recalled in the correct position in the sequence) were very similar to hearing people's curves, and secondly, that when a deaf person made an error it was likely to be a substitution of an item whose sign was visually similar. However, the study was conducted on only eight deaf people and the total number of intrusion errors appearing more than once in the study was only 26. Also, hearing people's memory span in words was 5.9 while the deaf group in sign was 4.9. Part of this may be attributed to the fact that the deaf subjects had to write down their responses, i.e. translate from the signs they saw, into words.

Klima and Bellugi (1979) report further developments in their work which give stronger support for the notion of a sign coding and indicate that the sign errors produced in writing down are duplicated when the response mode is signing by the subjects.

Kyle (1980b) reports some initial work on British Sign Language (BSL) as a code in short-term memory. Twelve hearing subjects were compared with 17 deaf people in an ordered recall task. There was a stimulus set of 10 pictures of simple objects for which there was an unambiguous sign. Hearing people had 3 conditions:

(i)   they saw 6 slides of the pictures in sequence;
(ii) they saw 6 slides of words for the pictures in sequence;
(iii) they heard 6 words of the pictures read to them

Deaf people were presented with conditions (i) and (ii) but with a different third condition: they saw 6 signs of the pictures in sequence. Presentation was at the rate of 1 per second and recall was ordered, i.e. they had to remember the first item first, then the second item, etc. All instructions were signed to the deaf subjects and responses were made by writing the serial number (1 to 6) in the space by whichever picture from the set of 10 had appeared in that position.

The results are as shown in Figure 4.1. The pattern of results for hearing people is as expected with words spoken being the best recalled, and it is possible to see the characteristic difference in the final serial position due to recall from something like the brief auditory store (precategorical acoustic store) discussed by Morton (1978). Deaf people do not show this difference as all their presentation was in one modality, i.e. vision, but it can be seen that something like the traditional serial recall curve is found, and there is a statistical difference showing that presentation in sign is significantly better than in word or picture ($F = 5.68$ $p < .025$). The equal recall in the final serial position probably reflects the use of a visual store to hold the final item without having to transfer it to a specific code. This would fit very well with the proposed visual store (post-iconic) which deaf children make much greater use of than hearing children (O'Connor and Hemelin, 1978).

Figure 4.1: Serial Recall by (a) Hearing Subjects (N = 12) and (b) Deaf Subjects (N = 17)

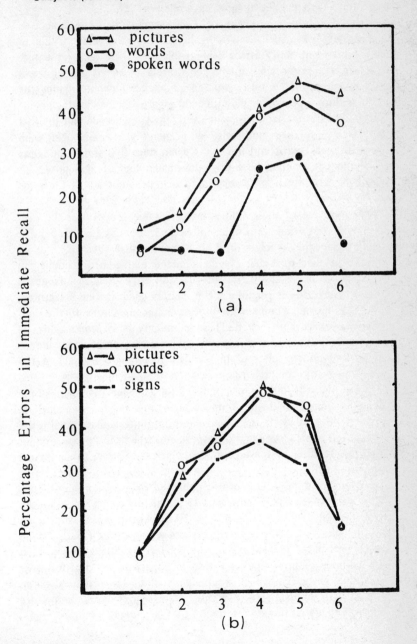

These results also agree well with Bellugi *et al*. (1974) in suggesting that the pattern of recall is similar for deaf people to that of the hearing, though there may be differences in representation.

In a second smaller study (Kyle, 1980b) reports that interference or suppression tasks, such as holding blocks of wood while trying to remember, significantly affect deaf people's recall of items presented. However, the reinforcing effects for hearing people of saying items as they appear, is curiously not repeated in deaf people signing the items as they appear. This is outlined in Figure 4.2. For hearing people better recall results from the salience of the speech code and the fact that as an item is seen and registered in memory; it is also being reinforced by speaking it and hearing it again since it is said aloud. Deaf people do not seem to have this additional effect of signing 'aloud', suggesting that visual or manual feedback does not act in the same way as auditory or articulatory feedback does for hearing people.

The outcome of these studies indicate some support for the idea of a code compatible with sign representation, but the code does not simply replace the speech code; it functions in a different way.

Some further work has been conducted taking into account the existence of bilingual hearing people who have used sign language from an early age. As part of a national study of sign language learning, groups of hearing people with professional connections to the deaf community have been tested. These are mainly social workers for the deaf. As well as memory measures, tests of signing ability were administered and groups selected for analysis accordingly. A part of the interpreting and comprehension test was used to select people. This consisted of a videotape of seven different deaf signers, signing information contained in pictures. These videotapes were made with a deaf audience. The subject's task was to translate into spoken English the descriptions signed on the videotape. Scoring was the proportion of the actual features on the tape in sign which the hearing subject translated into English.

The first hearing group formed consisted of eleven social workers, whose parents were deaf (mean age 43 years), and whose scores for the interpretation test were greater than 50 per cent correct. The second group consisted of eleven whose parents were hearing (mean age 35 years) but had an interpretation score greater than 50 per cent correct. The majority of this group had been working with the deaf for more than nine years. The third group consisted of inexperienced social workers with the deaf (less than three years) who had some knowledge of sign, but scored low on interpretation. They were 19 in number and

Figure 4.2: Serial Position Curves for Percentage Change in Recall —
(a) as a Result of Speech Articulation, and (b) as a Result of the
Suppression Task

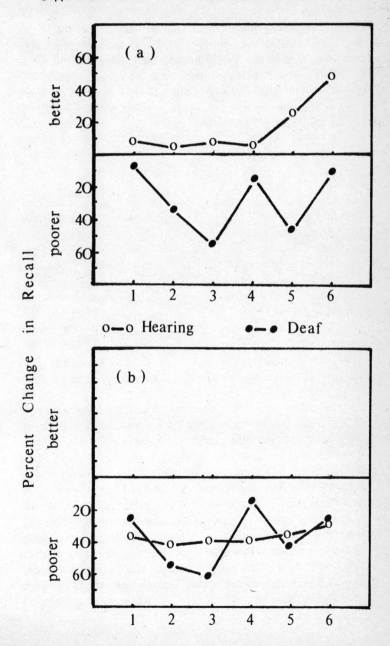

had a mean age of 34 years. The deaf group consisted of 14 prelingually deafened adults who use sign language (mean age 33 years). No reliable measure of hearing loss was available but all had difficult speech. Four of the group had deaf parents.

The study presented sequences of items on videotape at the rate of one per second. Items were either printed words or individual signs made without lip movement. Each list consisted either of all words or all signs. There were two sets of items balanced across the study and subjects had to write down on a grid the order number of the items from 1 to 6 according to where they had appeared in the list. All test lists had 6 items. Table 4.1 shows the design.

Table 4.1: Design of the Study

		Presented form on videotape	
		WORDS	SIGNS
Responses made on a grid of	WORDS	8 trials subjects speak words	8 trials subjects speak sign
	SIGNS (pictures)	8 trials subjects sign words	8 trials subjects make sign

All trials had 6 items in sequence; serial recall followed presentation of the last item.

Brief practice in the technique of writing down the order of the items was followed by eight practice trials where words were presented and subjects had to respond on a grid of 10 words, or signs were presented and subjects had to respond on a grid of 10 signs.

In the main part of the study, subjects were told either to sign the item as they saw it (and write responses on signs) or to speak each item (and write responses on words). The rationale of this technique was to attempt to produce code-switching of the type which would isolate the code used most efficiently for short-term memory. Subjects were therefore being offered the opportunity of a 'word' code or a 'sign' code.

Subjects' signing or speaking aloud was always matched to the grid presented for responding. So when the subject made the sign he would write down the order on a grid with pictures of the sign. When he spoke the order had to be written on a grid of words. It was hoped that this would tend to optimise the use of a sign code or a speech code. This proved to be a problem as it produced two response modes which were of unequal difficulty. The grid containing pictures of signs only partially captured a representation of the sign, because of the lack of movement, and was unfamiliar to both hearing and deaf subjects. This reduces some of the power of the comparisons where the response mode was compared and it is necessary to make relative rather than absolute judgements.

Deaf people scored more poorly in recall in this test than did the hearing groups, though overall recall was lower than normal because of the concurrent tasks of speaking or signing.

Subjects with error rates greater than 75 per cent were rejected. Mean percentage errors were 61 per cent for the deaf group (N = 14), 50 per cent for the bilinguals, 47 per cent for the good signers and 41 per cent for the inexperienced group. The difference between the groups is significant (F = 7.73 p $<$ .01) but may be partly explained by an age factor and by scores on a nonverbal reasoning test which follow the same trend. The inexperienced group were the youngest and most capable.

Comparison of presentation methods (seeing words versus seeing signs) independent of response mode showed significant differences in favour of words for bilinguals (t = 2.96 $<$ .01), good signers (t = 1.88, p $<$ .05) and the inexperienced group (t = 3.12 p $<$ .01), but no differences were apparent for deaf people.

In examining response mode the problem of the inequality of the tasks was encountered. Responses in words were better overall for all groups. Inevitably, then, any comparison of response mode (or code) will be a compromise which indicates the differences between modalities for deaf versus hearing, rather than exactly identifying the use of either of the specific codes. Nevertheless, there is a specific difference between deaf people and hearing people in relative performance (sign/speech) and it is worthwhile trying to express this. Figure 4.3 presents recall in sign mode as a percentage of recall in word mode. There is no significant difference between hearing groups, but a clear difference between deaf groups and hearing (t = 3.63, p $<$ .001).

These results on presentation mode and response mode fit into the theory which allows deaf people the sign code for short-term memory,

Figure 4.3: Recall in Sign as a Percentage of Recall in Words

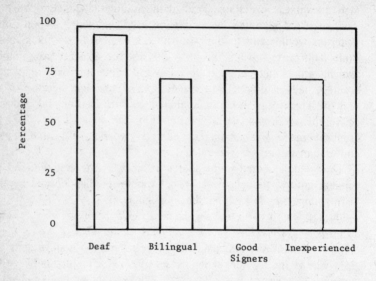

and hearing people a speech code, although one can argue this support is very much relative to this task. Deaf people's advantage in sign may be functionally dependent on the hearing subjects' better performance in a word mode. The precise demonstration of the sign code therefore remains somewhat elusive though clearly the findings may be interpreted consistently with its presence and use in deaf people's short-term memory. The relative deaf superiority in signs over words, when these are used as an output code, fits well into the idea that the articulation (or making of a sign) provides the basis of the code. However, this effect may not appear consistently when the input code is compatible, i.e. there will not always be the same effect (deaf people relatively better in signs than words) when the choice is between simple words being presented or simple signs.

For hearing people presentation in words is always better than in sign, while absolute difference in response mode always favours words. What is a little surprising is that there is no difference between bilinguals and the inexperienced, and this may be indicative of the simple nature of the sign/word translation, or the fact that these bilinguals do not try to internalise sign in this task.

Comparing recall when making the sign at presentation with recall when no instructions are given, deaf people's recall of signs is significantly better when not asked to sign concurrently with presentation ($t = 2.68$, $p < .02$). This repeats the finding reported earlier in Kyle (1980b) where signing overtly appears to interfere with the serial nature of this task. This adds to the notion that deaf use of a sign code is different from the use of a speech code, and we need to consider more appropriate tasks for its investigations. The principal reason for hearing people's advantage when speaking aloud is due to the added auditory feedback obtained. It therefore seems that this feedback is very different for deaf people. Either it interferes through the perceiving of movement in the periphery of vision, or else the kinaesthetic feedback upsets the internal representation. Therefore as well as having considerable difficulties in taking notes at a talk or in class, the nature of a note-taking exercise may at times interfere with the extraction of information. There is a great need to examine the most appropriate learning approach for education and using an adequate communication mode is only the first step.

In summary, this paper has considered three types of evidence concerning the existence of a sign code in representation and memory. From personal reports the existence of information storage in sign language form seems clear, though it requires more structured information if it is to be used in education.

Studies in semantic organisation as it affects writing and 'thinking' give support to representation in sign of a similar form to that of spoken language, though its output is clearly different, i.e. it tends to appear in sign language syntax, when deaf people write. Neurophysiological evidence suggests the general nature of difference in processing arising from deafness, which is almost directly consequential on auditory deprivation. Finally, short-term memory remains the most elusive of the areas of research, though from Klima and Bellugi's (1979) work on substitution errors, and some of the above study, there are grounds for belief in sign coding in short-term memory, but its natural function may be different from that of speech coding. This would suggest sign language as a vehicle for the conceptual processing necessary for, say, reading development but to maximise its effectiveness in the classroom, further investigation is required.

Conrad in this volume sets the question of to what extent we have considered the educational methodology necessary to teach deaf children even if we have adopted sign language as the means. W.R. Scott, a well-known teacher of the deaf, clearly sets out the lesson-planning required to teach through sign language. While maintaining that signs should be used as a means for education, and that they should gradually give way to written language, he clearly perceives the details of its use:

> We have already remarked that gesture language is very different in its character from written language and that the various relations expressed by conjunctions, prepositions, relatives and inflections are almost without equivalents in gesture language, while a single action where the eye, face and hands speak simultaneously represent at once an idea which could not be expressed without many words. (p. 134).

He accurately describes sign language as based in ideas and effectively demonstrates that the ideas in the complex sentence syntax of English can be broken up into idea units of simpler form which follow the sign language order or syntax. This syntax difference is comparable to the differences of other spoken languages from English, and should be used to support the teacher from the beginning of the child's education. He says sign language explains the concepts while Signed English may support English learning more effectively. However, his reasoning on the role of sign language in education is very simple:

> Sign Language then is used by teachers because it is the only common ground on which they can meet their pupils and where they can both understand each other, so that one can communicate and the other receive the knowledge to be conveyed. (p. 118)

Given our educational history and research knowledge, perhaps we should not be surprised that this was first written over a hundred years ago.

5 SIMULTANEOUS INTERPRETING

Peter Llewellyn-Jones

Interpreting for deaf people in Great Britain has traditionally been considered the province of the Welfare Officers or Social Workers for the Deaf. Indeed, as part of the training and qualification for this profession the act of interpreting from speech to sign and from sign into speech was practised and examined. With changing approaches to social work practice and training, the traditional qualification for work with the adult deaf, the Deaf Welfare Examination Board Diploma or Certificate was phased out, to be replaced in the mid-1970s by one-year post-qualifying specialist courses for generic social workers. Due in part to this change in training and in part to the swing from voluntary society based services to direct Local Authority based services for deaf people, fears regarding the supply and quality of interpreters for the deaf have grown. It is neither possible or particularly profitable to try to compare the interpreting services of today with those of 15 or 20 years ago, but it is true to say that as the deaf community becomes more aware of the opportunities open to it, both educational and social, the demands upon interpreters are increasing. The interpreters themselves have long recognised the need for, but total lack of, formalised training.

The shortage of suitably trained and qualified interpreters is not questioned and official recognition of this shortage was given in 1977 in the form of funding, by the DHSS, of the British Deaf Association 'Communication Skills Project'. Approximately one half of this grant was earmarked for the establishing of a Registry of Interpreters for the Deaf. The call for a registry, welcomed by the professionals and the deaf community, has brought with it demands for the setting of a minimum acceptable standard and a standardised assessment and training procedure.

There are, then, two problems immediately facing the interpreting profession:

1. What is the most suitable form of training?
2. How does one realistically assess interpreting skills?

89

Neither of these questions can be answered without first addressing the fundamental issue of identifying the skills required. Hearing sign users have tended to regard the problems of communicating with adult deaf people as unique. The deaf community have been viewed predominently as a handicap group, and sign language, not as a language but as a range of communication techniques, the particular form selected being dependent on the educational achievement and linguistic competence (i.e. literacy) of the deaf person being communicated with. These traditional attitudes towards sign language are now, however, being challenged. Linguists maintain that sign languages in fact meet all the requirements necessary for them to be regarded as real languages (Klima and Bellugi, 1979; Wilbur, 1979), and parallels have been drawn between the deaf community and minority language groups (Markowicz and Woodward, 1975). It is, therefore, not wholly inappropriate to set interpreting for deaf people into the wider context of foreign language interpreting, both to look at the similarities and to examine the differences.

Interpreters for the deaf are frequently called upon to interpret simultaneously from speech to sign language and vice versa, and this is usually regarded as the ultimate test of interpreting skill.

To look for similarities, or differences, in the functioning of spoken language and sign language interpreters, it is necessary to examine the (internal) processes involved. Moser's model (1978), a simplified form of which is shown in Figure 5.1, allows us to examine the psychological processes involved when simultaneously interpreting from one language into another. As interpreters must *both* listen and speak (or, in this case, sign) approximately 60-75 per cent of the time (Barik 1972 and 1973; Gerver 1972), the psychological processes involved with simultaneously interpreting are very complex. The interpreter, on hearing the original message (Source Language), starts to recognise and process the initial or surface features. By tapping his long-term memory store he recognises the combinations of sounds as individual words and, as more information comes in, his syntactic knowledge tells him that the words are coming in a certain order that at least is syntactically plausible, and therefore capable of making sense. His semantic knowledge immediately fixes meanings, or a limited choice of meanings to certain individual words and, coupled with the syntactic information, the meaning or possible meaning of the phrase. So far, providing the interpreter has native or near native competence in the Source Language, the process has required very little, if any, conscious effort. The more precise meaning of the phrase can only be determined by linking

Figure 5.1: A Hypothetical Model of Simultaneous Interpretation

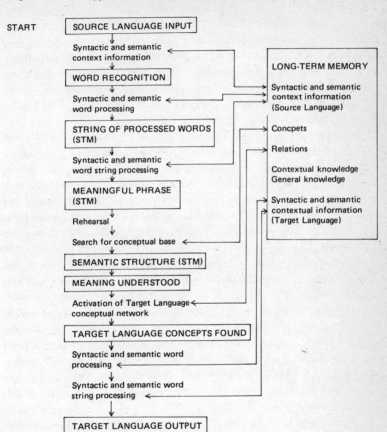

Source: After Moser, 1978.

it with contextual information already present in the long-term memory store. The more contextual information available, the more apparent and precise the meaning of the phrase and, consequently, the less effort required.

It is at this stage that the act of interpreting becomes more complex and hence more of a conscious effort than simply listening (see Figure 5.1). The interpreter is now part way through processing the initial information, but more has already started to come in, and this has to be stored somewhere until he can deal with it.

According to Miller (1956), on whose theories this part of Moser's model is based, Short-Term Memory (STM) or, as he calls it, Generated Abstract Memory, is an unstable temporary store where incoming information is held until it can be fully processed. If information is not processed, it is quickly lost, and there is ample evidence to show that lists of unrelated words or numbers without an underlying meaning are held for only a very short time. Miller states that the storage capacity of STM is 7 ± 2 items of information. This type of short-term memory would appear to explain why sign language interpreters feel under increasing pressure the more they fall behind the speaker. If the items of information so stored are in the form of words, to feel comfortable the interpreter would need to keep within four or five words behind the speaker. The results of the 'speaker-interpreter lag' observations reported below would seem to bear this out. These four or five words, however, may not include enough contextual or syntactic information for the interpreter to understand the message completely, especially if the two languages concerned have very different grammatical structures.

Moser suggests that the simultaneous interpreter overcomes the capacity limitations of short-term memory by using it more efficiently. By storing 'chunks' of information, rather than words, the interpreter is able to stay further behind the speaker, so enabling him fully to understand before attempting to reconstruct the meaning in the Target Language.

Although Miller's description of STM seems to account for some of the problems faced by interpreters, it does not make any allowance for, or offer any explanation of, the initial processing necessary to 'chunk' the information.

More recent work on sentence processing, as opposed to the remembering of unrelated words or numbers, suggests that a different process is in fact in operation. The notion of 'Working Memory' (Baddeley, 1979) seems to come closer to explaining the initial processing and, as will be discussed later, possibly sheds more light on the additional problems encountered by sign language interpreters (see Figure 5.2). After a cursory acoustic filtering, to discard non-meaningful auditory signals (noise, etc.), the incoming information is passed into the Working Store. The Executive scans the information and passes the meaning on to the long-term store. Contextual information from the long-term store programmes the Executive, telling it what to look for and what to reject. It is here that syntax is discarded – in other words, the exact wording of the Source Language is forgotten, and only the meaning retained. If, however, the Executive fails to extract the meaning on its first attempt, the information can be recycled through the Articulatory Loop and scanned again.

Figure 5.2: A Processing Model of 'Working Memory'

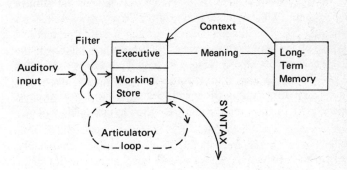

A similar process can be observed in children reading. When a sentence is not understood, a child will read it again out loud. Adults will do the same, but much more infrequently and usually silently, or subvocally. Heard information not readily understood can be 'rehearsed' in the same way, thus giving the Executive a second chance to scan for meaning.

In this model, the capacity of short-term memory does not appear quite as important, as information is processed and passed into the long-term memory fairly rapidly and effortlessly, the original wording of the Source Language, no longer needed, being discarded. It is only when information is not readily understood and the Articulatory Loop brought into service that capacity becomes relevant. This will be discussed later, but let us for now assume that the information has been processed and passed into the long-term store.

In Moser's model (Figure 5.1), the concepts, stripped of the hindrance of the Source Language, can now be related to the interpreter's knowledge of both the Target Language and the experience of the Target Language users. According to Seleskovitch (1978) an accurate interpreter preserves meaning, not words. It follows then, that the interpreter has to do more than simply reconstruct the message in a syntactically acceptable form of the Target Language. He must use his knowledge of the Target Language community, its culture and its experiences. To convey the exact *meaning* of the original message, he needs to find conceptual equivalents, not merely word equivalents. To give a simple example, a word-for-word translation of '. . . about the size of a loaf of bread . . .' from English into French would not convey the original meaning of the message. Bread, in France, is quite different both in shape and size to bread in England, so another example, but one that is equivalent conceptually, would need to be found.

The interpreter is now ready to select the most appropriate way of expressing the concepts, the form and style of Target Language being dictated by the needs and expectations of the audience. Some data collected on Sign Language interpreters is shown below. Let us attempt to examine the findings within the context of the hypothetical model.

Interpreter Effectiveness

As part of the research project 'Sign Language Learning and Use', the Sign Language Research team at Bristol University asked approximately 150 professional hearing sign users to complete a variety of measures relating to signing skill. A sub-group of approximately 16 of the more experienced sign users were also asked to simultaneously interpret a tape-recording of one 3-minute spoken passage into sign language. Three passages were used, matched for speed (120 words per minute), linguistic complexity and content, and the subjects were instructed to interpret them into the form of sign language they would normally use with a group of profoundly, prelingually deaf adults.

The signed interpretations were videotaped and the recording later played to panels of deaf people who did not know the interpreter. Only one interpretation of each passage was seen by each panel, who were required to complete comprehension measures based on information contained in the passages. The comprehension measures, in the form of multiple-choice questions, were administered in sign language with a standard videotape, and the responses marked on answer sheets. To account for variation between the deaf panels, a fourth standard interpreted passage was presented to each.

After discounting the judgements made by deaf panels scoring less than 70 per cent on the standard test passage, we were left with passages interpreted by a group of 13 interpreters — 6 of whom were native signers in that they had deaf parents (Group A), and 7 of whom were social workers with at least 7 years' interpreting experience (Group B).

All three passages were played to a hearing control group (N = 15), and the average comprehension score for each passage compared to the scores of the deaf panels receiving the information through interpreters. The score of each deaf panel was expressed as a percentage of the control group score. The results appear in Table 5.1.

Table 5.1: Comprehension of Interpreted Passages by Deaf Panels

100% = Comprehension of same passages by hearing control group

Group A — Native sign users		Group B — Non-native sign users	
Interpreter	Comprehension score (%)	Interpreter	Comprehension score (%)
1	95	1	83
2	83	2	71
3	59	3	65
4	53	4	48
5	48	5	41
6	40	6	35
		7	35
AVERAGE	63	AVERAGE	54

Although, because of the very small sample, this can only be considered as a pilot study, the amount of information lost during the interpretation gives cause for some concern. The figures quoted by Murphy (1978) for a similar study conducted with interpreters at California State University, show an average information loss of 16 per cent. Murphy concludes, however, that this loss is attributable to the basic language and educational deficiency of deaf people. It seems unlikely that language and educational deficiency account for much of the information loss in our results as all of the passages were clearly interpretable and understandable, as demonstrated by the few very high scores, and the comprehension tests were administered in sign language, the deaf judges therefore not being required to use English skills when responding. The discrepancies seem much more likely to result from (1) faults in the test design or procedure, and (2) the efficiency and skill of the individual interpreters.

The most frequent comment of the interpreters taking part was that the measures were artificial. They complained that without audience feedback it was impossible to 'pitch' the signed interpretation. This implies that interpreters are capable of using a wide variety of signing styles — the variety eventually selected being determined by overt expression of comprehension, or otherwise, on the faces of members of the audience. We are now in the process of measuring the effect of audience feedback on the effectiveness of sign language interpreters.

Time Lag

Three interpreters were selected from each group to examine the relationship between time distance behind the speaker and the overall comprehension score of their interpretation. The lag was measured by stopping the videotape at 20-second intervals and comparing the information being signed at that point with the words being spoken on the audio tape. The original passage was included on the sound track of the video recording.

Perhaps the most striking feature of the graphs in Figures 5.3 and 5.4 is the very low average lag shown by even the most effective interpreters. According to the foreign language interpreting model proposed above, much emphasis is put on the necessity for the interpreter to fully understand the message before he can even begin to reconstruct it in the Target Language. It seems surprising, then, that Interpreter A1 managed a particularly high score of 95 per cent comprehension (Table 5.1) while keeping, at most, 7 words behind the speaker and, for much of the passage, only 4.

A low average lag can be part explained by the interpreter's ability to predict. If the incoming information is being processed deeply enough within Semantic Memory, the contextual knowledge so gained allows the interpreter to make, usually accurate, predictions about any new information. This would seem to fit in well with the model

Figure 5.3: Lag (words behind speaker) against time (20 second intervals) — Group A — Native Signers

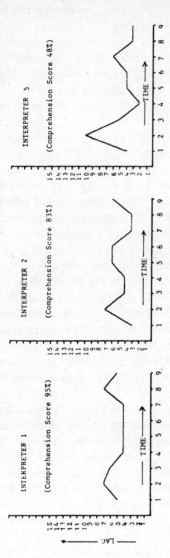

Figure 5.4: Lag (words behind speaker) against time (20 second intervals) — Group B — non-Native Signers

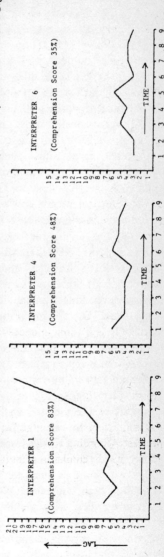

proposed in Figure 5.2 where the contextual information already stored programmes the Executive. This expectation would also speed up processing of meaning as the Long-Term Memory would already have a likely range of conceptual bases at its 'fingertips'.

However, we have still not accounted for the structural differences between the Source and Target Languages. Sign language has been shown to have a quite different syntax from that of spoken English (Klima and Bellugi, 1979) and a lag of more than four words would certainly seem necessary for the interpreters to totally restructure the message, even allowing for prediction.

The six interpreted passages were viewed again by a prelingually deaf native signer (fourth generation) who was asked to comment on the styles of signing adopted in each. It was immediately apparent that signers A1 and A2 were not, in fact, using sign language, but instead a Signed English version of the original message, slightly simplified but retaining a very similar basic structure. For example, Interpreter A1 expressed the original message '. . . who will be accompanied by up to 50 relatives' as '. . . WITH ABOUT 50 r.e.l.a.t.i.v.e.s'. (Words in upper case are glosses for signs and words spelled in lower case represent fingerspelling.) Signer A2 stayed even closer to the form of the original message, even fingerspelling such words as 'b.e . . . b.y. . . . u.p. . . . t.o. . . . etc.' There is much evidence (Conrad, 1979) to show that the average English competence of deaf adults is well below the hearing norms. How, then, using a basically English syntax, did Interpreter A1 manage to convey so much of the information? On re-examination of his interpretation we found numerous examples of supplementary or explanatory information being added in pure sign language, i.e. after rendering part of the message in Signed English he quickly repeated any difficult concept or structure in sign language. For example, after 'ABOUT 50 r.e.l.a.t.i.v.e.s' was added 'BROTHER, SISTER, MOTHER (AND SO ON)'. The bracketed words are an approximation in English of a gesture used to signify 'etcetera'. Being a native signer who has not only lived with but also worked professionally with deaf people for a great many years, he was able to use his intuitive knowledge of what is readily understood by deaf people to supplement and explain as necessary. Interpreter A2 did not attempt to supplement in this way and so some of the difference in information loss can probably be accounted for by the complexity of the English syntax used.

Interpreter A5, however, adopted an altogether different technique and attempted to interpret the message into sign language. His competence as a signer and communicator is unquestioned and his rendition was judged by the deaf informant as the most easily understood. His score of only 48 per cent comprehension (Table 5.1), however, suggests problems in adequately processing the information. Although starting rather too quickly he soon allowed the lag to increase until he was able to process sufficient information for him to reconstruct it into sign language and for the first 40 seconds he appeared to be functioning very effectively. Shortly after the second time check, however, he suddenly appeared to become conscious of the increasing lag between the speaker's original message and his signed interpretation. His facial expression slowly changed to one of panic and in a desperate attempt to 'catch up' he omitted several pieces of quite important information. By the fourth time check he was within two words of the speaker and, because of the lost information and hence lack of contextual knowledge, unable to both process sufficiently or predict accurately. He then attempted to allow a more realistic lag, but by time check 7 the interpretation had broken down again and for the remainder of the passage he reverted to Signed English, staying within three words of the speaker.

As we do not know the precise nature of 'Working', or Short-term Memory, it is not possible to state, with certainty, the reasons for the 'breakdown'. A possible explanation, however, is that as he became aware of the increasing lag he consciously tried to remember what was being said. According to the Working Memory model of Figure 5.2, this would bring into service the Articulatory Loop. This silent or subvocal rehearsal of the English syntax would undoubtedly interfere with his ability to simultaneously produce sign language. It would also slow down the processing of the new information thus increasing the lag even further. Baddeley (1979) suggests that the storage capacity of the Articulatory Loop is approximately 1½ seconds — i.e. is time-based, rather than dependent upon the number of items stored. By consciously trying to rehearse an increasing amount of information it is clear that the Articulatory Loop will soon be working to capacity and information is then 'forgotten'. It seems plausible, then, that Interpreter A5 is in fact making the mistake of actively listening to the words, or consciously trying to remember each sound, instead of concentrating on meaning and so allowing himself to process and understand relatively effortlessly.

By contrast, Interpreter B1 appeared to be at ease with what seems a quite erratic lag. In fact, the more linguistically complex the incoming information, the more lag he allowed before attempting to interpret. Even at time checks 8 and 9, when the lag reached an extraordinary 21 words, no information was omitted and, from his appearance at any rate, no discomfort or panic experienced. The loss of information is probably accounted for by his lack of mastery of the Target Language, and the deaf informant actually considered him to be the worst signer and 'very difficult to understand'. How, then, did he manage to achieve a fairly creditable comprehension score of 83 per cent?

He did not attempt to interpret into sign language as such, but instead adopted the strategy of extracting the meaning from the original message and re-structuring it into a very simplified Signed English form, using English constructions well within the capability of even quite poor readers. He was, from the point of view of the model in Figure 5.1, interpreting very effectively and hence able to overcome, to some extent at least, his lack of fluency in sign language. He quite sensibly chose a Target Language form that was within his capabilities. Interpreter B1's obvious ability to process and conceptualise with ease, coupled with Interpreter A5's knowledge of sign language, would, it appears, produce an extremely effective and efficient sign language interpreter.

Interpreters B4 and B6 both adopted the strategy of attempting to produce an accurate Signed English version of the message. Interpreter B4 tried, on occasions, to simplify, but seemed unwilling to allow enough lag to receive sufficient information and he invariably reverted to a sign-for-word rendition. An example of one such attempt occurred at time check 6. After a pause in the original message, which allowed him to catch up with the speaker, he then waited for sufficient information for him to begin his interpretation. He was obviously unwilling to wait long enough, however, and started signing after the sixth word.

The lack of effectiveness of these two appear to result from a combination of factors: (1) inability to process deeply enough; (2) inappropriateness of Target Language (when one considers the average English competence of the deaf community); and (3) lack of native or near native competence in sign language.

Number (3) was highlighted on several occasions by the inappropriate choice of signs and the lack of use, or misuse, of such basic features as directionality and placement.

It appears, then, that the 13 interpreters adopted one of the two basic strategies:

(1)   'Transliterating' from the spoken Source Language into a manually-coded form of the same language, preserving the

   original syntax by using, where possible, direct sign-for-
   word substitution.

(2) Discarding the wording and syntax of the Source Language
   and instead concentrating on expressing the meaning, rather
   than the form, of the original message, i.e. 'interpreting'.

One interesting point to note is that only one of the interpreters
actually attempted to interpret into sign language.

Appropriateness of Target Language

This is a topic of some controversy and revolves around the question
of whether sign language (as normally used by the deaf community)
is appropriate for formal settings. It is likely that arguments in favour
of the use of Signed English at conferences, church services, and indeed,
in education, stem from traditional attitudes towards the linguistic
status of sign language. These attitudes and possible reasons for them
are discussed in Llewellyn-Jones, Kyle and Woll (1979). It should be
noted here, though, that the work of Llewellyn-Jones *et al*. suggests
that the deaf community attach more status to sign language than to
Signed English. This finding is based on evidence from pilot studies
only, but if replicated would obviously have a direct bearing on appropriateness of Target Language.

  From another point of view, however, choice of Target Language
could have a bearing on interpreter effectiveness. Interpreter A1 was
the most effective interpreter in the sub-group described above. There
is evidence to suggest, however, that his Signed English interpretation
was only this effective because of his intimate knowledge, not only of
sign language, but also of the sign language community.

  It should also be noted that neither he, nor Interpreter A2 or, indeed, any of the more effective interpreters, stuck rigidly to the
wording of the original message. Although it could be argued that this
deviation is simply as a result of speed-induced paraphrasing, there
could be a more complex reason, linked to the nature of information
processing. Referring to the 'Working Memory' model in Figure 5.2
it is possible that the exact replication of the original message, by
silently mouthing, in fact brings into service the Articulatory Loop.
In this case the Loop is not triggered by the Executive as it would normally be, but by the action of mouthing itself, which, in effect, is
subvocalizing. We have already discussed how the constant use of the

Articulatory Loop may adversely affect processing. Although this theory has yet to be tested, it does seem to fit in with the experiences of sign language interpreters who, when under pressure, tend to whisper. This whispering, or vocalisation, appears to be an attempt at rehearsal, but rather than relieve the pressure it has the opposite effect. As the interpreter is now hearing his own voice, as well as that of the speaker, he becomes even more aware of the length of lag. A 'vicious circle' is then established and pressure mounts until the Working Memory is overloaded and the interpretation breaks down. A restructuring of the original message, however slight, would therefore appear to be a convenient way of avoiding this effect.

Conclusion

It would appear that the models proposed in Figures 5.1 and 5.2 do give a clear insight into processes necessary for effective sign language interpretation. Although largely transliterating, only by concentrating on the meaning of the passage was Interpreter A1 able to supplement his transliteration with interpretation and explanation in sign language. Interpreter A5, however, although expressing the message in a clearly understandable form — perhaps the most understandable — encountered problems in the 'Working Memory' (Figure 5.2) part of the model; problems that could, it seems, be overcome with suitable training and practice.

A thorough knowledge of (a) the target community and (b) its language are essential, as demonstrated by A1, and to some extent A5. Interpreter B1, 'the worst signer' and 'very difficult to understand', was fairly effective only because of his ability to cope easily with the processing necessary for him to relate the *meaning* of the message to his knowledge of the deaf community's English competence and experience.

The problem of appropriateness of Target Language has yet to be resolved. Interpreter A1 endeavoured to use Signed English where possible because of his stated view that sign language is not suitable for formal settings. On the other hand, the results of the pilot studies into the attitudes of the deaf community (Llewellyn-Jones, Kyle and Woll, 1979) appear to question this. It cannot be questioned, however, that a thorough knowledge of sign language as used by deaf people is essential even for interpreters following a rigidly Signed English approach. Such a knowledge, coupled perhaps with a keener awareness of the contextual information contained in the original message, would have averted the misuse of basic grammatical features of signed communication and reduced the number of inappropriate signs chosen.

In answer to questions posed at the beginning of this chapter regarding suitable training for sign language interpreters, it is clear that parallels can be drawn between spoken language interpreting and spoken to sign language interpreting. There are undoubtedly problems associated with the switching of modality, i.e. speech communication to visual/gestural communication, which are not accounted for in the existing models, but there are enough similarities in the processes necessary to both forms of interpretation for valuable lessons to be learned from foreign language interpreting techniques and training methods.

'Accurate interpretation' has traditionally been seen by sign language interpreters to mean adherence, not only to the meaning, but also to the form of the original message. The attitude of foreign language interpreters, however, is less rigid.

> It is not enough for the interpreter to merely understand the message and transmit it in its entirety; he must also *formulate it in such a way that it reaches its target* ... he explains the message to them more than he translates it. (Seleskovitch, 1978)

Any objective assessment of an interpreter's skills must test his ability to convey accurately the *meaning* of the original message, but he must also convey it in a way that is acceptable to the target audience.

PART TWO: LINGUISTIC ASPECTS

INTRODUCTION

Bencie Woll

Until recently, linguists included among the essential characteristics of a human language the use of an auditory-vocal channel (Hockett, 1955) or claimed that having command of a language involved knowing sound-meaning correspondences (Chomsky, 1965). This insistence on sound as a basic feature of language arose in the first instance from the emphasis of linguists on correcting the view that written language was the highest form of language. Their establishment of spoken language as primary led them in turn to a curious ignorance about sign languages. Sapir sums up the position of linguists in the first half of the twentieth century:

> Still another interesting group of transfers [from spoken language, like writing and Morse Code] are the different gesture languages of deaf-mutes, of Trappist monks vowed to perpetual silence, or of communicating parties that are within seeing distance of each other but are out of earshot. Some of these systems are one-to-one equivalences of the normal system of speech; others, like military gesture-symbolism or the gesture language of the Plains Indians of North America (understood by tribes of mutually unintelligible forms of speech), are imperfect transfers, limiting themselves to the rendering of such grosser speech elements as are an imperative minimum under difficult circumstances. In these latter systems, as in such still more imperfect symbolisms as those used at sea or in the woods, it may be contended that language no longer properly plays a part but that the ideas are directly conveyed by an utterly unrelated symbolic process or by a quasi-instinctive imitativeness. Such an interpretation would be erroneous. The intelligibility of these vaguer symbolisms can hardly be due to anything but their automatic and silent translation into the terms of a fuller flow of speech.
>
> We shall no doubt conclude that all voluntary communication of ideas, aside from normal speech, is either a transfer direct or indirect, from the typical symbolism of language as spoken or heard or, at the least, involves the intermediary of truly linguistic symbol-

ism. This is a fact of the highest importance. Auditory imagery
and the correlated motor imagery leading to articulation are,
by whatever devious ways we follow the process, the historic
fountain-head of all speech and of all thinking. (Sapir, 1921,
p. 21)

In the quotation above we find the combination of an insistence that
spoken language is primary, with a recognition that the 'spoken-ness'
of it is not.

Since 1960, however, a number of different interests have converged
to focus attention on sign languages. The first was the interest of
William Stokoe, at Gallaudet College in Washington, DC, in describing
American Sign Language from the approach of American structuralist
linguists. His early work, including *Sign Language Structure* (1960) and
A Dictionary of American Sign Language on Linguistic Principles
(1965), remains the basis of most sign language notation and description of the internal structure of signs. The *Dictionary* was the first
to be arranged by signs rather than by English translation.

A second centre for sign language research was established by Ursula
Bellugi and Edward Klima in San Diego with the aim of describing the
acquisition of American Sign Language by children. They discovered
on the way that the process of acquisition could not be described without first more fully describing the language that was being acquired.
A great deal of work has come from them and their colleagues, particularly in the area of sign morphology (Klima and Bellugi, 1979).

Other linguists have also involved themselves in sign language research, and centres for the study of sign languages have been established
in France and Britain as well as in the USA. This immense growth of
interest in sign language research has forced a wider recognition of the
appropriate place of sign languages among other natural languages.
This research has highlighted both the similarities and the differences
between spoken and sign languages, reorientating linguists to the role
of the medium, whether auditory-articulatory or visual-gestural, in
defining the form of a language (see Kavanagh and Cutting, 1975).
It is now known, for example, that the limited set of simultaneous
components (cheremes) which go to make up the internal structure
of a sign — location, handshape, movement and orientation — combine
and contrast with each other in the same way that a limited set of
linear components (phonemes) combine to form the words of spoken
languages. (See the Appendix to this volume for a fuller description

of the notation of the internal structure of signs found in the chapters in this section.) Research has also shown the richness and complex structures of sign languages, and the wide range of inflections (Siple, 1978; Friedman, 1978).

A further area of research has been the role of non-manual behaviours, such as facial expression and body movement, in conveying meaning and sentence structure (Baker, 1978b; Liddell, 1978). Linguists have also described the sociolinguistics of sign languages, such as variation among different users of the language and attitudes of users to their language (Woodward, 1976; Markowicz, 1979; Deuchar, 1977), in terms of vocabulary and grammar.

As well as forming the first collected body of work on BSL, the chapters in this section combine to shed light on more general issues of language, for example the extent to which the properties of spoken languages that we take to be intrinsic to language are merely artefacts of the auditory-articulatory medium of communication. We are also now beginning to address the question of how much sign languages differ from each other.

Deuchar firmly places BSL among other languages from a sociolinguistic perspective, through a discussion of variation. Factors such as age, sex and region are shown to relate to variation in a number of linguistic features of the language. She also discusses the problems of obtaining linguistic data, problems which are pertinent to all researchers in sign languages.

With Brennan's chapter we move from sociolinguistic aspects of BSL to grammatical features. In this and the following chapter, the concern is to outline a number of syntactic and morphological processes. It is in these areas that contrasts may most clearly be drawn between spoken and sign languages. While formal categories may be similar in these two language groups, the visual-manual medium has important effects upon the realisation of these categories. Brennan discusses BSL structure in terms of its complex aspectual system, introducing features such as classifiers and modulation.

Woll's chapter is concerned with another area of meaning in BSL: questions. Just as in spoken languages, special devices identify questions as formally distinct from other types of sentences, and Woll, in this chapter, as Brennan does in her chapter, devotes attention to the role of non-manual components of sign discourse, in this case, the facial expression, head movements, and postures found in questions.

Evans's chapter, the final one in this section, links the topics of the preceding chapters with issues in communication and education. The growth of linguistic interest in sign languages has been clearly associated with dissatisfaction with traditional approaches to the education and language development of deaf children. An understanding of the linguistics of BSL is a prerequisite to making informed choices about educational methods.

The chapters in this section combine to give a preliminary view of the linguistics of British Sign Language. In contrast with the linguistic analysis of English, this is only at its beginning. Nevertheless, the contributions in this section provide an overview of current research and the basis for future work.

6 VARIATION IN BRITISH SIGN LANGUAGE

Margaret Deuchar

This chapter is based on the assumption that variation is a fundamental characteristic of language. No language used in a community is uniform or static: all languages are variable and constantly changing. Recent work in sociolinguistics has made it possible to account for variation in language by relating it to social factors such as the personal characteristics of the speaker (e.g. social class, age, sex) and features of the situation (e.g. formal or informal). This approach to language has come to be known as 'variation theory'. Variation in language can be found at several levels: the lexicon (or vocabulary), the phonology (or sound system, in spoken languages), and the syntax (or the way in which words or signs are put together).

Linguistic research into spoken language has not always followed the approach of variation theory; in fact this is a relatively new departure. Highly respected work on English, for example (cf. e.g. Chomsky, 1965), focuses on an idealised homogeneous variety of the language without any reference to social context. Variability in the language according to social factors is ignored. This makes the task of the linguist easier in writing grammatical rules, and may arguably have been essential for the theory of grammar to advance at all. However, it is only in research into standardised, high-prestige languages that people can generally agree on what the idealised variety of the language should be. In the case of English it is the standard written language, with its clearly defined sentences. However, sign language has no generally accepted written form, and even no standard unwritten form, at least in Britain. Because of the lack of an idealised variety in BSL, we cannot ignore the existence of variation or the importance of the social context. We have to undertake the ambitious task of describing it in all its varieties, and of trying to account for that variation.

In what follows I will report on my attempt to relate variation in BSL at various levels of the language to social factors, and will compare this to similar research on English and ASL. My report of research in BSL will include discussion of some of the problems of data collection and analysis posed by the variation theory approach.

In English, variation at the level of lexicon is perhaps the most obvious to the lay person; it is well known, for example, that people living in different parts of the country use different words. One word whose usage is related to geographical area in Britain is 'lass'. This is used by some people living in Scotland and northern England, whereas people in southern England would generally use 'girl'. Variation in lexicon according to region (word geography) was of interest to linguists before variation theory in its present form was developed. The survey of English dialects, which began in 1946, involved the investigation of regional variation in vocabulary, and it was discovered, for example, that the term for 'cow-house' or 'cow-shed' varies according to region. While the latter terms are in common use in southern and central England, 'shippon', an older word, is used in parts of Devon and Cornwall and northwestern England (cf. Wakelin, 1972).

James Woodward was one of the first linguists to apply variation theory to research in ASL. In investigating black southern signing in Georgia, Woodward (1976) was able to relate variation in the lexicon to the social factor of race. For example, while white Georgia signers made the sign PREGNANT with interlocking hands extending from the trunk, black signers used an older sign, made by touching the chin twice with an open, spread hand.

In Britain, users of BSL are as aware as users of spoken English that there is variation at the lexical level. It is well known, for example, that people use different signs for the same thing in different parts of the country. A good example is the sign for 'university', which is made with a clawed hand over the heart in the Lancaster area, but in other ways in other parts of the country. Another part of the lexicon of BSL which seems to show obvious variation is the number system, and it would be interesting to know to what extent this variation can be accounted for by social factors. In a preliminary investigation at Lancaster Deaf Club, where I asked people to count from 1-10, there were ten different systems in total for only 14 informants. All informants counted from 1-5 identically, but the variation began at the number 6. Among signs for 'six' alone, I found three variants: (1) with the thumb; (2) with the little finger; and (3) with the right index finger on the left fist. Their distribution is shown in Table 6.1. The only clear generalisation that can be made from the data is that the third variant was produced only by people who were over 40, and who had been educated in the north-west. So age and region of school may both be significant factors. The sample investigated was too small for any more general statements to be made, but variation in numerals would seem to merit further investigation.

Table 6.1: Distribution of Variants of SIX

Variant	Sex	Approximate age	School
(1)	F	65	Margate
(thumb)	F	25	Preston
	M	25	Preston
	M	70	Edinburgh
	F*	50	Birkdale
(2)	F	40	Preston
(little finger)	M	40	Preston
	M	40	Leeds
	F	20	Boston Spa
	F	20	Boston Spa
(3)	F	65	Burnley
(right index	F*	50	Birkdale
on left fist)	M	50	Preston
	M	40	Preston
	M	40	Preston

* This informant produced both (1) and (3) variants.

Numerals are a particularly feasible area of the vocabulary to investi-
gate because one can ask direct questions about them, simply by
asking people to count, with little risk of distorting the data. This is
not possible for all areas of vocabulary; it is difficult to elicit taboo
or swear signs, for example. Also when eliciting items that do not
form part of tight semantic systems (as do numerals or, say, kinship
terms) it is difficult to avoid using an English word. When asking about
the sign for 'university', for example, I had to fingerspell the word.
Although most people gave me signs, two people gave me a fingerspelled 'u', which might have been influenced by my own fingerspelling.

The lexicon is one level of the language at which variation can be
found, but in research on English, there has been most interest in
variation at the phonological level (see Labov, 1972b). This is probably because phonological phenomena are more generalisable than
lexical phenomena (cf. Woodward, 1976, p. 213), and more frequent
than syntactic phenomena. To give an example of research conducted
on British English, Trudgill (1974a) conducted a survey of the English
spoken in Norwich, and focused on phonological variation in relation
to factors such as social class, sex, and formality of the situation

('style'). One phonological variable he was interested in was (h). /h/ may be deleted in Norwich English at the beginning of words, as in 'hat' pronounced [æt] rather than [hæt]. Deletion of /h/ was found to be related to two factors: social class and formality of the situation. The higher the social class of the speaker, and the more formal the situation, the less the /h/ would be dropped. The reverse was also true: the lower the social class of the speaker and the less formal the situation, the more the /h/ would be dropped. In casual speech, all speakers would drop their 'aitches' some of the time, but working-class speakers did it more than middle-class speakers. So each factor, class and situation had a separate effect on the deletion or non-deletion of /h/.

In sign language research we can also look for variation at the level of phonology, if we define phonology as the system of units below the level of the sign. As Klima and Bellugi (1979, p. 43) say, 'A simple lexical sign is essentially a simultaneous occurrence of particular values (particular realisations) of each of several parameters'. The major parameters are hand configuration, place of articulation and movement, while minor parameters include orientation of the hands and number of hands used.

In ASL Woodward (1976) was able to relate variation in one or two hand use for certain signs to factors of both age and race. Older signers used more two-handed variants of the signs than younger signers, and black signers used more two-handed signs than white signers.

In BSL, I investigated phonological deletion and its relation to social factors. As Battison (1974) has shown, phonological deletion of various kinds is possible in ASL, and this is true of BSL also. For example, deletion of tab, or place of articulation, seems to be possible where the tab is the nondominant hand, and especially where the tab is a flat hand or fist. For example, I have often seen the sign RIGHT (citation form ⊔ℬ⌐⊔Ȧ⌐⌣˟) made without the passive hand, and I have also observed CHRISTMAS (citation form ⊓Ä⌐⊔ℬ⌐˟⧛) without the passive fist. Deletion of more marked or less common tab handshapes seems less frequent, but may nevertheless occur, as in e.g. FATHER (citation form ⁗⊢Ӏ⌣⁗ Ӈ⌐⌣) without the two-finger tab. If this kind of deletion is indeed less frequent than the other, there may be a good linguistic reason; a more marked or less common handshape conveys more information than a less common one, so that its loss would have a more serious effect on communication. A type of deletion which involves less information loss than tab deletion, and which also seems to be more frequent, is the deletion of one hand from an otherwise two-handed sign. This happens particularly in two-handed signs where the hands are identical in handshape and movement, but where they do not touch one another, e.g. GIVE, HOSPITAL, HOLIDAY.

As well as linguistic factors affecting frequency of phonological deletion in BSL, it seems likely that there will be social factors, especially formality of the situation. In more formal situations, where more attention is paid to one's signing, I would expect less deletion than in informal situations. I tested this hypothesis in relation to hand deletion in two-handed signs on the basis of 30 minutes of film data (from Reading Deaf Club) in two settings: a church service and a deaf club social evening. I looked at all signs which were either two-handed or had two-handed variants, and which did not involve contact of the hands, and noted whether deletion had taken place. (Signs showing deletion when one of the hands was occupied were excluded from consideration. 'Deletion' is a term used for convenience of description, and is not meant to imply necessarily that the two-handed form of the sign is more basic or underlying than the one-handed form. The important point is that there is variation between one-handed and two-handed forms of signs according to the setting.) As shown in Table 6.2, out of about 100 signs in this category from each setting, 50 per cent had deletion of one hand in the informal setting (deaf club social evening), while only 6 per cent had deletion of one hand in the formal setting (church service). To give some examples of individual signs in both settings: GOOD occurred 6 times in the formal setting, always with two hands, and it occurred 28 times in the informal setting data, of which 21 had only one hand; HAVE occurred 6 times in the formal setting, of which 3 had two hands, and it occurred 4 times in the informal setting, always with one hand only. So whether you look at individual signs or at the general category of two-handed signs, you find more deletion in informal settings. Further investigation is needed here to see to what extent deletion is governed by linguistic factors or social factors other than formality of situation.

The third level of the language at which variation can be studied is syntax. In American English, for example, work done on the speech of Detroit, USA (reported in Trudgill, 1974b), investigated the use of non-standard multiple negation as in 'I don't want none', occurring instead of the standard 'I don't want any'. It was found that this variation could be related to two social factors: class and sex. Working-class speakers used more multiple negation than middle-class speakers, and men used it more than women. This demonstrates that syntactic as well as phonological variables can be related to social factors.

Table 6.2: One-hand Deletion in Two-handed Signs (Reading Deaf
Club)

	Setting			
	Formal		Informal	
	No.	%	No.	%
Two hands	104	94	45	50
One hand	7	6	45	50

In ASL, Woodward and DeSantis (1977) also investigated negation, in particular the use of negative incorporation in the American and French sign languages. In both sign languages, certain signs can be made negative by incorporating a special movement into the sign. In ASL this involves an outward, twisting movement of the hand from the place the sign is made, so that e.g. GOOD becomes BAD in this way. For signs which allow it, negative incorporation is an alternative to several other means of negation, such as the addition of a separate sign, NOT, which can be juxtaposed with the sign instead of the negative being incorporated. Woodward and DeSantis found that there was variation in the use of negative incorporation in ASL (i.e. it was not always used as the means of negation in signs where it was possible), and they were able to relate this to both linguistic and social factors. One of the linguistic factors was the feature ± face: signs made on the face (e.g. GOOD) were more likely to undergo negative incorporation than signs made on the body (e.g. HAVE). One of the important social factors was region; signers living in the northwest of the US were more likely to use negative incorporation than signers living in the northeast. In French Sign Language (FSL), which has a similar form of negative incorporation, Woodward and DeSantis found the same linguistic factors affecting negative incorporation, but different social factors. Region was not a significant factor, but sex was; women used more negative incorporation than men in FSL.

In BSL, formality of situation seems to be an important factor affecting variation at the level of syntax as well as at the phonological level, as discussed above. We know, for example, that the syntax of BSL shows more influence from English in formal than informal situations (cf. Deuchar, 1977; Lawson, this volume). For example, English word order is more likely to be reflected in the order of signs in a formal meeting than it would be in an informal conversation. So a sentence signed WE WILL MEET TOMORROW in a formal situation, following English word order, might be signed informally as TO-MORROW MEET WILL. Another area of syntax which seems to be affected by formality of situation is negation. In formal signing, addi-tion of the sign NOT (◻ 🖐 ⌐ 🖐 ⌐) seems to be the most fre-quent means of negation, as in, for example, WE SHOULD NOT, but in informal signing, NOTHING (◻ F ⌐ ⌐ F ⌐ ᶻ˩) is used more frequently, as in e.g. YOU COME NOTHING HERE ('You didn't come here'). Other means of negation in informal signing are simultaneous head-shaking as in e.g. UNDERSTAND ('I don't understand'), and negative incorporation. (head-shake)

The situational factor is so strong in sign language that it has been suggested for both ASL and BSL (cf. Stokoe, 1969; Deuchar, 1977 and 1978; and Lawson, this volume) that they exhibit diglossia (cf. Ferguson, 1959), having separate varieties for formal and informal situations. This would clearly imply an overriding importance for the situational factor, which is an empirical question. In order to investi-gate the effect on variation in BSL syntax of factors other than formality of situation, I conducted a pilot study in Lancaster Deaf Club, attempting to relate use of negative incorporation in the verbs KNOW and LIKE to factors such as age, sex, occupation and school attended.

Negative incorporation in BSL is similar to the phenomenon in ASL and FSL, as investigated by Woodward and DeSantis (1977). In BSL it occurs in a similar, limited set of verbs. These verbs include WILL, KNOW, LIKE, WANT, BELIEVE, and AGREE. All these signs can be negated by an opening and upward (or downward) movement of the hand, but may also be negated by alternative means, such as the addition of NOT or NOTHING to the verb, as described above. Because negative incorporation occurs in only a limited set of verbs, and because it is only one of several means of negation in these verbs, data collection in this area is quite problematic. My study will serve to illustrate some of the problems involved in research on variation in syntax.

In order to investigate the usage of individuals and to try to relate this to social factors, I chose interviews as the method of data collec-tion. The interviewer was a member of the deaf club, and all inter-views were observed by me. At the beginning of the interview signers were asked about their approximate age, how long they had lived in

Lancaster or anywhere else, which school they had attended, whether
the school was residential, at what age they had left school, and what
their current or past occupation was. They were then asked a series of
general knowledge questions, having been told that the questions were
just for fun, not to test their ability, but to see what signs they used in
their replies. The questions asked were designed so that the respondents
would be likely to know the answers to some, though not all of them,
and the actual purpose of the questions was to elicit equivalents of 'I
don't know', where the verb KNOW would show either presence or
absence of negative incorporation. The general knowledge questions
were followed by a few questions about likes and dislikes, designed to
elicit sign equivalents of 'I don't like'. Respondents were shown pictures of celebrities, drinks and food, and asked their opinion of tele-
vision programmes and the interview was then concluded. The interview
was conducted with nine people as a pilot study, and the results were
then examined.

Table 6.3: Negative Incorporation in KNOW (Lancaster Deaf Club)

Subject		Negative variant of KNOW		
Sex	Age	KNOW (NEG)	KNOW NOTHING	NEVER KNOW
F	65	3	0	0
M	45	2	2	0
M	45	4	0	0
M	60	3	0	0
F	55	0	0	1
F	50	2	0	0
F	35	9	0	0
F	40	3	0	0
M	70	0	0	0

N.B. Only sex and age of subjects are given for interest, as no other information
proved to be relevant.

The results (see Table 6.3) show that the method of data collection
was not entirely successful, and so needs to be improved. In response
to general knowledge questions which they could not answer, signers
did not necessarily use any negative form of KNOW, but often shook
their heads or looked puzzled. However, out of eight people who did
use some negative form of KNOW at least once, six people used KNOW

(NEG-Inc) (KNOW with negative incorporation) categorically, i.e. they used no other means of negation with KNOW. One person varied between KNOW (NEG-Inc) and KNOW NOTHING, and another used NEVER KNOW once, with no other occurrences of KNOW. The problem in analysing these data is that the number of occurrences per person of negative KNOW was highly variable, and often small, ranging from nine to nil.

Elicitation of a negative form of LIKE was even less successful, partly because people expressed likes in preference to dislikes, possibly out of politeness, and partly because they used other terms for dislikes, such as RUBBISH, or head-shaking. The small amount of data obtained for each verb meant that it was not possible to relate the results to the social factors on which I had information for each individual.

A general problem affecting the results was no doubt the presence of the hearing observer. This had the effect that, despite requests to sign, some signers did more mouthing than usual, and others even used their voices. This raises the question of the Observer's Paradox (cf. Labov, 1972c) or how to observe people signing as they would if they were not being observed. Labov has pointed out that the presence of an observer makes a situation more formal, and affects the language used correspondingly. An interview situation is also likely to be defined as formal, and in this study the combined influence of the interview situation and the presence of the hearing observer probably made the linguistic behaviour formal.

So how can one solve the problem of the Observer's Paradox in sign language research? One obvious solution is for the hearing researcher to adopt a lower profile, and not to be present at all during data collection. This should become increasingly possible as more deaf people become involved in sign language research. The other problematic effect, that of the interview situation, is more difficult to deal with. One might argue that we should dispense with the structured interview completely when investigating informal signing, and observe and record only naturally occurring signing. This approach seems reasonable for investigating variation at the level of phonology, since the forms with which one is concerned occur very frequently. However, certain syntactic variables, such as negative incorporation, do not occur so frequently, and so have to be elicited in a more structured way. The problem, as posed by Labov (1972c, p. 117) is 'how to enrich the data of natural conversation by minimal intervention'. This problem remains to be solved for research into variation in syntax in general, both in spoken language and in sign language.

So far I have discussed problems of data collection in connection with research into sign language variation, but I have not given any consideration to data analysis. I do not intend to discuss it here at great length, partly because problems of data collection have to be solved before data analysis can take place, but it seems worth making a few points. There is in fact some controversy about the appropriate methods of analysis for variable data, and in particular whether variable rules are an adequate way of capturing language variation.

A variable rule looks like a rule of generative grammar, except that the probability of its application depends on certain linguistic and/or social factors. To give an example, phonological deletion of one hand in a two-handed sign in BSL might be captured by a variable rule in the following way:

$$\text{ØDD} \longrightarrow \left\langle \text{ØD} \right\rangle \Big/\Big/ \left\langle \begin{array}{c} \text{Informal} \\ \\ \text{Formal} \end{array} \right\rangle$$

$$(- \text{ contact})$$

Informal: $p < .5$
Formal: $p < .06$

This rule says that in signs with two hands (two 'D's in notation), one hand will be deleted variably. The probability of deletion taking place will be .06 in formal situations, .5 in informal situations. These figures are based on the actual percentages of deletion in the data on film mentioned earlier. So one way of analysing the data is to use it to formulate rules which will predict future linguistic behaviour in relation to factors such as the formality of the situation. Not all those working in variation theory agree with this approach, however, and some, for example, prefer to look in more detail at the linguistic data itself before relating it to social factors. The latter approach is taken by Woodward in his work on ASL. Variation theory is still in a formative stage as far as methods of analysis are concerned, and since the discussion is too complex to be reported briefly, the literature on the subject (e.g. Sankoff, 1978) is best consulted at first hand.

In this chapter I have tried to show how variation theory is an appropriate and interesting way of approaching sign language research. Although there are many unsolved problems both of data collection and data analysis, the search for solutions will hopefully serve the dual purpose of increasing our knowledge of BSL as used in the deaf community, and of enriching linguistic theory.

Acknowledgements

Thanks are due to members of Lancaster and Reading Deaf Clubs for providing the data, and to Sue Foster for helpful comments on an earlier version of this chapter.

7 GRAMMATICAL PROCESSES IN BRITISH SIGN LANGUAGE

Mary Brennan

For the non-signer, seeing British Sign Language (BSL) can be rather like switching on the radio and hearing an unfamiliar spoken language. The listener, at first, simply hears a confusion of sound, then gradually begins to discern some kind of patterning. Often, however, that patterning is filtered through the person's own native language system so that importance may be given to features of the new language which are trivial, while essential aspects are ignored. Similarly, hearing people try to find patterns in BSL which are already familiar. They try to make sense of BSL in terms of English. Such an approach is difficult to avoid, even for those of us researching into the language, yet it can result in a highly distorted view of the nature of the linguistic system.

The dangers of distortion are increased because in looking at BSL through English, we bring with us assumptions based primarily upon our knowledge of spoken language in general. Yet sign languages are expressed in a quite different medium; they are gestural/visual systems, produced by movements of hands, face and body and perceived by the eyes. All language mediums impose particular constraints on the nature of the linguistic system, hence the recognisable differences between spoken and written forms of languages. More positively we can look for ways in which a linguistic system exploits the medium in which it is expressed. The visual/gestural medium has allowed BSL to develop in ways which would be quite impossible in English and hence quite unexpected to hearing people. Deaf people may also have assumptions about the structure of their own language which are based on the status of spoken language within the wider hearing community. It is just as difficult for a deaf person to describe the processes and mechanisms at work in his own language as it is for hearing people to give an account of the role of auxiliary verbs or case relationships in English. As fluent English users, we do not need to stop and think about how the language works and if we do, we may end up being very puzzled. Similarly, the fluent BSL user manipulates the complex patterning of the language, often without realising that it is complex. In research on BSL both deaf and hearing groups have to learn to look at BSL in a new way.

Since the development of research into different sign languages, there have been important changes in the name given to the linguistic medium used in signing. The older term, the *manual* medium, is clearly inadequate since this suggests that the hands alone create the meaningful patterning in sign languages. Certainly the hands have a special role to play, but other types of gesture, including fine movements of the eyes, mouth, face, head, shoulders and body may also be used in a regular and systematic way; hence the use of the term *gestural* in place of manual. The addition of the term *visual* to the label focuses attention on the way in which sign languages are perceived. Present research indicates that patterning within sign languages is affected not only by the physical possibilities of production articulators (head, arms, hands, etc.) but also the characteristics and limitations of visual perception. One clear example is that more detailed refinements of handshape and movement occur closer to the central point of focus, while signs made on the periphery tend to use grosser and more recognisable options.

More recently a third word has been added to the label for the linguistic medium, *spatial*. Sign patterning occurs in space, and we therefore need to understand the dynamics of space and the possibilities of space. At first, this may seem a rather obvious point; of course sign languages occur in space but why should that be particularly important? The main answer to this question lies in the contrast between the temporal patterning of spoken languages and the primarily spatial patterning of sign languages. In spoken languages words occur in time, one after the other, and they can be analysed in sequential terms. Thus word order is crucially important in a language such as English. In a sense, spoken words also occur in space: they are produced in one place rather than another, in a particular linguistic and situational context.

Just as spoken language occurs both in time and space, so sign language exploits both temporal and spatial patterning. Signs do occur one after the other, and sequential order may be important, but *where* signs are located spatially and *how* they execute systematic patterning in space can be just as significant as *when* they occur. Moreover, at any one point in time, several linguistic forms can be produced simultaneously. One of our informants produced a signed sentence which could be translated as: 'I used to sit and stare at the teacher without understanding a thing.' If one freezes the film at exactly the right moment, all of that information can be encapsulated, although of course the signed utterance can only be fully understood in context. The initial gloss of that single moment would probably be the sign LOOK; how-

Example 7.1: 'I used to sit and stare at the teacher without
  understanding a thing.'

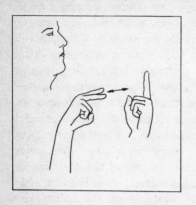

ever, on closer examination, we can note several other important
features of the sign production. The left hand, index finger extended,
is pointing outwards away from the signer's body, indicating the
object of the sign articulated by the right hand; given the context we
know that this form refers to the teacher. The right hand produces
the sign LOOK, but rather than using the neutral, unmarked form of
LOOK which has the V handshape (index and second finger extended)
with palm facing left, moving outwards, the signer changes the orientation of the sign so that the fingers point outwards and slightly upwards
towards the left hand. Thus the exact form of LOOK, as well as indicating the object (the teacher), incorporates information about the
subject; the subject was a child who had to look up at the teacher's
face. The body stance, shoulder position and head position all emphasise and reiterate this information, as the shoulders are held back,
the head is slightly tilted and the eye gaze is directed towards the
imagined position of the object. However, this is not all that is happening; the facial expression is also providing vital information indicating
that the child could not understand a thing. Viewed in slow motion,
and occurring across the same time stretch as the manual signs noted
above, the head tilts to the side and the tongue, with tip curled inwards, protrudes slightly. This is a non-manual sign which means
something like 'can't be bothered'. To describe major grammatical
processes in BSL, therefore, reference must be made to these three
features of sign conversation, namely manual production, non-manual
gestural production and exploitation of the signing space.

It should be clear from the above example that at any one time in a sign language utterance, several different systems may be working together simultaneously. Different types of information are packed into the utterance in different ways. The danger is that an observer expecting the types of patterning found in spoken language will note only the activity of the dominant hand, and gloss the whole utterance as LOOK. This kind of gloss completely underestimates the range of grammatical categories and processes realised in such an utterance.

The term grammatical process is a somewhat wide one and obviously this chapter can only focus on one small area of grammar. The following comments will therefore concentrate primarily on morphological processes, i.e. modifications in the forms of individual words which produce regular changes of meaning. However, the traditional distinction between syntax and morphology is not so easily applicable to sign language. The above example has shown that several different systems of options may be operating at one and the same time, and it is not always easy to decide whether a particular feature should be regarded as syntactic or morphological. If we accept that the internal structure of individual signs is composed of particular realisations of the parameters of position, handshape, orientation and movement (see Appendix), then a systematic change in any one of these aspects accompanied by a regular change in meaning may be classed as a morphological process.

Example 7.2: Incorporation of Subject

a. Right.   b. I'm right.

The neutral or unmarked form of the sign CORRECT (Example

7.2a) is produced by bringing the closed fist of the dominant hand into contact with the flat palm of the non-dominant hand. However, in signed utterances the actual position and orientation of this sign may vary according to the subject: in 'I am correct' (7.2b) the sign is made on the chest with palm facing inwards. In both cases explicit reference to the subject of the sentence by the use of a separate sign may or may not be made. The orientation of the sign provides information on who or what the subject is, so the notion of subject is *incorporated* into the form of the sign. It is important to note that our evidence suggests that if the subject is made explicit, then there are restrictions on the options available depending upon the choice of subject. It is probably ungrammatical to produce 'You are correct' by using the pro-form YOU with index finger pointing *away* from the signer and then to produce a form of CORRECT in which the orientation of the palm is directed inwards *towards* the signer and the hand contacts the chest. There is thus concord or agreement in the grammatical sense between the subject and the form of the verb or adjective in such cases. This concord may be just as obligatory as the concord which operates in English. Indeed, as the notion of agreement is actually rather limited in English as compared with many other spoken languages, we may find that agreement rules are more pervasive in BSL than in English.

While the location changes in CORRECT seem to be directly morphological, other aspects of location may be viewed syntactically, in that we must take account of other items in the utterance and recognise the relationships that exist among them. The table at the end of this chapter lists a number of syntactic processes. In the example, 'He walked towards the two people', one hand produces the sign for TWO PEOPLE (extended and spread index and second fingers pointing upwards), while the other produces the sign for WALK (extended and spread index and second fingers pointing downwards, and moving alternately with whole hand moving forward (see Example 7.3). If we ignore the other item in the utterance we could misinterpret the sign WALK as 'walk away', 'walk out' or simply 'walk'.

A more fundamental difficulty relates to establishing criteria for distinguishing the basic units of sign language. In a spoken language like English, grammatical processes operate at different levels and across different stretches of utterance. Yet in BSL it is not always easy to identify such units as words, phrases, clauses or sentences. Certainly some kind of 'chunking' is apparent and can be signalled by such features as pause, the extension of a sign, the holding or freezing of

Example 7.3: 'He walked towards the two people.'

a sign in a particular position, or allowing the hands to come to rest. In other cases it is more difficult to decide on the boundaries between units or on the nature of the units which are distinguished. In English we know that different kinds of processes operate in the noun phrase and the verb phrase; the distinction between nouns and verbs and noun phrases and verb phrases is crucially important in any elaboration of grammatical rules. Of course, in BSL, it is also possible to distinguish classes and units but we are still at a very early stage in establishing comprehensive criteria. An example may illustrate this point. One of our informants discussing the situation in Northern Ireland comments that this conflict is passed on from generation to generation. He uses a sign in which the first two fingers of each hand are extended together and the two fingers of the right hand are placed over the left (as in the British 'f'), the two hands then move downwards in steps. This sign is sometimes translated as 'tradition', 'hereditary' or 'generation' depending on context. For example, if it is produced beginning at a point close to the ear and then moving downwards to the right, it means 'hereditary deafness' (see Example 7.4). In the Northern Ireland example, the signer extends the sign and follows this by a one-handed sign, using the flat hand with palm upwards, also moving down in steps. In one short sample of text he uses GENERATION four times either with or without the one-handed sign following. It could be suggested that the sign glossed as GENERATION is a noun and the one-handed sign is a verb meaning something like CONTINUE or CARRY-ON. However, it is clear from the occasions when the one-handed sign is omitted that the verbal element of continuity is also expressed in the first sign. Yet the observable difference between the unmarked form of GENERATION and the marked form meaning 'It is passed on from generation to generation', is very slight and can probably be described only in terms of emphasis.

Example 7.4: Related Meanings

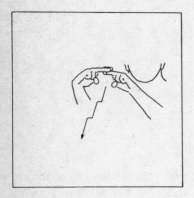

a. Hereditary deafness

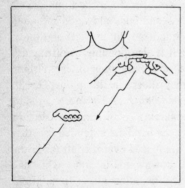

b. Carried on from generation to generation

c. Hereditary

Klima and Bellugi (1979) have commented that they found their original clues to the nature of morphological processes in ASL by looking at the idioms used by deaf signers. In our research at Edinburgh we have videotaped 30 informants in pairs. As well as using structured materials and asking the informants to undertake specific tasks, we have tried to provide opportunities for spontaneous conversation. Since all our informants are profoundly deaf people from deaf families, utterances which would probably be classed as idioms occur frequently.

We too are finding these idioms a source of information on sign modification and patterning. The term idiom itself is open to different
interpretations. There is a tendency to class any item which cannot
be easily translated into English as idiomatic. If we take a wider view
and see idiom as usage specific to a particular language, then we begin
to see why idioms are so important. They make use of features which
are specific to sign languages and not spoken languages. Because there
are no one-to-one glosses for these, the researcher is forced to try
to make sense of them without reference to English It is worth noting
that hearing people with a limited knowledge of signing tend to ignore
idioms; they concentrate on what can be translated easily into English
and thereby lose much of the richness of patterning within the language.

An examination of idioms provides information, among other things,
on the existence of specific *classifiers* in BSL: these are pro-forms (like
pronouns) in which the handshape of the sign provides information on
the type or class of referent. The pointed upright index finger may be
used to stand for PERSON, the flat hand palm down for CAR and the
whole hand with spread fingers upright for PEOPLE. A few examples
of the use of the PEOPLE classifier may help to illustrate this (see
Example 7.5). The italicised sections in the English translations represent meanings expressed by a sign which makes use of the PEOPLE
classifier. However, the actual sign may be varied by the use of one
or two hands, the positioning of the hand(s), the movement of the
hands and accompanying facial or non-manual gesture. In 5a the
sign begins by making use of the two hands moving down and forwards with fingers flickering. Then the left hand is formed in the
shape of a tunnel (fingers together, hand bent at major knuckles),
and the right-hand fingers, still flickering, move underneath. In the first
sentence of 5b two-handed signs are used; firstly the hands are
positioned in front of the signer's body, right hand resting on left,
fingers spread, the left hand moves forwards and the right hand backwards with long up and down movements. Both hands then move in
a symmetrical semicircle. In the second sentence of 5b only one hand
is used, the fingers flicker and the hand is moved in a slight arc in
front of the body. In 5c a two-handed sign is used with one hand
moving back and the other slightly forward. What we have here are
recognisable and regular changes which give information that in a
language like English would need to be expressed by accompanying
adverbials of time, place manner and degree.

Such examples also give us a clue as to why Kegl (1979) has

Example 7.5: Classifiers

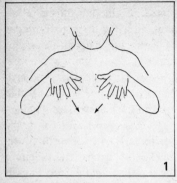 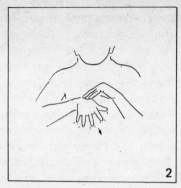

a. When the sirens went, *all the people rushed*[1] *into the air raid shelter.*[2]

 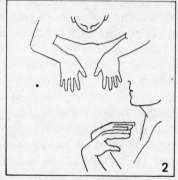

b. There were *crowds of people there,*[1] *throngs of Catholics.*[2] *Mingling amongst them*[3] were some Protestants.

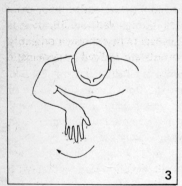

c. I think *far too many people* want to join the badminton group.

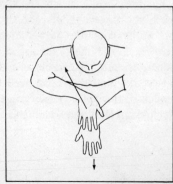

suggested an analysis of ASL verbs in terms of classifiers and motion. The difference between 'one person went' and 'the people went' may simply be in the choice of classifier; the movement is similar for both.

The Edinburgh BSL project is concerned primarily with the grammar of BSL and within that huge field we are hoping to find specific information about tense and aspect in BSL. We wish to examine how information about time is encoded in the language, and how verbs are modified to express temporal information. However, we are using the terms tense and aspect in a fairly wide sense, because we recognise that there are numerous ways in which such information can be encoded. The distinction between tense and aspect is difficult to characterise, yet it is a vital distinction. Comrie (1976), in his study of aspectual systems in many different languages, describes aspect as being concerned with 'the internal temporal constituency of the situation'. Tense, on the other hand, is deictic; it places an action or event in relation to some particular temporal reference point, such as the present moment. Having placed an action at a particular point in time we can still view it in different ways in terms of its own temporal structure. We can see it, for example, as ongoing, recurring or complete. In 'He was singing yesterday', and 'He is singing tomorrow', the singing occurs at different points in time, yet in both cases we choose the same aspectual option of progressive, indicating ongoing activity.

One of our tasks is to discover to what extent these different temporal notions are grammaticalised in the language, and to what extent they are lexicalised. Many languages express deictic time relations by means of accompanying adverbials rather than changes in the form of the verb. In English we tend to use both and in many cases temporal adverbials are obligatory even though verb modification is present. In BSL deictic time reference appears to be expressed primarily by time adverbials, while aspectual contrasts are realised by systematic modifications of the verb. In English the difference between 'simple present' and 'habitual' is carried by the adverbial:

Now he comes to the front.
He always comes to the front.

In BSL the presence of the adverbial ALWAYS seems to demand a modification of the verb form by repetition. As yet we do not have enough evidence to show whether such modification is compulsory or merely probable. In the BSL forms for:

I've never seen him before.
I see him often.

we would expect to find modification by repetition in the second example, but not in the first.

The kinds of modification employed to express aspectual constraints mostly involve changes in the movement parameters. In the earlier example of STARE the sign LOOK is held in space so the sign means 'look at for a long time'. The whole action of the sign can be repeated to indicate 'looking at again and again'. In a signed utterance meaning 'They were all talking for ages', the sign TALK may be repeated again and again and articulated in a semicircle in front of the body (see Example 7.6). The semicircle may express continuity but may also incorporate the subject of the sentence. This incorporation of clause elements such as subject, direct object, indirect object, complement and adverbial within the form of the verbal element appears to be one of the most pervasive features of BSL and other sign languages.

At this stage it is not easy to define the limits of aspect itself. What is clear is that much of the information carried in the verb form would be expressed in English by adverbs of duration, degree, extent, frequency, time and place. The difference between 'I agree fully' and 'Well I agree but . .' can be indicated in the modification of the sign AGREE. In the first example, there is a single definite movement, in the second several shorter movements. In both cases facial and body expression will also be important. The table at the end of this chapter summarises a number of the processes discussed above.

At this stage in the analysis of our data we are able to recognise many different types of modification, but as yet we are unable to specify classes of verbs which are associated with one type of mechanism rather than another. We know, for example, that some verbs such as MEET are reversible, in that it is possible to change the orientation of both hands. Others can be located at different points in space, e.g. WALK, FLY. However, there are cherological restrictions here. LOOK has many variations including, for example, a sign meaning 'they all look at me', in which the two hands with first two fingers in the form of V turn inwards to point towards the signer (see Example 7.7). Such a modification involving changes in palm and finger orientation is impossible with the semantically related sign WATCH. However, the two hands may be moved towards the signer rather than away, so that there is modification by movement.

In WATCH, one hand is placed on top of the other, and it is

impossible to turn the hands inward. In the same way, many signs which involve contact with the head or body, such as LIVE and KNOW, cannot be located at different points in space. During the course of our research we hope to be able to provide detailed elaboration of the specific classes of verbs. We also hope to show which items have compulsory accompanying non-manual information.

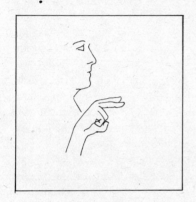

Example 7.6: Incorporation of Clause Elements

a. Look at for a long time.

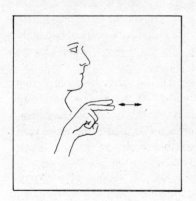

b. Look at again and again

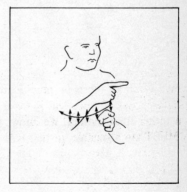

c. They were all talking for ages.

Our early analyses of the data collected on videotape suggest that BSL has a variety of grammatical processes which allow the realisation of the traditional grammatical categories of tense, aspect, number and person. (The table at the end of this chapter shows a variety of these).

More than this, BSL is able to exploit its manual-gestural-spatial medium in ways which are quite unknown in spoken languages and hence particularly fascinating.

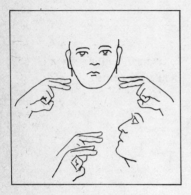

Example 7.7: Verb Classes

a. They all look at me

b. *They all watch me.

c. They all watch me.

* Non-occurring form.

Grammatical Processes in BSL

A. Person/Number

1. Incorporation of Subject

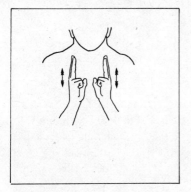

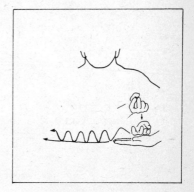

They were all dead.   They were all sitting.

2. Incorporation of Object

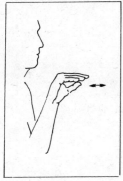

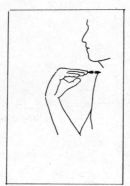

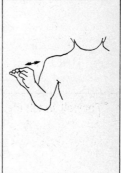

a. I remind you   b. You (singular) remind   c. I remind him.
(singular)   me.

3. Incorporation of Subject and Object.

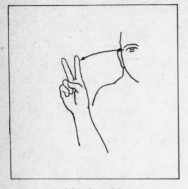

a. I look at him.

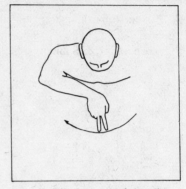

b. I look at you (plural).

c. He looks at me.

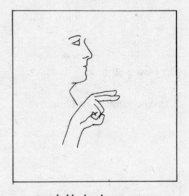

d. He looks at you.

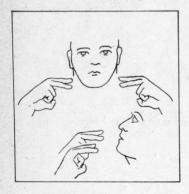

e. They look at me.

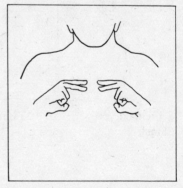

f. They look at each other.

B. Locatives (cf. English adverbials of place)

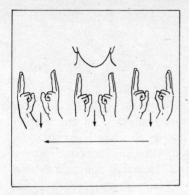

a. They sat in rows.

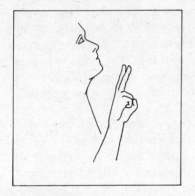

b. He looked up.

c. He looked around.

8 QUESTION STRUCTURE IN BRITISH SIGN LANGUAGE

Bencie Woll

Until fairly recently, something called 'language', which was defined as consisting of sound units composed of phonemes, and characterised by its referential function, was treated as the core of human communication. All other behaviours found in the context of human communication were called 'nonverbal', meaning nonvocal or non-linguistic, and were considered to be subordinate, peripheral and unsystematic (Baker, 1977). The central assumption of this approach was that 'language' alone was primary in communication. These assumptions have been strongly challenged in recent years. For example, Crystal (1969) had asked 'why should prosodic or paralinguistic patterning be judged by phonemic or morphemic criteria?', and he suggests an arrangement of behaviours along a 'most-least' linguistic continuum, rather than classifying some as nonlinguistic. 'Language' in this new approach becomes one system of interaction among several potentially simultaneous interacting modalities.

If we wish to look at some particular area of human communication, then it would be useful to select an area where we can see the modalities interact. Questions provide a meeting point for interpersonal and referential behaviours, taking place in a number of modalities simultaneously, formally distinct from other utterances.

To understand the structure of questions in BSL, we might first see how the description of questions forms a part of linguistic research in spoken languages. Traditionally, linguists make a distinction between three major types of sentence: declarative (statements), imperative (commands), and interrogative (questions). Greenberg, in his research on linguistic universals (1966), suggests three ways (for all spoken languages) in which questions are marked as distinct from other sentence types; firstly, by an interrogative particle; secondly, by a difference in intonation pattern; thirdly, by a difference in word order. Any or all of these three characteristics may be found in combination. These types of distinctive marking are illustrated below with examples from English. Since English and BSL are so unlike, any features we find in common suggest that some linguistic universals also apply to sign languages.

Example 8.1: Table of Question Types in English

Sentence	Question Word	Special Intonation	Special Word Order
a. (no English examples)	+	−	−
b. You're going?	−	+	−
c. Have you got a pencil?	−	+	+
d. It's at what time?	+	+	−
e. What have you got?	+	+	+
f. Can you leave now?	−	+	+
g. When can I get you?	+	+	+

The table shows for each question whether there is a special question word, a special word order, and a special intonation. In the examples given in 8.1, a diagrammatic line has been used to show where there are rises and falls in pitch. Most important, the use of intonation to mark questions shows that important distinctions in the meanings of sentences may be signalled through a different modality, 'pitch', rather than through articulated sounds. Note, too, that examples 1b and 1d suggest surprise as well as questioning.

There are two major groups of questions in English, which can be referred to as 'wh-' and 'yes/no' questions. 'Wh-' questions are characterised by incorporating the words 'what', 'why', 'which', 'how', 'who', 'where', 'when', as in the questions, 'When are you leaving?', 'Who took the book?'. 'Yes/no' questions are those which can be answered with 'yes' or 'no'; 'Is it 10 o'clock?', 'Would you like a cup of coffee?', etc. Both these sorts of questions are characterised by occurring with two special features. The first is called inversion of the verb, as illustrated below.

> John can drive.
> Can John drive?

The auxiliary verb 'can' is moved to the beginning of the sentence. Where there is no auxiliary verb, 'do' is added and moved in the same way.

> Does John drive?

In 'wh-' questions, the 'wh' word appears at the front of the sentence before the auxiliary verb.

> John can drive a lorry.
> What can John drive?

The third special feature that occurs in questions is special intonation. This is found in all the sentences in Example 8.1. Intonation in general is an interesting phenomenon. It extends over relatively long stretches, unlike the sound units or words of a language. Intonation patterns in a language are among the very first patterns which a child learning a language can respond to and produce, but they are among the most difficult for second language learners to perfect. Also, and this is a problem for describing intonation, the writing systems of most languages give a very inadequate representation of intonation.

Questions in BSL

It may be assumed, in the first instance, that questions exist in BSL, as they do in other languages, and that they fulfil the same functions; and this assumption is supported by the existence of signs such as ASK, ANSWER and QUESTION, as well as signs such as INTERVIEW, which is derived from the sign ASK.

Wh—Questions

Some questions occur with certain lexical items (wh-questions) just as in English. A list of these is given here with English translations (see Example 8.2). It should be noted that there is no one-to-one correspondence between a sign representation and its English translation; some single signs can only be translated by two or more English words (see Appendix for explanation of symbols). The list in Example 8.2 is not exhaustive.

In English, the 'wh-question' words are linked in form to each other. They all begin with 'wh-' (with the exception of 'how', although historically it too began with 'wh') and several are linked to non-question words such as the pairs 'where-there', 'what-that', 'when-then'. In BSL too, some 'wh-question' signs are linked to each other and to other non-question signs.

If we compare some of the 'wh-question' signs we see that the same handshape and movement occur in WHEN, HOW—MANY and HOW—OLD; all have five fingers extended, separated, and wiggling (5). This handshape and movement also occur in the sign MANY. The location of WHEN is the same as the location of signs such as YESTERDAY, TOMORROW and EVERYDAY. The location of HOW—OLD is also the location of AGE and OLD, and the location of HOW—MANY is the same as MANY. We can thus see links both among 'wh-question' signs and between these signs and others with related meanings. These links are indicated in Example 8.3. The internal elements of these signs, such as handshape and location, have general meanings themselves. This sort of analysis can also be performed on other kinds of signs such as verbs of motion. For example, in the sign MEET, the handshape 'upright index finger' ( ) denotes 'one person'; the movement 'approaching'. In the sign DEPART (one person from another), the handshape is the same as MEET; the movement indicates that one person is moving and that this movement is away from the other.

The appearance of a 'wh-question' sign does not suffice to form a question. These signs may also be used as relative pronouns, similarly to the way they are used in, and probably influenced by, English. (See Lawson, this volume, for a discussion of the influence of English on BSL.) In Example 8.5, recorded in a conversation between a deaf and a hearing person, the sign WHEN at the beginning of the utterance only introduces an English-type relative clause (see Carter, 1980; Carter and Woll, 1980, for a discussion of BSL relative clauses). Only the second clause, marked with arrows, constitutes the utterance as a question.

Example 8.2: Wh- Question Signs (see Appendix for explanation of
notation)

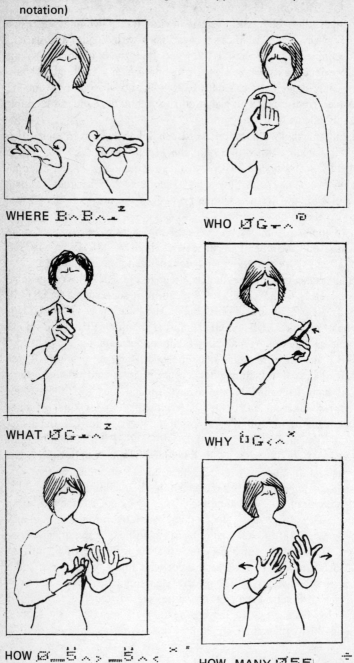

WHERE B∧B∧⌐ᶻ

WHO ∅G⊤∧ᴿ

WHAT ∅G⊤∧ᶻ

WHY ∅G‹∧ˣ

HOW ∅⎯5∧›⎯5∧‹ ˣ "

HOW-MANY ∅55⊤∧ ÷&

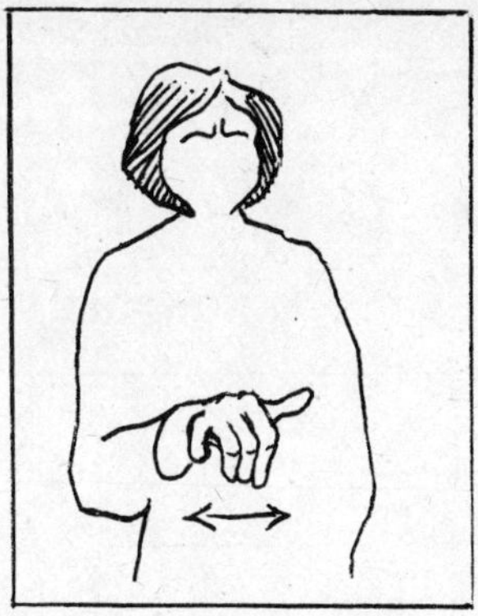

WHICH

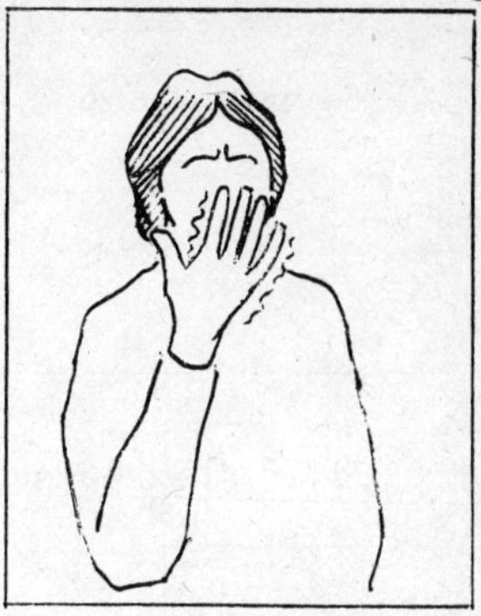

HOW–OLD

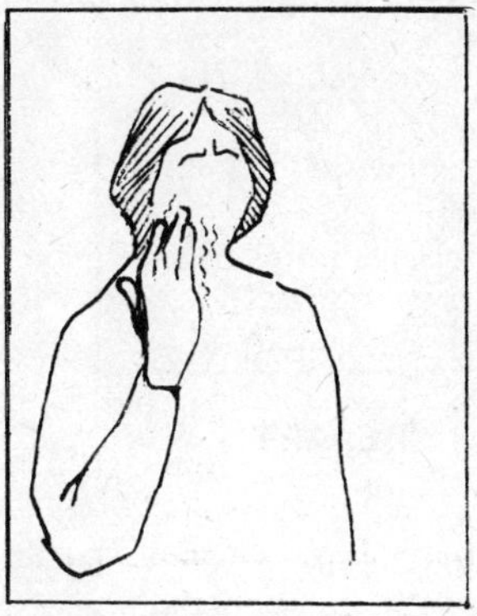

WHEN

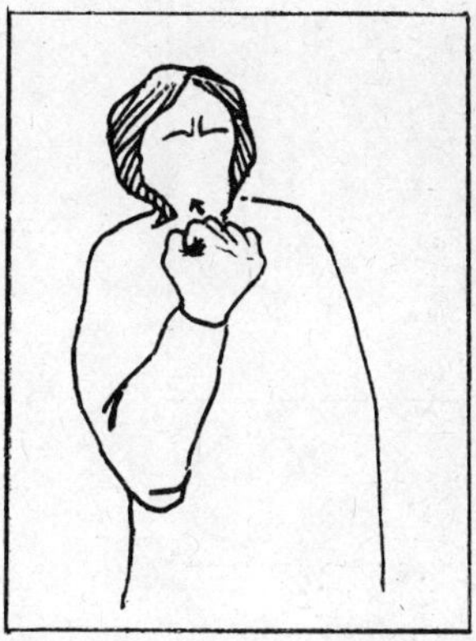

WHAT–DATE

Example 8.3: Classifier Incorporated into Question

	Location			Question Sign
Handshape 5 incorporated into	*Time	3	=	WHEN
	*Quantity	Ø	=	HOW—MANY
	*Age	1	=	HOW—OLD

Example 8.4: Classifier Incorporated into Verb

MEET   DEPART

Signers are therefore able to recognise that the presence of a particular manual item does not necessarily characterise an utterance as a question. Other features of an utterance must be available to a signer to recognise it as a question, and the information used by signers to decide if an utterance is a question will be discussed later in the section of this chapter on non-manual components.

A number of examples are given (see Example 8.6) of 'wh-questions' in BSL utterances. As can be seen from the examples, 'wh-' signs occur at either the beginning of a clause, at the end of a clause, or both at the beginning and at the end.

The type of structure indicated in which the same sign appears both before and after a particular stretch of signs, is called bracketing (examples 8.6 b, d, f, h, j and l). Bracketing marks constituent boundaries in a variety of constructions in BSL, for example, in noun phrases: SHIRT WHITE SHIRT, and adverbials of time: ONE—WEEK WORK BRISTOL ONE—WEEK. We therefore may conclude that bracketed 'wh-question' signs apply to the entire stretch of signing around which they occur. The extent of the question marker — the whole clause — signalled by the bracketed 'wh-question' sign, is paralleled by other clause-length markers which will be discussed in the section below on non-manual components.

Example 8.5: Utterance Containing Question

GLOSS: WHEN HER SISTER AND BROTHER TRAVEL CAR—
                  THERE / p·a·t STAY ONE—WEEK / COME SELF /
                  HOW—LONG HER SISTER SAY THERE //

                  └ - - - - - - - - - - - - - - - - question - - - - - - ┘

TRANSLATION: When her sister and brother travel there by car and Pat stays
                  one week and then comes back on her own, how long will
                  her sister stay there

Example 8.6: Wh-Questions

a. WHERE YOUR FATHER GO
   where will your father go

b. WHERE GO WHERE
   where is she going

c. WHO GO WITH
   who will she go with

d. WHO INDEX SEE WHO
   who will she see

e. HOSPITAL NAME WHAT
   what's the name of the hospital

f. WHAT WORK WHAT
   what work does he do

g. WHY BAR
   why (did you like) the bars

h. WHY YOU GO INDEX
   AMERICA WHY
   why did you go to America

i. INDEX AMERICA HOW
   TRAVEL INDEX INDEX
   how did you travel between here
   and America

j. HOW TRAVEL INDEX HOW
   how did you travel there

k. WHEN INDEX GO THERE
   when will she go there

l. WHEN GO HOLIDAY WHEN
   when will she go on holiday

Yes-No Questions

'Yes-no' questions, unlike functionally similar questions in English, are not distinguished formally in terms of manual sign order from other sentence types. That is, one cannot tell from a sign gloss that an utterance is a question. A number of optional manual markers may be used to distinguish questions, and these are treated below as manual shift regulators.

Baker, in a study of turn-taking in ASL (1978b), has enumerated a set of devices which signal generally that one signer is relinquishing his turn or 'handing over the conversation' to the other. These devices are found at the end of sign utterances. Baker's list includes:

1. Holding hand or hands out, fingers pointing away, palm up, heel of hand higher than fingertips (B ∴ ⌄)
2. Indexing the addressee (i.e. pointing)
3. Prolonging the duration of the last sign
4. Index finger raised, palm away from body, held still or with finger moved from side to side (☑ G ⊥ ∴ ᶻ) the same as the sign WHAT

The same manual shift regulators can be found as optional devices in BSL, however, apart from their general use as shift regulators, the distinctiveness of these devices as question markers is not clear. As questions formally signal that a turn is to be relinquished, and that the other participant is to respond, these features may merely mark this shift and not indicate a more specific question marker. One exception is item 4 above. The sign WHAT may appear at the end of 'yes-no' questions. Interestingly, the ASL sign WHAT (similar in form to BSL WHERE) may also function in this way (Joan Foreman, personal communication). The use of WHAT in this way is limited to rapid discourse among native signers, and this suggests that WHAT functions as a sort of basic question marker.

Example 8.7 consists of drawings and translations of 'yes-no' questions, and the parallel non-question sentences. Looking at the manual component of these examples, we see no evidence as to sentence type. Yet signers recognise the utterances in column B as questions, and the utterances in column A as statements. To understand how signers recognise these as questions one must look, not at the hands, but at other components of signing, in the same way that to understand fully questions in spoken language, one must move away from examina-

Example 8.7: Facial Expression Determines Yes/no Questions

A. Statements

It's a woman.

OK.

B. Questions

Is it a woman?

OK?

tion of strings of words and listen to intonation.

Non-manual Components of Questions

Stokoe *et al.* (1965), Bellugi and Fischer (1972), Baker (1977, 1978b) and others have observed that non-manual activity is used in forming 'yes-no' questions in ASL. All agree that a particular facial expression, head position and body posture signal 'yes-no' questions. If throughout the signing of a sentence the head and shoulders are leaned forward, the chin is forward enough to keep the face vertical, and the eyebrows are raised, the sentence will be interpreted as a 'yes-no' question. Liddell (1978) points out that facial expression and body posture play the *determining* role in the identification of 'yes-no' questions in ASL since facial expression and body posture alone can signal a 'yes-no' question, but generally the hands alone will not.

An examination of 'yes-no' questions in BSL shows that they are accompanied by just those features described for ASL 'yes-no' questions, as the contrast between columns A and B of Example 8.7 shows. (One-sign utterances have been chosen because of the limitations of still pictures.) Eyebrows are raised, and chin, head, and shoulders are brought forward for the duration of the question. Furthermore, in the same way that there may be a prolongation of a sign at the end of a question (see the list of manual shift regulators above), so too there may be a prolongation of these non-manual features at the end of a question.

If the combination of eyebrow raising and forward movement of the head and body constitute utterances as 'yes-no' questions, might the same be true for 'wh-' questions? It has already been said that the presence of one of a specific group of signs is necessary, but not sufficient to identify an utterance as a 'wh-' question. The non-manual components of 'wh-' questions appear to be just as complex as, but different from, those found with 'yes-no' questions. While there is special marking with eyebrows and body for 'wh-' questions, the eyebrows are knitted, and the shoulders are hunched as well as forward. In the same way that the combination of features described before were essential for the identification of an utterance as a 'yes-no' question, so too the combination of features described above permits the identification of an utterance as a 'wh-' question.

In example 8.5 quoted earlier, it was claimed that only part of the utterance, starting with HOW–LONG, could be interpreted as a

Example 8.8: Other Facial Expressions

hands: pʰʻu

a.　eyebrows: knit

　　body: no change

Explanation: Speaker unsure of what the letters PHU (partially hearing unit) stand for

hands: NOTHING HANDLE NOTHING SQUARE

b.　eyebrows: knit

　　body: shoulders hunched

Explanation: Speaker can't guess identity of object in game of 20 Questions and is puzzled

hands: ONLY 3 HOUR

b.　eyebrows: raised

　　body: shoulders back

Explanation: Speaker is surprised at how short a time someone spent skiing on a skiing holiday question. Examination of the videotape shows that the marking of 'wh-' question expression described above begins during the slight pause after SELF, and continues until the end of the utterance; this is indicated in example 8.5 with the dotted line between the arrows.

One must not assume, of course, that other utterances occur with absolutely no facial expression at all. Rather, question facial expressions are marked as *distinct* from other facial expressions. Other utterance types may incorporate facial expression as an essential part of their meanings, for example, negatives, where the manual component may be the same as in a non-negative sentence, but the head is shaken while the manual signs are articulated. Like questions, the negative marked by head shaking occurs throughout the duration of the sequence being negated.

Other utterance types resemble questions in interesting ways. A number of these are shown in Example 8.8. In all three examples, and as with negatives and questions, particular information about the speaker's attitude is being conveyed non-manually. 8a and 8b may be interpreted as showing puzzlement; 8c as showing surprise, and the elements of facial expression which signal this — knitted brows and raised brows, respectively — are parts of the same facial expressions we find in questions in BSL. This resemblance should not be considered entirely fortuitous. We have discussed for BSL and English *how* people ask questions; one might also consider *why* they do so. Functionally, questions are a means of labelling a speaker's uncertainty and simultaneously seeking a reduction of it. We have seen how in English, certain intonation patterns associated with questions may, in combination with normal word order, suggest surprise or puzzlement (Examples 8.1b and d). Although research on questions in sign language discourse is only in its beginnings, this area may provide some clues for understanding how utterance interpretation takes place during conversation.

Summary and Theoretical Perspectives

We have examined certain features of questions in sign language. While linguistic research on BSL is less than five years old, some of the findings here provide support for the description of British Sign Language as an independent natural language, similar in some ways to spoken languages and other sign languages, and unique in other ways. Research on questions in BSL can also help to suggest fruitful approaches for spoken language research.

Research on spoken conversation has centred on 'communication' as the phenomenon in which 'language' carries certain weight and 'nonlanguage' carries certain weight. In sign, one channel of this 'non-verbal' behaviour (manual) takes on the role of primary linguistic carrier, fairly well matching the characteristics of 'language'. However, while the nonmanual aspects of sign communication are more intrinsically crucial, more encoded, than nonverbal behaviour in spoken language conversation, they share many similarities with the nonverbal behaviours of spoken conversations and thus seem to be located on the same 'more or less' linguistic continuum but further towards the linguistic end. As a consequence, in the context of sign conversation, the line distinguishing the special subset 'language' becomes blurred (Baker, 1977).

The most important features of sign language which encourage the view of nonmanual behaviours as part of the language is their use in serving major linguistic functions in the absence of manual behaviours which could have served that function. These multi-channel, systematic behaviours work together, not as independent systems that just happen at the same time, but as behaviours mutually relating at all levels.

9 PSYCHOLINGUISTIC PERSPECTIVES ON VISUAL COMMUNICATION

Lionel Evans

This chapter is concerned with communication problems in the education of children with such severity of deafness as to preclude satisfactory development of language through hearing. It centres on lip-reading, fingerspelling and signing as substitute media of communication, and considers these in relation to aspects of language acquisition, cognitive processing and teaching methodology. These are problems of interest, not only to educators, but also to psychologists and linguists, and the paper aims to provide an introduction to research and practice.

It sets out to explain empirical findings, to evaluate their implications and to suggest hypotheses for further research. It also includes some discussion of the relevance of this information to the construction of a theory of visual language development for deaf children. As there are some differences in the present understanding of terms for visual media, it is necessary to define the terms as used. It is also important to know how these media are used in education. The chapter is structured as follows:

1. Visual/gestural communication — a description of lip-reading, fingerspelling and signing.
2. Educational practice — current trends.
3. Linguistic and educational effects — an explanation of experimental findings on the efficiency of visual communication media and some effects upon linguistic and educational growth.
4. Theoretical and practical implications — an evaluation of implications for language and cognitive development and teaching methodology.

Visual/Gestural Communication Media

In this description of lip-reading, fingerspelling and signing, definitions are offered of the terms as used in this paper. These media may relate, in varying degree, to spoken language, and they are explained here in relation to English. Mention of their use in educational practice will follow, and research findings on their efficiency and developmental effects will also be dealt with later, but this section does include brief reference to study of them as systems of communication.

Lip-reading

The normal communication of spoken language for hearing people is a vocal-auditory process (i.e. it is expressed by voice and received by hearing). For deaf people this becomes a vocal-visual process. They receive spoken language by lip-reading, which involves the perception of the shapes and movements of speech sounds.

Visual reception of speech through lip-reading is less complete than auditory reception of speech through normal hearing. Apart from such environmental factors as distance of viewing or speed of utterance, two main influences on reception are 1) the restricted visual characteristics of speech sounds and 2) the compensatory use of linguistic cues.

Whereas speech sounds are all audible with normal hearing, the corresponding shapes and movements for lip-reading vary in degree of visibility, and some are virtually undetectable. A review of American studies of this problem (Markides, 1977) indicates a continuum, from the most visible vowels to the least visible consonants.

There is also a problem of visual similarity (Bruhn, 1942; Berger, 1970, 1972; Burchett, 1950; Clegg, 1953). Some speech sounds are indistinguishable from others, and these are referred to as *homophenes*. Experimental studies suggest that, for practical purposes, the speech sounds of English reduce to four homophenous groups of vowels (Fisher, 1968) and four homophenous groups of consonants (Woodward and Barber, 1960; Woodward and Lowell, 1964).

It has been estimated (Hardy, 1970) that two-thirds of English speech sounds are either invisible or indistinguishable from at least one other. They combine to produce homophenous words (for example, 'man, pat, bad'). Estimates of the proportion of homophenous words in English range from 40 per cent to 60 per cent (Bruhn, 1949; Wood and Blakely, 1953; Vernon and Mindel, 1971). In isolation, such words can not be identified purely visually. In lip-reading of continuous speech they have to be differentiated through the linguistic context.

Fingerspelling

Fingerspelling is a manual-visual means of transmitting the written form of a language. Hand and finger shapes, or formations, correspond to the alphabetic symbols of individual letters. These combine sequentially into configurations to represent whole words. As there is one-to-one equivalence between the graphic and manual symbols, fingerspelling has word-for-word correspondence with reading and writing. The term fingerspelling covers both expressive and receptive aspects, so that it is necessary to distinguish between fingerspelling production and fingerspelling perception.

As there are different written alphabets, so there are many different forms of fingerspelling. The present-day manual alphabet used most widely by deaf people in Britain is a two-handed form, but the majority of the different alphabets now in use in other countries are one-handed forms. There is something of a worldwide trend towards the one-handed form as used in the United States, or in a slightly modified form as the International Manual Alphabet. This is the case in countries which previously had their own traditional one-handed alphabets, such as Scandinavian countries, as well as countries which are introducing fingerspelling into educational practice for the first time, such as Malaysia.

Signing

Signing is a generic term describing forms of communication in which the use of gestures predominates, ranging from those which are themselves languages to those which are codes for transmitting spoken languages. Signing (in the context of English-speaking communities) can be placed into three main categories: 1) sign language 2) manual English, and 3) Signed English systems.

Sign Language   Sign language uses signs to convey information usually carried by words of spoken language. There are many sign languages used by the deaf people of different countries. Of these, American Sign Language has probably received the most extensive linguistic examination, and is used as the example for this description. The growing body of information provides some understanding of the properties of sign language, at levels corresponding broadly to the phonology, morphology and syntax of spoken language. It is not intended to review research into the structure of sign language, but brief mention will be made of some features which may have a bearing on language acquisition and teaching methodology.

Whereas the morphemes of spoken language are made up from the combination of phonemes, signs have their substructure of manual elements which combine to form meaningful units. Stokoe (1960,

1978) has proposed three formational aspects, referred to as *cheremes*, which distinguish a sign from all others: 1) the place where the sign is made, termed the tabula (abbreviated to *tab*); 2) the shape and orientation of the hands, termed the designator (*dez*); and 3) the movement of the hands, termed the signation (*sig*). It has been pointed out further (Battison, 1974) that these elements combine according to formational rules in American Sign Language (for example, both hands moving independently have identical shapes and movements, whereas one hand remains stationary for signs with different shapes for the two hands).

A sign language may appear to have a small lexicon in comparison with the vocabulary of a spoken language used in a literate community. American Sign Language (Frishberg, 1977) is known to be continually expanding, through such features as the initialisation of existing signs to provide more specific meanings. Basic signs are modified by changing the hand shapes to the one-handed fingerspelling formations corresponding with the initial letters of the English words represented (for example, the sign for CLASS is modified to represent the words TEAM or GROUP by using the ·t· or ·g· handshapes, respectively.

Although the actual 'manipulation' of signs has been shown to be a slower process than articulation of spoken words (Bellugi and Fischer, 1972; Grosjean, 1979a), it has been suggested that the rate of expression of conceptual propositions in sign utterances is not significantly different from spoken sentences (Bellugi and Fischer, 1972). This may be due to compensatory linguistic properties which offset motor constraints in signing. The grammar of sign language is derived partly from such features as changes of timing, movement or direction of the signs. Grammatical information which is added sequentially in English is achieved in sign language by simultaneous encoding and internal modulation (for example, the signs for 'I see you' and 'you see me' are differentiated purely by directionality of movement (Brennan, this volume). Although different from English grammar, such spatial grammatical features would seem to be specifically adapted to a manually produced and visually perceived language.

Manual English   Another variety of signing is used by deaf people to express themselves more closely to English language. The conceptual signs are used in conjunction with fingerspelling to approximate the syntax of English. This is the style of signing usually attempted by hearing people. This approach is sometimes referred to as signed English, but as fingerspelling is an essential, non-redundant component, this is not a strictly accurate term. The signs alone do not carry the English syntax, and this system is more logically described as *manual English*.

Signed English Systems   There are, however, a number of contrived systems designed to provide an exact signed representation of spoken English. They differ from manual English, as just defined, in that they do not depend upon fingerspelling, but rely entirely upon signing, and are thus more accurately described as *signed English systems*.

A contrived system of signing English was first devised in 1934 and developed over the next 40 years into the Paget-Gorman Sign System. This highly structured system has basic signs for words of a common theme, with specific identifying gestures. A number of new signed English systems evolved in the United States in the 1970s. Seeing Essential English (Anthony, 1971) is a lexicon of signs which aims to give each English word a distinct sign. Linguistics of Visual English (Wampler, 1971) is also a lexicon of signs, intended to represent morphemes. Signing Exact English (Gustason, Pfetzing and Zawalkow, 1972) provides a sign for each word or basic concept, and is rather closer in structure to American Sign Language. In general, these systems invent new signs, modify existing signs, and create affixes, verb endings, plurality and articles. They do not depend upon fingerspelling, although they may use the principle of initialisation for closer sign-to-word correspondence.

A somewhat different approach is that of the system known as Signed English (Bornstein, Hamilton, Saulnier and Roy, 1975). This is not just a system for representing English, but also a carefully thought out and well supported instructional programme to assist in the acquisition of language competence by young deaf children. It sets out to provide an easily learned gestural system to parallel the language of pre-school children. It uses 'sign words' taken mainly from American Sign Language, and 'sign markers' which represent common English word form changes (for example, the one-handed fingerspelling formations for ·d· and ·s· to indicate past tense and plurality, respectively).

Educational Practice

Definitions have been given of the main *media*, or means of communicating linguistic information. Speech, hearing and lip-reading are termed *oral media*, whereas fingerspelling and signing, which use the hands, are known as *manual media*. In addition to these 'live', inter-personal, means of communication, there are of course the *written media* of writing and reading. Speech and writing are expressive media and hearing, lip-reading and reading are receptive media, but the terms fingerspelling and signing are used for both expression and reception. It is useful, particularly in the context of language acquisition, to refer to those media, whether oral, manual or written, which can be received visually without any dependence upon hearing, as *visual receptive media*.

The term *method* describes the way in which media are used in teaching. Thus an *oral method* relies upon speech, hearing and lip-reading. A *manual method* uses fingerspelling or signing, although it is usual for these to be used in conjunction with oral media, so that the term *combined method* is more meaningful. It is invariably implied, also, that the written media are included in any teaching method. In this paper, *methodology* is used with a wider meaning for the study of the aims, content and evaluation of teaching methods.

Educational *practice* is used as a broader term to describe the way in which one or more teaching methods are used within a school. This may be an oral method only, a combined method only, the use of different methods at different stages, or the selective use of oral or combined methods for different children.

It is probably true to say that, in the past, the majority of British schools for the deaf aspired, at least officially, to use oral methods of teaching. A major recent development has been the integration into ordinary schools of partially hearing children who, by educational definition, follow a normal pattern of language development. When properly assessed and classified, partially hearing children, irrespective of degree of hearing loss, should be capable of learning language on the basis of hearing and lip-reading of speech, and thus benefiting from pure oral practice.

The children now placed in the schools for the deaf tend to have profound prelingual deafness and are unable to understand speech by hearing. These children must rely upon visual reception of language. During the 1970s there was a growth of interest in the use of manual media in the education of such children, and some schools have intro-duced combined teaching methods. The term *Total Communication* is being applied to such an approach, which uses fingerspelling and signing in conjunction with speech and lip-reading, together of course with written media and the use of amplified hearing where possible.

The systematic use of combined oral and manual media is, however, by no means new, and has been applied, as the *simultaneous method*, in the United States for more than a century. The term Total Communication has itself been used previously in a semiotic sense (Mead, 1964), but it has more recently acquired a more specific application to communication for deaf people. An official definition, agreed by the Conference of Executives of American Schools for the Deaf (1976) as 'a philosophy incorporating appropriate aural, manual and oral modes of communication in order to ensure effective communication, with and among hearing-impaired persons', emphasises Total Communication as an eclectic attitude to the use of the appropriate media to suit the needs of the individual deaf person and the particular situation. Nevertheless, since Total Communication was introduced in the late 1960s into educational practice, at the Maryland School for the Deaf (Denton, 1970), it has acquired the connotation of a teaching method.

Some impression of the possible development of the trend towards the fuller use of a combined method in Britain may be gained by examining the growth of Total Communication in the United States. A survey of teaching methods (Jordan, Gustason and Rosen, 1979) based upon responses from 642 different American schools or mainstreamed classes (corresponding to partially hearing units in Britain) with a total population of 31,285 hearing-impaired students, revealed that by 1978 nearly 65 per cent of the classes reported using Total Communication, as opposed to nearly 35 per cent using pure oral methods.

Linguistic and Educational Effects

Recent study of the results of the traditional approach to education of deaf children in Britain has added to an interest in the use of teaching methods using manual media. In due course it may be possible to study the long-term effects of combined methods on linguistic and educational development. In the meantime, studies can be made of oral and manual media for transmitting linguistic information, and American research has already examined some aspects of their use with young deaf children.

The research findings can be examined in terms of the 'negative evidence' which indicates the limitations of mainly oral teaching, and the more 'positive evidence' of the greater efficiency of combined media for transmission of linguistic information and the effects on linguistic and educational development.

Conrad (1979) has reported on the attainments of a virtually complete population of hearing-impaired school leavers completing their education in the predominantly oral educational system of England and Wales. He found that acceptable levels of linguistic and educational attainment have not been achieved. Apart from its effect upon general educational development, the justification for an exclusively oral method of teaching must rest essentially upon its capacity to promote oral perception, oral symbolisation and oral production of language. Conrad's investigation has shown that these specific aims for oral teaching, as reflected in actual attainments in lip-reading, internal speech and speech intelligibility, have not been realised for hearing-impaired children in general.

With regard to the limitations of lip-reading, Conrad concluded that deaf children exposed to lip-reading up to school leaving age did not perform better in lip-reading tests than inexperienced hearing children. This was consistent with American studies which discovered that subjects with normal hearing performed as well as (Di Carlo and Kataja, 1951; Berger, 1972) or better than (Lowell, 1957; Butt and Chreist, 1968) deaf subjects on lip-reading tests. Within groups of hearing-impaired subjects, it has been found that ability to understand language through lip-reading declines with increasing hearing loss (Simmons, 1959; Evans, 1965).

Comparisons of the efficiency of lip-reading with combined media for understanding English have also provided consistent results. In an early American study (Johnson, 1948) severely deaf students had better test scores through fingerspelling than lip-reading. Subsequent studies carried out in the United States (Klopping, 1971), in Scotland (Montgomery and Lines, 1976) and in England (Savage, Evans and Savage, 1981), have all shown significant advantage in language reception through fingerspelling combined with lip-reading over pure lip-reading, and further significant advantage for the combined use of signing and fingerspelling in conjunction with lip-reading. A recent British study (Grove, O'Sullivan and Rodda, 1979), in which deaf subjects used either pure oral or combined media according to their own personal preference, also found combined media to be superior for transmitting various types of linguistic material.

For information on the place of signing in language development it is necessary to look to American studies. There is evidence to suggest that young deaf children generate an esoteric gestural system (Schlesinger and Meadow, 1972; Goldin-Meadow and Feldman, 1978) and that deaf children can express similar semantic functions in their spontaneous signing as hearing children at the same stage. It has been suggested that the early language development of deaf children in signs can at least parallel that of hearing children in words (Bellugi and Klima, 1972; Nash, 1975), and indeed there are reports of children of deaf parents using signs earlier than the normal age for first words (Wilbur and Jones, 1974) and the use of two-sign utterances at age ten months (McIntire, cited in Wilbur, 1976).

American studies have provided evidence of the effects of manual communication on educational attainment. The use of fingerspelling as part of teaching method facilitates reading (Hester, 1963), and also written language and lip-reading (Quigley, 1969).

Comparisons have also been made of the subsequent linguistic and educational attainments of deaf children of deaf parents brought up using manual communication with deaf children of hearing parents brought up using pure oral communication. Studies of carefully matched groups of subjects concluded that early manual communication leads to significantly better levels of educational attainment (Stevenson, 1964), lip-reading (Stuckless and Birch, 1966) and written language and social development (Meadow, 1968).

In the interpretation of such results it is necessary to consider the possibility that the deaf children of deaf parents are more likely to have hereditary type hearing loss and thus a lower chance of central nervous system defects which can confound the handicapping effects of hearing loss. A study which controlled for this factor, by using only deaf children of hearing parents for whom there was positive evidence of hereditary deafness, confirmed the superior attainment for those children using manual communication (Vernon and Koh, 1970).

The overall findings of these American and British studies reveal the limitation of pure oral methods of teaching, indicate the superiority of combined media using fingerspelling and signing over lip-reading for transmitting linguistic information, and suggest that the early use of sign language and the later use of manual English, whilst having no adverse effect on lip-reading or speech intelligibility, provide the severely deaf child with an advantage in linguistic and educational development which is maintained throughout school life.

Theoretical and Practical Implications

The findings of research into visual communication have implications for understanding problems of language acquisition, cognitive processing and teaching methodology. It has been shown that in the visual reception of speech there is incomplete sound-to-shape correspondence, resulting in a preponderance of homophenous words. Lip-reading is therefore inadequate to transmit the correct syntax of English. The visual gaps and ambiguities have to be filled through knowledge of the language, probably in the way that reduced accoustic speech information can be recognised through anticipation of linguistic sequence (Shannon, 1948; Denes and Pinson, 1963; Fry, 1964), and this explains the tendency for hearing people to score better than deaf people on tests demanding understanding of spoken language through lip-reading alone. It has been claimed (Craig, 1964) that lip-reading, as a code for reception of an already learned language, cannot exceed the limits of linguistic knowledge, but it has been demonstrated further with deaf children, through their superior performance in manual English (Savage, Evans and Savage, 1981), that lip-reading fails to reach their actual level of linguistic competence.

In pure oral practice, for children unable to receive language through hearing, lip-reading is expected to function as the language acquisition medium. As the visual pattern of speech is less than isomorphic with the auditory pattern, lip-reading is inappropriate for acquiring original competence of English. Thus, as Vernon (1974) points out, in the pure oral method prelingually deaf children '. . . are expected to learn language through a process which presumes they already have language skill' (p. 96). Conrad (1977a) concluded that the evidence of his study of lip-reading ability of deaf school-leavers '. . . suggests that the education of profoundly deaf children is at present theoretically ill-equipped to teach English [at least] as a first language by means of lip-reading' (p. 65). It is necessary, therefore, to recognise the place of lip-reading as a communication medium of greater value when language competence has been established. Lip-reading also has a special role for communicating with people who lack expressive skills in manual media, which in itself is good reason to encourage its development through continuous use in conjunction with fingerspelling and signing in manual English.

Where fingerspelling has been used in education, it has usually been introduced to deaf children after they have developed some skill in reading and writing. It has thus been learned as a transfer from written language, which in turn is a secondary representation of the primary language competence in whatever form acquired. The correspondence between the manual and written alphabets allows accurate transmission of English, within the individual's limits of literacy. The high accuracy level for reception of words in isolation (Savage, Evans and Savage, 1981) gives fingerspelling a special role in teaching methodology as a 'lexical tool' for learning technical terms and names and for reinforcing the orthographic pattern of new words.

Research findings with older children at school have shown that more linguistic information passes when signing is added to finger-spelling. Signs, which directly represent referents, can substitute for the content words, which convey the semantic information. They do not, however, represent all function words, which add to the grammatical structure of English. As the function words are usually short, and as word length affects visual reception (Taafe and Wong, 1957; Erber, 1971), they cannot be perceived readily through lip-reading. It has been found experimentally that guessing of function words of spoken language is dependent upon whole semantic structure using cues from further away in the sentence (Treisman, cited in Herriot, 1970). This may confound the problem of understanding function words through lip-reading, as longer sentences are more difficult to lip-read (Morris, 1944; O'Neill, 1954; Clouser, 1976). These short words can, however, be transmitted accurately through fingerspelling. The implications are that these media have complementary roles, signing for conveying content words, and fingerspelling for conveying function words, together representing the syntax of English.

A further potential contribution of fingerspelling to manual English is the process of initialisation of conceptual signs to provide a more specific meaning corresponding to English words. This is now an established feature of American Sign Language (Frishberg, 1977), but it is questionable whether the process can be incorporated as naturally into British Sign Language using two-handed fingerspelling. Whereas one-handed fingerspelling formation can be applied (to the *dez* hand or hands) in either a single-handed or a double-handed sign, a two-handed formation may not be so readily applied to a double-handed sign, at least without violating the natural rule (as explained by Battison, 1974) of two independently moving hands having identical shapes. This question of compatibility between the cheremic structure of signs and the fingerspelling formations would seem to be a relevant linguistic factor in any comparison of one-handed and two-handed fingerspelling.

The growing research into its structure supports the claim that BSL is a language in its own right and not a representation of spoken language. As a language, it may be expected that it can be internally symbolised to promote cognitive processing. The work of Ahlgren

(1977) in Sweden offers some tentative support for this possibility. She suggests that the early stage of sign language is easier for deaf children to learn than the early stage of spoken language is for hearing children, for the reason that visual perception normally has a place in linguistic and cognitive development. Brown (1977), in an American study, also had findings to suggest that sign language is superior to spoken language for the acquisition of an initial lexicon and attributes this to the iconicity of the early signs, which facilitates short-term memory.

This type of evidence provides a case for the early use of sign language with young deaf children, but if English is to be their eventual target language there arises the question of how a transfer from sign language to English can be made. Research findings support the use of oral and manual media, in what is now widely understood as the Total Communication approach to education, but this is, strictly speaking, only an optimally efficient combination of media for language communication. What is of particular importance is to know how these media should be introduced and integrated into an optimally efficient sequence for language acquisition.

The present state of understanding of visual media permits the formulation of a tentative theoretical framework for such a strategy. The research findings indicate the early use of a sign language lexicon, incorporating such features as iconicity and spatial grammar, to promote original language competence and to provide a cognitive input. Systematic emphasis upon lip-reading would be more effective when some degree of English language competence has been gained. Written language and fingerspelling would occupy intermediate places within the infrastructure of the developmental sequence.

PART THREE: COMMUNICATION ASPECTS

INTRODUCTION

Margaret Deuchar

The two previous sections of this book have focused on the psychological and linguistic consequences of deafness. In both sections it has been shown that research into the language of deaf people can contribute greatly to our knowledge about language in general. Deafness provides us with further insights into the way in which language is related to cognition, and into how language can be structured in a visual medium. The emphasis is thus on deafness as a valuable resource rather than as a pathological condition.

However, we must not lose sight of deafness as involving people, and in particular people belonging to a minority group within a predominantly hearing society. Deaf people live simultaneously in two worlds: that of the hearing and that of the deaf. Most deaf children are born into hearing families, so that their first contact with deaf people may be when they go to school and meet other deaf children. The teachers, however, are hearing, and the children have to acquire the language and norms of hearing society while belonging to their own deaf peer group. Deaf children may not know many deaf adults until they leave school and join a deaf club, thus becoming fully fledged members of the adult deaf community. At the same time, however, they emerge into the mainly hearing world of employment and responsibility, where they often have to survive independently of other deaf people. Deaf people thus have to function simultaneously within a majority and a minority culture, each having different modes of communication.

All the chapters in this section deal with communication and deafness within the context of a hearing society. Lawson considers the defining characteristics of the deaf community and the effect of English on sign language; Colville discusses how our knowledge of BSL can help us to improve sign language teaching techniques; Denmark illustrates the consequences of lack of communication between hearing parent and deaf child; Gregory and Mogford describe the progress made by deaf children in acquiring the language of their hearing parents; and Edmondson discusses communication in the deaf school classroom.

What is the deaf community? As Lawson says in her paper, 'The principal identifying characteristic appears to be a knowledge of sign language'. BSL is the native language of most of those who belong to the British deaf community. BSL is not based on English, but has grown up spontaneously among deaf people in schools and deaf clubs. However, because of the communicative norms of hearing society, and the low prestige of BSL, sign language is influence by English. This influence is particularly clear in formal signing, and Lawson suggests that there is a continuum from 'pure' BSL to English. Varieties of signing between the two extremes are, she suggests 'pidgins', charac-terised by mixed structures. The term 'pidgin' is descriptively useful here, though we may replace it with a more precise or accurate term when more is known about pidgins and the phenomenon of language variation in general. Lawson's chapter is particularly valuable in that it is one of the first by a native signer. The combination of her signing competence and membership in the minority group which she is des-cribing gives added credibility to her analysis.

Colville's paper also shows the benefit of his personal experience, in his case as a hearing member of the deaf signing community through having deaf parents. He demonstrates how attitudes to BSL and lack of knowledge of its structural properties have given rise to poor tech-niques for teaching sign language to hearing people. Sign language has been taught as if it reflected English structure, and not in the form in which deaf people use it. Colville makes some practical suggestions as to how BSL can be taught without reference to English, exploiting the possibilities of the visual medium.

Denmark's paper highlights the communicative difficulties of deaf children with hearing parents. He writes from the point of view of a hearing psychiatrist dealing with deaf patients. His research aimed to account for the fact that young deaf people are more likely to have behaviour and adjustment problems than their hearing counterparts. He concludes that one of the most important factors accounting for this is poor communication between hearing parents and deaf children in their early years. This problem could be solved, he says, by better parent guidance, including the provision of opportunities for learning sign language. Denmark suggests finally that good parent/child com-munication in the formative years of a deaf child's life could prevent mental health problems from occurring later.

Gregory and Mogford also deal with communication between hearing parent and deaf child, though from the point of view of lang-uage acquisition. They study vocal communication only, in order to

compare deaf with hearing children. They find not only that deaf
children acquire words at a slower rate than hearing children (which
one might expect), but also that the words learned are different.
Deaf children tend to use more words relating to actions and social
interaction, while hearing children use more words describing the
environment. The reasons for these differences are not clear, though it
might be worth approaching them within a Hallidayan framework
(see Halliday, 1975). Halliday suggests that the 'instrumental', 'regu-
latory' and 'interactional' functions of language are all acquired in
the first phase of language development, while the 'informative' function is only acquired later. So the greater use of the 'instrumental',
etc., functions by the deaf children in Gregory and Mogford's study
could be interpreted as indicating that they were still in the first phase
of vocal language development, while the hearing children had reached
a later stage. However, we shall probably not have the full picture
until research has been conducted dealing with visual/gestural as well
as with vocal communication, and with deaf children of deaf as well
as of hearing parents. (For preliminary studies in the UK see Dalgleish
& Mohay, 1979 and Maestas Y. Moores, 1980).

Edmondson presents a personal view of communication in the deaf
school classroom, based on his own observation. He expresses anxiety
that the pre-conditions which he considers necessary for language
learning are not being met, and suggests that British Sign Language
as used by deaf adults should be introduced into the classroom in
preference to Signed English. He presents some speculative views on
the importance of adult language input for a child's language 'achievement', and on the extent to which language input is or should be
variable. These ideas remain to be tested by further research.

The research presented in this section indicates that the communication of deaf people must be studied in the context of their position as
minority group members who also have to function in a hearing world.
Deafness is at least as much a social as a physical handicap, for deaf
people are expected to adjust to the communicative norms of the
hearing majority even though they are ill equipped to do so. If hearing
people could be made aware of the need to adapt themselves to the
communicative mode of the deaf, rather than the reverse, then the
social handicap of deafness could be minimised.

Further research into communication and deafness should provide the
information necessary for hearing people to adjust to the communicative
needs of the deaf. In addition, it should have the effect of affirming the
identity, worth and communicative richness of the deaf community.

10 THE ROLE OF SIGN IN THE STRUCTURE OF THE DEAF COMMUNITY

Lilian Lawson

This chapter will cover three main areas: the deaf community and its structure and functions; the British Sign Language-to-English continuum; and sign language variation. Attitudes of members of the deaf community towards sign language and its variation will also be mentioned.

Deaf people are separated from the hearing society around them, and from the culture that belongs to that society, because of a physical feature: lack of hearing. They therefore belong to a minority group. Deafness means that speech and hearing cannot be the primary means of group social interaction. However, the desire to belong to a group, the desire for social contact, is no less strong in deaf people than it is in normal hearing people. Deafness isolates deaf people from the social group of which they would otherwise be members because of their residence and work, and is also the main cause of the formation of special social groupings of deaf people. Such groups have existed from at least the introduction of special education in Britain in the last century. At that time the medium of instruction was sign language, or at least a manual communication method.

The sign language of schools for the deaf has the flexibility and expressiveness typical of any language used for the natural communication of daily thoughts, feelings and needs of a close-knit group of people. Pupils leaving a school for the deaf continue their association with each other and with pupils from other deaf schools in different parts of Britain. The means by which they carry on that interchange of thought, so necessary for full social interaction, has always been the language of signs. Thus, sign language, namely British Sign Language (BSL), while undergoing growth and evolution, has become a vital part of the culture of the British deaf.

It is the pleasure gained from mixing with other deaf people that makes one remain a member of the deaf 'in-group' — the British deaf community. So powerful is the attraction of social interaction with deaf people that others, on making contact with the deaf but who have no skill in BSL, learn to sign and become members of the community.

These latecomers are the post-lingually deaf, orally educated deaf and deaf people who are educated in schools for the hearing.

The British deaf community is held together by such factors as self-identification as a deaf community member, language, endogamous marital patterns, and numerous national, regional and local organisations and social structures (see Figure 10.1). These factors have been defined as responsible for the formation of the American deaf community (Croneberg, 1976; Markowicz, 1979; Woodward, 1975, 1978). Not all hearing-impaired and deaf individuals belong to the deaf community; some prefer to identify themselves with the larger 'hearing world' and try to belong to that group. The deaf community comprises those deaf and hard-of-hearing individuals who have a common language, common experiences and values, and a common way of communicating with each other and with hearing people. A person's actual degree of hearing loss (audiometric deafness) is not important in determining that individual's identification with and acceptance by the deaf community, though some loss of hearing must have occurred at a fairly early stage. The principal identifying characteristic appears to be a native knowledge of sign language. For the deaf in Britain it is BSL, just as it is American Sign Language (ASL) for the deaf in America and so on.

Members of the deaf community usually attend special schools for the deaf. A large number of these schools are residential institutions where deaf pupils eat, sleep, study and play together — isolated from their hearing counterparts. After leaving school, deaf people tend to work together at those limited places which employ deaf adults. Most of the adult deaf marry within the deaf community. Throughout their school and adult years the deaf are also drawn together by numerous sporting opportunities (e.g. sports meetings of the SDASA and the BDASA), regional meetings (e.g. BDA council meetings), school re-unions, social activities such as those arranged by the local deaf clubs, etc. The result is that the deaf have formed a cohesive and mutually supportive community.

The majority of deaf people have two hearing parents. As these parents use a language (spoken English) that the deaf child can neither hear nor consequently use with much fluency, communication with family members is limited. It is at school among peers that most personal and social information develops (sharing occurs and close relationships are established), all through a language specially shaped fo the eyes rather than the ears (visual/manual channel), and a language passed on by deaf parents whose deaf children then teach other

Figure 10.1: Categorical Classifications and Factors of the Deaf Community

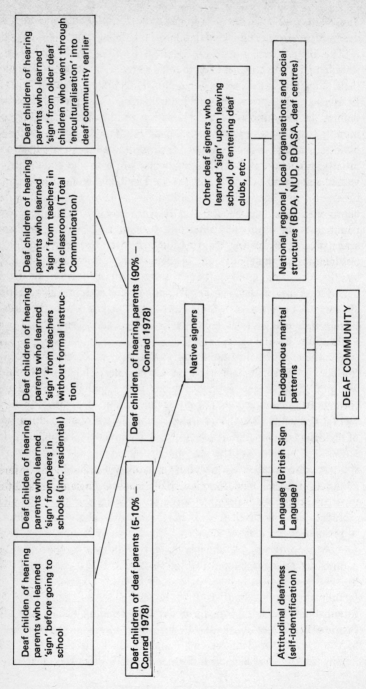

deaf children how to use the language.

At the heart of every community is its language. This language embodies the thoughts and experiences of its users and they, in turn, learn about their culture or heritage and share in it together through their language. Thus deaf people achieve this through British Sign Language.

From the above it may be inferred that attitudinal deafness (self-identification as a member of the deaf community and identification by other members as a member) appears to be the most basic factor in determining membership of the deaf community. Attitudinal deafness is associated with appropriate language use. The language situation in the British deaf community can best be described as a diglossic continuum between BSL and English. Deuchar (1977), using a classic paper on diglossia by Ferguson as a model, has pointed out the existence of diglossia in the Reading deaf community (which is more or less identical to other deaf communities in different cities of Britain):

> ... this superposed variety is termed 'High' or 'H' by Ferguson and the other 'Low' or 'L'. While 'H' is used in public, formal settings such as church, school and in news broadcasts, 'L' is used in more private, informal settings such as conversation among friends. (p. 349)

The notion of diglossia was first extended to two other sign language communities, that of ASL and Danish Sign Language (DSL) (Deuchar, 1977). From her research in Reading, Deuchar found that the notion of diglossia was also found in BSL:

> ... two structurally different varieties of sign are used for different functions in the deaf community of Reading, England. In addition, in this case, the differential structure is related to the differential functions of the varieties, in that, while 'H' is constrained by the spoken language of the dominant culture, English, with its associated auditory medium, 'L' is constrained by and also exploits the visual medium which deafness causes it to use. (p. 356)

Brennan pointed out that like English, BSL had many different varieties and could probably best be thought of as a continuum (see Figures 10.2 and 10.3).

The deaf adult will make his choice of appropriate variety according to the kinds of factors, e.g. topic, purpose, participants, etc. However, the deaf person will take into account not only the status or role of the participants but also such factors as whether or not they are deaf and whether or not they use any form of manual communication system. Many deaf people will also have the further choice of using a variety of English in conjunction with BSL. In conversation with a profoundly deaf adult, the individual may choose to use BSL alone; in conversation with a hearing person, he may use a variety of BSL in conjunction with a variety of English, in other cases he may choose to use English alone. (Brennan, 1978, pp. 4-5)

Figure 10.2: The BSL—English Continuum

English   BSL

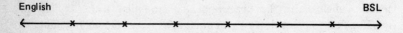

Crosses on the continuum between BSL and English indicate the varieties of BSL from which the deaf individual will make his choice of appropriate variety according to the kinds of factors; topic, purpose, participants, etc.

Signing that approaches English along the continuum serves as the formal variety in the diglossic situation and tends to be used in formal conversations such as church services, classroom teaching, platform speaking and with hearing people. Signing that approaches BSL tends to be used in smaller, informal, more intimate conversations and among the deaf signers themselves. Many signers have remarked that English is superior to BSL because BSL has been often regarded as ungrammatical and improper or non-existent. Signers generally feel that 'grammatical' and 'proper' English should be used instead of BSL for teaching in schools for the deaf. A few deaf teachers are using the manual representation of English (i.e. Signed English), and many deaf people prefer to see lectures and formal conversations in Signed English. Yet they use BSL unconsciously in their informal conversations with other deaf people at home, in deaf clubs, places of employment and in school playgrounds without any reservations. Much formal grammatical description has been done of English, in its spoken or written form, but only relatively recently has any research on BSL been undertaken. Some signers feel that standardisation is necessary, but their language situation is in fact as normal and stable as in other diglossic communities.

Figure 10.3: The Diglossic Continuum Between British Sign Language and English

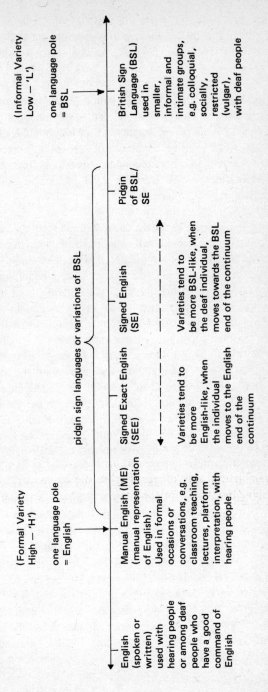

Along the continuum there are varieties of language, ranging from BSL at one end of the continuum to Signed English at the other. These varieties might be called 'pidgins'. According to Woodward's (1973) definition:

> pidgin languages are reduced in structure, contain a partial mixture of structure of two to several languages, and contain structure common to none of the languages in the communication situation. Pidgins are not native languages of any of the users. Pidgins are used primarily in restricted social situations for communicative purposes and are not generally used for socially integrative and personally expressive functions.

The notion of pidgin sign English as referring to varieties on the continuum intermediate between ASL and English comes from Woodward, and this approach can be adopted to describe the similar British situation. Such pidgin languages in use are: Signed Exact English, Signed English. Signed Exact English is near the English end of the continuum because it retains many of the grammatical rules of English; for example, inflection markers, the use of the copula, syntax and articles, to name but a few. Signed English is further away from the English end of the continuum than the previous variety because it does not retain inflectional markers in signing though it may retain the use of copulas, articles and syntax. Both these varieties retain the spoken (or silent spoken) English lip pattern throughout the signing and therefore lipreading is important. However, in BSL, spoken English is not used and instead the mouth movements of native signers are not necessarily related to the usual lip-reading patterns of spoken English.

Signers will possess varying ranges of competence on the BSL-Signed English continuum (see Figures 10.4 and 10.5). Native signers will be competent in the varieties near the BSL end and, depending on their command of English, will have greater or lesser competence in varieties approaching the English end. Non-native signers will have more competence in varieties approaching English than in those approaching BSL. However, all signers will get as close to the BSL end of the continuum as their competence allows in informal situations, and will approximate the English end as far as possible in formal situations. Signers whose competence extends along the whole range of the continuum are rare: many native signers, for example, will use 'pure' BSL in informal situations and a variety of pidgin sign English in formal situations (e.g. Signed English).

Figure 10.4: Diglossic Continuum: Characteristics of Sign Varieties Illustrated by English Glosses

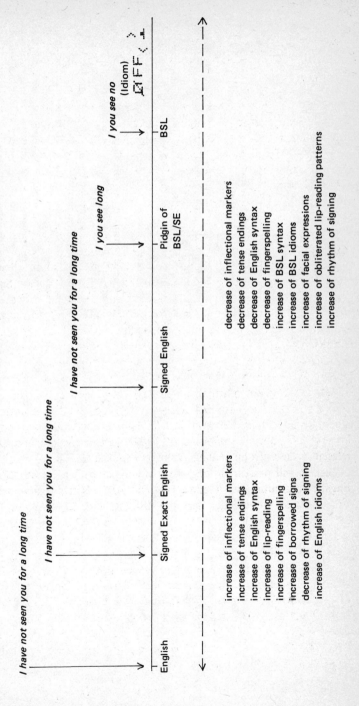

Figure 10.5: The Diglossic Continuum Between BSL and English: Attitudes and Status of Variations of Users

	Manual English	Signed Exact English	Signed English	BSL/SE	BSL
← →					← →

1.	Deaf children of hearing parents with a good command of English and signers who learned 'sign' post-lingually tend to use more English-like varieties.	Deaf children of deaf parents and other native signers tend to use more BSL-like varieties.
2.	When conversing with hearing people, they tend to use more English-like varieties and may even use spoken or written English.	When conversing with hearing people, they tend to use the formal variety of signing which is further away from the BSL end of the continuum.
3.	When conversing with hearing people — if the topic is political or formal, if the participants are hearing or formal people, or if the purpose of the conversation or situation is formal — they tend to use more English-like varieties, or vice versa.	When conversing with deaf people — if the topic is political or formal, or if the participants are hearing or formal, or if the purpose of the conversation is formal — they tend to use the formal variety of signing, or vice versa.
4.	The signers tend to use more fingerspelling which is increasingly conducted in the English word order.	Native signers tend to use less fingerspelling along the continuum and in the fingerspelling the English syntax changes to that of BSL.
5.	They tend to favour SE or SEE in classroom teaching.	They tend to disapprove of the use of SEE but approve the use of SE in classroom teaching.
6.	They tend to understand the pidgin sign varieties better than pure BSL.	They tend to understand the pure BSL better than the pidgin sign varieties.
7.	If the education received, literacy skills and kind of employment are of a high standard, the signers tend to prefer to use the English-like varieties.	These factors do not matter for the native signers and instead it is the social background which matters. If the signer comes from a deaf family more use is made of BSL-like varieties than would be the case for native signers from different backgrounds.

The attitudes of native signers towards the use of BSL or the status of BSL in the deaf community tend to be more positive than those of non-native signers. Among native signers, the deaf children of deaf parents and deaf children who learned to sign when very young at deaf schools, there is a more favourable feeling towards the use of 'pure' BSL in schools for the deaf. However, the attitude of some deaf signers who have excellent competence in English and who became deaf at the age of about six years or upwards, tends to be one of repugnance towards the use of BSL in schools and they have referred to it as a 'dumb language' or a 'stupid non-language'. Disapproval is also shown by some deaf signers who learned to sign upon entering a deaf club and these deaf people usually cannot use the 'pure' BSL variety because they did not acquire BSL when they were very young. They may nevertheless admit that BSL is the native language of the deaf community in Britain and also that its usage is a powerful cohesive bond resulting in unrestricted and relaxed exchanges of thoughts, ideas and feelings between members of the deaf community.

Generally all deaf signers assume that BSL is used only at home or in deaf clubs while a formal variety of BSL, such as Signed English, is preferable to BSL as the medium for formal conversation with hearing people and for platform interpreting at conferences, meetings, churches and lectures. This is because they have been told, for too long, by teachers and others in authority that signing is disgraceful and must not be used in public. It is naturally bewildering for many deaf signers to be informed now that BSL is a real language consisting of proper signs, previously thought improper, in contrast to the kind of signs (including borrowed English and initialised signs) which were considered superior by the hearing social workers and missioners of the deaf and some teachers for the deaf. However, most native signers are opposed to the notion of hearing educationalists inventing or creating signs specifically for classroom teaching or borrowing words from English which are supposed to have no equivalent in the BSL vocabulary. Such invented signs are 'for', 'the', 'a', 'of', the 'to be' verbs, and the 'to do' verbs. These signs are regarded by the native signers as odd or even ridiculous.

Some native signers have been known to change their opinions if a teacher of the deaf or a sign language teacher takes the trouble to explain the need for created signs in classroom teaching. The same kind of understanding attitude can be found in signers when they are told about the specifically created signing systems such as Makaton for mentally-handicapped children, etc., because they are sympathetic and touched to know that BSL can be useful and an aid to less fortunate children. However, native signers are generally against the use of the Paget-Gorman System and the Rochester Method in schools for the deaf because they were not consulted for their views on manual communication in schools and they are wary of the possible new creation of sub-cultures of deaf people using different signing systems and unable to mix with each other upon leaving school.

As well as varying in terms of approximation to, or distance from, English, BSL also has lexical variation, which means that there are different signs for the same English word. The lexical variation occurs either where there are differences in the signing of groups of people living in different geographical areas (e.g. SCHOOL in Glasgow and Edinburgh; WHO in Glasgow, Edinburgh and Dundee; SUGAR in Scotland and South of England; NIGHT in Glasgow, Dundee and Aberdeen; SAY in Glasgow and Edinburgh, etc.), or when there are religious groups like the Catholic deaf community and the Protestant deaf community in Glasgow using different signs (e.g. WEAK, HELP, WAY, FAMILY, READY, DAUGHTER, etc.). In the deaf Catholic community some signs were based on the Irish Catholic one-handed manual alphabet and so were initialised signs. Deaf signers have remarked that they are happy with lexical variations which they compare to the 'dialects' of spoken English in different towns and only a minority wish for universality in BSL in Britain. These lexical variations often come about via the schools for the deaf. At such a school, the young deaf children learn the particular variety of BSL which is characteristic of the locality or religious group. The school is also a source of local innovations as each generation of schoolchildren comes up with some new signs of modifications of old signs. A great many of these signs are shortlived, but some survive and penetrate into the local adult sign language system. Certain signs, however, which originate at shcool are not transmitted because they carry distinct overtones of childishness and immaturity (e.g. WONDERWOMAN and 125 mph TRAIN).

Diglossia serves important functions in the deaf community by maintaining social identity and group solidarity. No overt attempts by hearing people should be made to change the social situation of the deaf community as they, being outside this community, do not share the values and experiences common to the members of the deaf community. Plans that hearing people evolve for deaf people are often totally inappropriate as a result of cultural differences and, therefore, if bilingual education is promoted solely by hearing people, it will probably fail. No social changes (and bilingual education is a social change), should be attempted without adequate knowledge of all the possible social ramifications involved. Sociolinguistic studies of the local deaf communities are absolutely necessary, and these studies must include the consideration of the attitudes of deaf people, deaf parents and deaf schoolchildren towards the local and/or standard language varieties used; towards diglossia; and identification of the local sign varieties in use.

Since research into BSL has begun so recently, we can look forward to exciting developments. It is to be hoped that these developments will promote the full and active participation of all deaf people in both the British deaf community and in British society as a whole.

11 THE INFLUENCE OF BRITISH SIGN LANGUAGE STRUCTURE ON COMMUNICATION TEACHING TECHNIQUES

Martin Colville

The title of this chapter could give rise to the misconception that the structure of British Sign Language (BSL) had been fully analysed and recorded. Unfortunately, this would be incorrect, but preliminary work on BSL and research on American Sign Language (ASL), Swedish Sign Language (SSL) and Danish Sign Language (DSL), seem to indicate that to enable students to learn to communicate effectively with deaf people, recognition must be given to the known grammatical features and properties of the language. It is these features in particular which allow people to communicate with each other easily and fluently.

The traditional way of teaching sign language has been to put signs of BSL into English word order. This immediately creates in the student's mind the impression that BSL follows the grammar of English and the student allows those natural aspects of communication, known in the hearing community as 'nonverbal' aspects, to be suppressed. It is of vital importance that teachers of sign language recognise that students must be encouraged to retain those nonverbal aspects and to develop those special nonverbal features which are an integral part of BSL structure. Even if the student wishes to use BSL signs in an English word order (Signed English) this does not mean that he must omit these nonverbal factors. Previous teaching of BSL and Signed English has been hampered by the lack of knowledge about BSL and also by the negative attitudes about BSL from both the hearing and deaf communities.

It is my intention, firstly, to try and explain my own development in using BSL and how attitudes can be and are created and, secondly, to show how the use of known features of BSL have helped students to a greater facility, use and understanding of both BSL and Signed English. My own use of both BSL and Signed English stems from the fact that I have deaf parents, my father being born deaf and my mother becoming deaf after acquiring speech and English grammar. In my own recollections of my childhood I have some very clear impressions of my own attitudes which have undergone changes through the years. As a child I always regarded my mother as the highly intelligent member of the partnership. She could speak, read and write, while I considered my father to be inferior because he could do none of these things. I used to wonder why my father bought a daily paper when I was told he could not read, but I soon found out that his reading was confined to the sports results. Similarly, his writing, when he did any, was in a beautiful clear script, so surely he could write, but again I found out that his writing was usually confined to single words. If he tried to write longer messages it became unintelligible because he did not follow English word order.

My childhood seemed to follow the classic pattern of most hearing children of deaf parents, in that I had to interpret for them. If I was called upon to do any interpreting which had direct relevance to the family situation, it would usually be for my mother who had accepted the role of being the person who made any contact with the hearing community. This, I am sure, helped to create in me a recognition and an attitude that English was superior to BSL. Important decisions concerning the family were conducted in Signed English and probably there were times when I was more aware of the immediate situation and the decisions made than my father. Once again this helped to create in me a feeling that my mother's way of communicating was best and my father, because he could not read and write, had to be pitied and sympathised with.

What I failed to recognise was that my method of communication with my parents was substantially different for both of them. I had totally failed to see that I was using two languages. I had the misconception that what I was using with my father was an inferior form of English. If I modulated a sign to expand or clarify a meaning for him, it was just something I was used to doing because he wasn't clever enough to understand English. Yet modulation is not an *ad hoc* means of explaining something in greater detail, it is a grammatical feature of BSL which must be recognised and incorporated into any teaching programme. Example 11.1 shows how the base sign TALK could be modulated to describe a conversation, where the signer was talking for a long period at high speed.

To communicate with my mother, I just organised the signs I used with my father into English word order and incorporated an exaggerated speech lip pattern. With my father I changed the way in which I signed, because I wanted to ensure clear and understandable communication. This means changing the order of signs and using a different type of lip pattern, as a number of signs require facial expression and lip patterns which are not congruent with speech lip patterns.

Other signs *require* the speech lip pattern, as that has become part of the sign.

Example 11.1: Base form of TALK

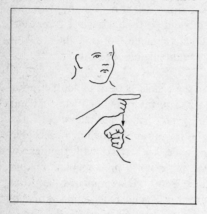

Example 11.2: 'Talk on and on.'

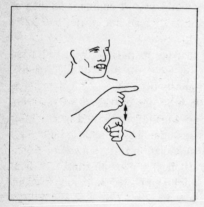

One thing I found confusing, but not disturbing, was that sometimes if I had been talking to my father, in what I thought was the inferior form of English, and then tried to explain the same thing to my mother in Signed English, I found my supposedly less intelligent father telling my mother what I had said because she had been unable to understand me. This other way of communicating was, and still is, a highly effective way of conveying complex information to my father without misunderstanding. Yet I was still under the impression that it was inferior.

Example 11.3: Sign Incorporating Speech Lip Pattern: HOME

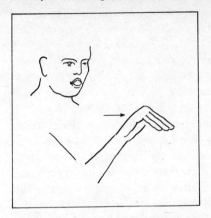

Even though I was unable to understand what was happening, I had recognised that if I wanted to communicate with deaf people who were either looked upon as uneducated or had unintelligible speech, then I would revert to what I now know to be BSL. This was giving me the grounding to communicate fluently with the majority of deaf people. The use of BSL made me recognise the importance of being prepared to use all the parts of my body, especially my face, to transmit the message I was conveying. For adequate communication with deaf people I had to be able to follow the messages that were being conveyed by their faces and body and be able to give positive and negative reactions myself so that there was no breakdown in our conversation.

Unfortunately, I was still under the impression that what I was using was not language and this impression was maintained by those deaf people who were fluent in using English. When I entered professional work with the deaf, it was still my firmly held belief that it was possible to teach deaf children and adults to communicate by the use of Signed English and that it was possible to minimise the use of BSL because I believed it was ungrammatical and therefore not a language. My contact with teachers of the deaf helped to maintain this view, because I saw teachers using Signed English very successfully. What I failed to recognise was that the successful teachers had managed to incorporate many of the rules of BSL into their Signed English, therefore easing the problems of communicating with a deaf child. They had a basis of communication in BSL before they started to teach Signed English. Some of these teachers were the children of deaf parents, but others had no connection with the deaf world and had developed their signing skills by regularly visiting deaf people or centres for the deaf. They had recognised that to sign fluently with deaf people they had to learn a second language and the only way to do that was to mix constantly with the users of the language.

While a course of sign language can and should give you the basic rules of a language, it cannot give you the fluency you require; *that can only be achieved by constant use with deaf people themselves*. The provision of sign language courses throughout the United Kingdom is very patchy and teaching techniques and methods are different from one area to another. Tutors vary from social workers with the deaf, to teachers of the deaf and to deaf people themselves. There are no regulating authorities to check that the teaching is meeting any required standard. The British Deaf Association in its Communication Skills Programme has organised the first teaching courses for teachers of sign language and this trend must be welcomed and encouraged.

Following discussion with tutors and from personal experience I believe the majority of courses are well intentioned but inadequate, with teachers falling back on three traditional techniques:

1. The use of fingerspelling.
2. The use of outdated publications showing signs.
3. The teaching of one sign for one English word.

The paucity of information and material is frightening and teachers using the above techniques often find themselves running out of ideas very quickly. Likewise, some teachers develop material of their own, but this is usually based on English word order, including the safe old prop of fingerspelling which helps to encourage the student to rely upon it to the detriment of signing skills. Often teachers will create sentences that are possible in Signed English, but not in BSL. In my own experience, I have found myself apologising when a question was asked about how to sign a sentence which was not possible to produce in Signed English. There were in fact ways of signing it in BSL clearly and explicitly but this was 'ungrammatical' and therefore unacceptable. So ways of easing the communication problems between parent and child, teacher and child, social worker and client, and friends and relations were hidden from them.

It is important to make teachers of sign language, teachers of the deaf, social workers with the deaf, parents, friends and relations, aware of the legitimacy of BSL, and also deaf people themselves must be helped and taught that BSL is a language. Rather than denigrating their own communication, deaf people need to become more aware of the rightful status of their own language.

Teachers of sign language have indicated that the traditional method of teaching sign language raises a number of problems:

1. An over-reliance on fingerspelling.
2. The domination of their mother tongue (English) over certain aspects of sign language grammar.
3. Ignorance and suppression of aspects of BSL structure which are essential even to a fluent Signed English system.
4. The inability of students to read fingerspelling and fingerspelling patterns as used by deaf people.
5. The inability of students to understand deaf people when they sign to each other.
6. The inability of deaf people to understand the communication patterns used by the students even though students have developed excellent Signed English skills.
7. The failure of the teacher to give students sufficient opportunity to develop their skills.
8. The high drop out rate of students owing to the teacher failing to recognise the importance of small classes.

This led me to rethink radically how I was going to teach Signed English and even now I must stress that my methods are undergoing constant evaluation and change. This is occurring because we are becoming more aware of the rules of BSL, but a planned and structured teaching programme is still a long way off.

My first decision was to postpone the teaching of fingerspelling until as late as possible. This could be as late as the seventh or eighth week of teaching, but sometimes it is necessary to introduce it sooner because students have made contact with deaf people. Even the way of teaching fingerspelling can have beneficial results in how the student is able to produce and understand fingerspelling (Colville, 1980; and there is a video teaching tape available from Moray House College of Education, Edinburgh, covering some of the issues). The manner in which fingerspelling is taught can affect the student's progress. It is important to stress the difference between fingerspelling patterns as they appear to the producer, and as they appear to the receiver. Students typically have enormous difficulty in interpreting fingerspelling, yet manual alphabet charts sometimes confuse rather than aid the student by showing some symbols from the receiver's point of view and some from the producer's.

Secondly, I try to maintain the aspects of nonverbal communication which students already have, but seem to be repressed once a person starts to learn Signed English. This approach also forms the basis of the work on teaching communication skills produced by the Sign Linguistics Research Group in Newcastle, under the leadership of Dorothy Miles. Their teaching methods also avoid using English as the communication medium in the classroom, stressing instead an immediate immersion into nonverbal methods of communication. Some aspects of the role of nonverbal communication in BSL are briefly covered in Brennan, Colville and Lawson (1980). They have also been described by Bergman and Hansen (personal communication, 1980) in terms of the articulators of sign language:

> The two hands
> The head
> The eye gaze
> The facial expression
> The shoulders
> The body

Brennan *et al.* (1980) concentrate on the role of the manual articulators, i.e. the two hands, in the production of signs. The roles of the other five articulators in BSL are still being investigated. In many situations one or more of the five articulators may be used in the production of a sign or sign utterance. If the learner ignores such features he may distort or misunderstand the language of the deaf person.

Examples 11.4a and b show the importance of facial expression and manner of articulation. 11.4a with neutral facial expression means STRIKE; if the movement of the hands is extended and facial expression is modified, as in 11.4b, the meaning of the sign is changed to REVOLUTION.

At the commencement of teaching it is imperative that the teacher ensures that he is able to give sufficient time to each member of the course. Therefore teachers should restrict the size of their course to a maximum of twelve people. I recognise that this can cause problems for those teachers who are bound by Further Education regulations, but if the teacher selects his students and has developed his teaching materials he should have no problem with students dropping out. This enables the teacher to do justice to himself and the students by giving sufficient individual time to each student.

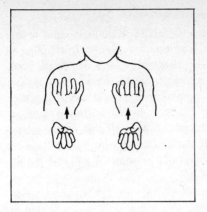

Example 11.4: The Role of
Facial Expression and Manner of
Articulation in Modulation

a. Strike

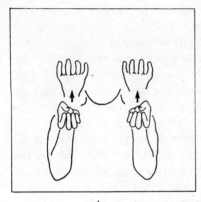 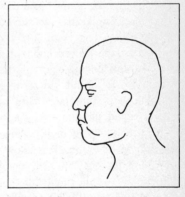

└──────── b. Revolution ────────┘

The rapport between student and teacher can and should be encouraged by allowing students to recognise that they will be asked to
do things which they are capable of performing. Initially students
should be given a name sign, so that both students and teacher can
immediately relate to each other by a sign and not have to rely on
speech. By this, further instructions can be given by the teacher, as
shown in the next exercise.

The students' ability to retain their own skill of using nonverbal
modes of communication is vitally important. One method is to have
a list of approximately 20 words on individual cards, including Love,
Hate, Pleasure and Vanity. These words are handed around the group,
and the teacher by pointing to two students and using their name signs
is able to ask one student to convey what is on the card to the other,
by the use of facial expression alone. It is interesting to note that there

is an approximate guess correct rate of between 45-50 per cent. The words are then handed around again, but the student is able to use body, face and hands to convey the word. This time the guess correct rate can be as high as 75-80 per cent. However, what is more important is that the students will sometimes use the correct base form of a sign, especially when the form of the sign is closely related to the natural gesture, with the correct amount of expression and feeling in the sign, facial expression and body movement. Often with this one exercise, particularly if the words have been selected well, the teachers will be able to show the students how some of the rules of BSL can be incorporated.

If the words 'fear' and 'terror' have been used, then quite often the students will use the same base form but will employ different strengths of expression. From this the teacher can show how the body moves backwards and the shoulders try to bend away and the face shows varying degrees of fear and terror. At the same time, it can be shown that the clawed hands denote tension in a sign. Similarly, the word 'sympathy' often brings the body forward and the face and the action of a flat hand can show gentleness and care. In sign language this ability to show more than one piece of information at the same time is called simultaneity. The teacher may show the use of localisation in BSL, by demonstrating the pronouns I and YOU in the appropriate direction. This allows plurality to be shown for the first time. The teacher can also demonstrate the possessive pronouns MY and YOUR (singular) by telling a student his name sign and accompanying it with MY and YOUR (see Example 11.5).

Using these exercises we are able to show students, simply and quickly, sign language rules which they should retain when they go on to use Signed English instead of trying to teach these rules after the student has learned individual signs in conjunction with English word order.

Other useful exercises which help this development towards a recognition of the rules of sign language, vital to communication with deaf people, are:

1. Filling in the picture.
2. Spot the difference exercises.
3. Concept cards.

Example 11.6 illustrates a 'filling in the picture' pair of drawings. The teacher splits the students into pairs, one with the full picture and the other with the outline. The student with the full picture must then convey the information contained in the picture to the other student who will then draw in the information conveyed.

Example 11.5: Related Personal and Possessive Pronouns

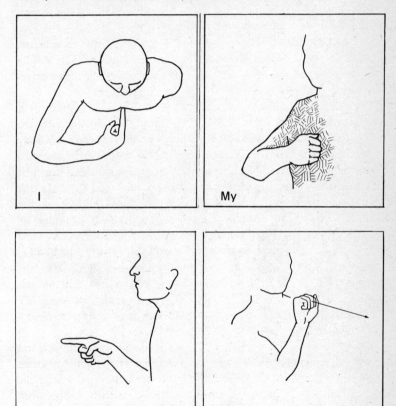

Example 11.7 illustrates 'spot the difference' exercise. Here they must compare the information in their pictures with as much detail as possible.

Concept cards are the third type of exercise. They are invaluable to teachers because they can be used for all levels of proficiency. They can be used with pairs or by having one student who sits at the front

Example 11.6: Filling in the Picture

 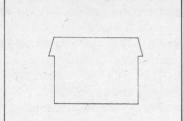

Example 11.7: Spot the Difference

of the group and tries to convey all the information contained in the picture. A typical concept card is illustrated in Example 11.8. For this concept card a beginner might give the following information about the card, that there is:

> a table; 2 benches; 4 plates; 4 drinks; sandwiches;
> a mother; a father; 2 children; a dog

How that information is conveyed at first is not important except that the group recognises what the student is describing. For example a beginner might show that there are two people by raising two fingers and pointing to himself. Then he might try to distinguish the two people by taking the most noticeable features of the two individuals. This could be the breast of the female and possibly by giving the man a beard. The teacher should note how the student presented the male/ female contrast or if their demeanor changed for each person. The teacher can then show the signs used by the deaf community, such as MOTHER, FATHER, MAN, WOMAN, ADULTS. With other parts of the presentation, the teacher can illustrate localisation, showing how the benches are placed along side the table and the plates placed upon the table in the correct position. This exercise demonstrates how deaf people use space and how important it is for the placing of a sign that it relates to previous signs.

Example 11.8:
Concept Card

    With such simple exercises the teacher can introduce: localisation, simultaneity, number, possession, placement, spatiality, and modulation. All these must be recognised if the student is to be able to produce and receive BSL and Signed English with deaf people. In addition students must be taught to overcome the tendency to simply focus on the hands. When they are learning to perceive sign language, they must train their eyes to stay in the area of the signer's face. If they allow their eyes to wander, especially following the hands, they will lose information conveyed by the rest of the body and face. If they focus on the face they will find that the hands will stay in their field of vision and they will receive the whole message rather than just part of it.

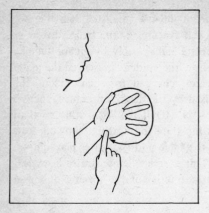

Example 11.9: Non-equivalence in English — BSL Translation: Three signs for the English word 'about'

a. ABOUT: on a topic

b. ABOUT: approximate amount

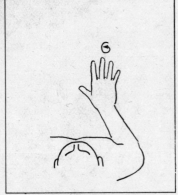

c. ABOUT: general area

It must also be recognised by teachers of BSL that it is not sufficient to be fluent in a language, but that they have a responsibility to know and understand the grammar of the language they are teaching. Personally I am learning all the time and developing ideas and changing methods constantly. Teachers of sign language have failed to acknowledge that one of the major characteristics of BSL is the existence of different signs for the same English word. Attempts are still being made to mould sign language and Signed English into English patterns. No one using BSL, or Signed English with BSL signs, would consider changing the plural YOU to the singular YOU just because there is only one word for YOU in English, any more than one would reduce

Example 11.10: Signs with Related Meanings

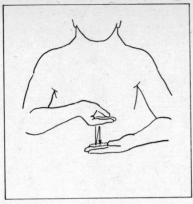

Money

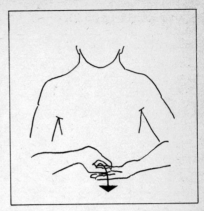

Pay

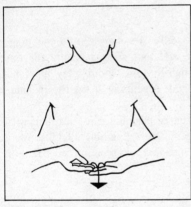

Buy

Wages

Spend

Example 11.10 cont.

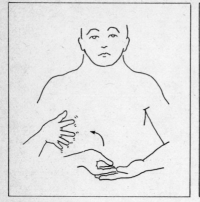
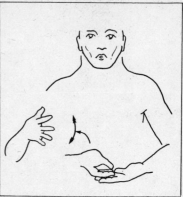

How much?   Expensive

French 'tu' and 'vous' to one word only. Teachers should encourage students to be more aware of the different signs available for one English word. For example, the English word 'about' may be translated by at least three different signs depending upon the meaning and context (see Example 11.9).

The teacher may also take advantage of teaching groups of signs with related meanings, rather than unrelated lists. Example 11.10 shows a number of signs; the relationship of meaning is as seen in their common derivation.

Conclusion

This paper is only intended as an introduction for teachers of sign language and it is hoped that it will stimulate teachers to think about their teaching methods and materials. I would also make the plea that teachers should consider whether they can introduce deaf people as teachers to share the teaching in their classes. It is their language that we are teaching and not only will it help the students, but also deaf people deserve the opportunity to learn from us, especially the formal rules of sign language, so that they can become more effective teachers.

12 A PSYCHIATRIC VIEW OF THE IMPORTANCE OF THE EARLY USE OF SIGN LANGUAGE

John Denmark

Psychiatric Services

Deafness, whether partial or profound, congenital or acquired, gives rise to problems of communication. Profound deafness from birth or early age presents an enormous barrier to the development of speech and verbal language and many of those with this type of deafness have severe communication difficulties.

Communication is of vital importance in psychiatric diagnosis and treatment so that in the case of those who suffer from early profound deafness these processes can be extremely difficult and time consuming. If diagnosis and treatment are to be effective it is essential that psychiatric workers are aware of the psychosocial implications of different types of deafness and have facility in manual methods of communication.

The development of psychiatric services for deaf persons in the United Kingdom began in 1964 when a fortnightly outpatient clinic was first held at the University of Manchester. Four years later an inpatient unit of 24 beds, 12 for each sex, was opened at Whittingham Hospital, Preston. In the same year another clinic, held monthly, was started in London. In 1979 another psychiatric unit for the deaf was established, also in London (Denmark and Eldridge, 1969; Denmark and Warren, 1972).

Patient Population: Types of Deafness; Types of Problems

Our services were developed on the premise that prelingually profoundly deaf persons required workers with the special skills mentioned and it was initially assumed that we would deal with prelingually profoundly deaf persons who were in addition mentally ill. However, patients with other forms of deafness — the partially hearing, those with deafness of later onset, those with additional handicaps such as blindness, and indeed those with communication problems of other aetiology — have been referred. Moreover, it was soon obvious that they also could benefit from assessment and treatment by workers with experience of deafness and its problems and who are willing to give time and effort to overcome the communication difficulties.

Mental illness affects deaf people just as it does those with normal hearing and many of the patients referred to our services suffer from mental illness which is coincidental to their deafness, e.g. from neurotic reactions and from functional and organic psychoses. However, in other cases the presenting problems appear in whole or in part to be a consequence of their deafness, and of these the largest group are children, adolescents and young adults with problems of behaviour and adjustment.

Behaviour and Adjustment Problems

Many young people are referred to our department because of their immature and irresponsible behaviour. Some are referred by schools because of their difficult behaviour or poor progress, some are referred because of their difficult behaviour at home, some are referred because of their poor work records, while others are referred by the Courts or by their legal advisers because of deviant behaviour.

Many of these young people have common features as follows:

1. They are severely or profoundly deaf.
2. They are without speech or their speech is difficult to understand.
3. They have poor verbal language.
4. They are educationally retarded.
5. They are emotionally immature.
6. They are covertly or overtly rejected by their parents.
7. Their parents have very limited ability to communicate with them.
8. Their parents have very little insight into their problems.
9. Their parents have received little counselling, whereas the guidance they have been given has often been unrealistic and over-optimistic.

As more and more young deaf people with behaviour and adjustment problems were admitted to our department it became apparent that special programmes needed to be develoepd and that disciplines other than medicine and nursing needed to be involved. In particular it was apparent that many of these young people required 1) further education to improve their communication skills and to develop social competence and 2) individual and group therapy to gain insight into their own difficulties and deficiencies. Moreover, it also became apparent that parents required training in manual methods of communication to enable them to communicate with their children. Programmes aimed at helping these young people were developed and are now an important part of our work. The unit now also employs not only the usual psychiatric workers but two social workers and two teachers in addition. Extensions to the original unit include classrooms, an occupational therapy department and a seminar room for group therapy.

The development of these special programmes has undoubtedly benefited many young maladjusted deaf people and enabled them to take their place in society. However, it soon became clear that the difficulties of some of these young deaf people were not necessarily the direct result of their handicap but were possibly the result of 'mismanagement'. It was obviously a lamentable indictment of the system that we found it necessary to advise the parents of a twenty-year-old man how to communicate with him.

Research

As a result of our experience we decided to undertake a research project to attempt to determine whether behaviour and adjustment difficulties were typical of the deaf population at large and, if so, to try to ascertain the factors responsible (Denmark *et al.*, 1979). The research was undertaken jointly by the staff of our unit and the Social Research Branch of the Department of Health and Social Security.

The Investigation

The effects of deafness depend upon such factors as degree of hearing impairment, age and rate of onset and the presence of other handicaps. We felt it was extremely important, therefore, to obtain a homogeneous sample of deaf adolescents whose deafness was profound and prelingual, who had no additional physical or intellectual handicap and who had suffered no social, cultural or educational disadvantage other than that resulting from their deafness. By selecting adolescents who had attended schools designated for deaf children we expected that all our sample would be profoundly deaf. Further rigorous criteria of acceptability were also drawn up.

The instruments used in the research were:

1. A test of functional hearing.
2. A test of intelligence.
3. Tests of educational achievement.
4. An interview schedule for the adolescent.
5. An interview schedule for their parents.
6. A rating scale of the adolescent's current behaviour to be filled in by parents.
7. A test of parent/adolescent communication.

Findings

Seventy-five adolescents, 40 male and 35 female, were included in the final study. Their mean age was 18 years 8 months.

Hearing Status   Pure tone audiometry is the commonest method of assessing hearing. However, the results of such tests do not correctly reflect the functional hearing ability of the individual. For example, a person may be profoundly deaf on pure tone audiometry but may be helped by an aid or aids to hearing to the extent that he/she can learn to discriminate speech auditorily. For this reason, and in spite of the difficulties in collecting audiometric data, a functional hearing assessment test covering seven levels of hearing loss devised by Schein and Delk (1974) was employed.

All our respondents had attended schools designated for deaf children. Surprisingly, only 43 of the 75 respondents had a hearing loss equivalent to 70 decibels or more which is approximately the 'cut off' level used by other studies of deafness to distinguish profoundly deaf people from those with partial hearing (Conrad, 1976). Our sample of 75, therefore, comprised 43 profoundly deaf and 32 partially hearing respondents.

Educational Achievement   Previous studies of the literacy and numeracy skills of deaf children in the United Kingdom have shown that their achievements in these areas are poor (Rodda, 1970; Conrad, 1976; and Ives, 1976), and our results mirror these findings. Only 5 per cent of both the profoundly deaf and partially hearing groups combined had a vocabulary reading age of 11 years or more, and 8 per cent of both groups had a vocabulary reading age of less than 7 years.

Behaviour and Adjustment   The parents of the adolescents were asked to volunteer information about any aspect of their children's behaviour which had given cause for concern and which was, in their opinion, a direct result of their child's deafness.

We found an extremely high incidence of behaviour problems in all periods of the subjects' lives. The types of problems were similar to those identified by other workers (Basilier, 1964; Rainer and Altshuler, 1968; Myklebust, 1964; and Remvig, 1969). Temper and aggression were identified by the largest number of parents as characteristic of their child, while a considerable number of parents felt their children to be withdrawn.

Effects of Adolescents' Behaviour   We also studied the effects of the adolescents' behaviour on their parents and how the parents coped with such behaviour. In the profoundly deaf group, 27 out of 43 (65 per cent) parents reported adverse effects at the pre-school stage and 25 out of 43 (58 per cent) at the post-school stage. In the partially hearing group the picture was similar with 21 out of 32 (65 per cent) experiencing adverse effects at the pre-school stage and 14 out of 32 (43 per cent) at the post-school stage. Some parents reported having to seek medical help because of the strain of coping with their child's behaviour.

Communication   One of the major objectives of our study was to evaluate the communication skills and abilities of young deaf people. The methods of communication used at different stages and in different situations were studied by means of a questionnaire completed by parents, while the communication abilities of the adolescents were studied by means of a Test of Communication. A high proportion (65 per cent) of children in the profoundly deaf group, used oral methods when talking to their teachers. Surprisingly, the percentage of partially hearing children using oral methods in class was much lower (47 per cent). Outside class, however, freed from the constraints of the formal teaching situation, practically all children in both groups used combined oral and manual methods, and for the main part these included sign language. Their preference for the use of manual methods is understandable as the study showed that only 9 per cent of the profoundly deaf group had speech and lip-reading skills which were sufficient to enable them to talk easily with hearing people. In comparison, 37 per cent of the partially hearing group achieved this level of competence.

Extreme difficulty in talking to hearing people was the base-line of achievement for the partially hearing group, while 16 per cent of the profoundly deaf teenagers were totally unable to talk to the man in the street. These results strongly support the theory that it is the partially hearing children in schools for the deaf who constitute the majority of the 'speaking' deaf school leavers.

A Test of Communication Skills was designed in order to measure objectively the communication skills of the adolescents. The test measured the ability of the parents to communicate with their children and compared this with those of social workers for the deaf, trained in manual communication methods. The results show that even though the social workers were complete strangers to the adolescents the use of manual methods enabled them to communicate with them more effectively than their own parents.

Parent Counselling and Guidance   The realisation that their child is deaf is invariably a very traumatic experience for hearing parents and feelings of anxiety, depression and guilt are common. Parents can be helped to cope with their feelings, however, by counselling and guidance.

Counselling is the skill of listening to people and allowing them to express themselves in order that they may see their problems more clearly. Counsellors must have a thorough knowledge of the dynamics of interpersonal relationships. Guidance differs from counselling in that the person receiving the guidance is given a number of options and through discussion comes to decide upon certain modes of action.

Counselling and guidance are in practice inseparable. They should be undertaken by professional workers trained in counselling and with experience of all aspects of the handicap including a knowledge of the psychological and sociological implications of that handicap and of services available.

Approximately half of the parents in our study dealt with their children's problems entirely on their own, and of the remaining parents the majority received assistance only from friends, relatives and other untrained sources. A minimal amount of support was received from professional personnel.

Twenty-eight (65 per cent) out of 43 parents of the profoundly deaf adolescents had no contact at all with social workers, while only 2 parents had contact of a regular or lasting nature. A large number of parents said that they had never heard of social workers and yet only a small number of parents felt that they had not needed any help.

Thirty-one out of 43 parents (71 per cent) of the profoundly deaf group and 23 out of 32 parents (71 per cent) of the partially hearing group received no help at all regarding the behaviour problems of their children.

Conclusions Like their hearing peers some young deaf people present problems of behaviour and adjustment. However, this study appears to confirm the results of others, that there is a higher incidence of such problems amongst young deaf people. Indeed, our study strongly supports the theory that disturbed young deaf people referred to our department show many of the characteristics of the deaf population at large and are probably, therefore, only the tip of a much larger iceberg. The study also shows that at the age of 17 years or more, and after approximately a dozen years at school, the majority of prelingually profoundly deaf children have very poor achievements. Many have poor oral communication but, more important, their own parents are often only able to communicate with them at a very superficial level. Effective communication between parent and child is vital if the child is to develop normally.

Behaviour and adjustment problems in both the hearing and the deaf population are in many instances a reflection of the individual's immaturity. Many young people with problems of this nature eventually mature and make a satisfactory adjustment. However, this study appears to indicate not only that there is a higher incidence of such problems amongst young deaf people which result from poverty of experience, but that other factors, some of which are capable of modification, are operable also.

The behaviour characteristic listed most frequently by parents in this study was that of frustration. Understandably, if a child experiences desires but is unable to express them, he will feel frustrated. If a parent wishes to teach her child normal standards of behaviour, and the child cannot understand what is being said, the parent will also experience frustration. Most important the child cannot learn. It needs to be clearly understood that before any child, deaf or hearing, can be taught anything there must be effective communication. As oral communication is dependent upon verbal language, the teaching of deaf children by this method cannot be undertaken in the long preverbal period. Difficulty in communication can affect not only the child's development but also the emotional and physical stability of the mother.

We attempted some assessment of the effect of the deaf child's behaviour upon parents. In both the profoundly deaf and partially hearing group the majority of parents reported adverse effects, while a number were so seriously affected by the strain of coping with their child that they required medical treatment.

In spite of the difficulties experienced in coping with their deaf child, one of the most significant findings of the study was the lack of professional support for the families. When the parents were asked why they had had no contact with such professional staff, the most frequent response was that they had never realised that such support was available or that they had never been approached. Very few parents felt that such help was not necessary, and clearly in the light of the problems described, it would almost certainly have been beneficial. Parents, it seems, are often not consulted over the vitally important issues which affect the whole future development of their child and indirectly affect the whole family. They are often relegated to the role of observers. When questioned about the advice they received on communication methods, several parents in our study echoed the feelings expressed by the late Mrs Lee-Katz, one time President of the International Association of Parents of Deaf Children. She wrote:

> Parents say they would have been willing and anxious to develop new modes of communication — sign language — in the very beginning, if only the need had been presented to them. They state that while it may have been true that many of their questions at the start revolve around the acquisition of speech, lipreading, and going to a normal school, it was incumbent upon professionals to enlighten them at this point in time, and not join them in perpetuating an impossible dream. (personal communication)

Education begins at home, but in the case of deaf children, education cannot begin until effective parent/child communication is established. Many parents in our study believed that if they themselves had been taught sign language it would have been a considerable aid to communication with their child, and certainly they would have welcomed more realistic guidance on this subject. Some parents sought instruction in sign language. Sadly, most found none available.

Looking to the Future

The potential of deaf children can vary enormously. A child with a significant hearing loss may be able to benefit from an aid to hearing to the degree that he can learn to discriminate the sounds of speech. Such a child, if he is of good intelligence and has a stable and supportive family, may well achieve oral success and be successful academically. On the other hand, a prelingually profoundly deaf child with no useful residual hearing who is also intellectually handicapped, with the best help in the world, will not only never develop auditory language but may not have the potential to acquire any useful verbal language. Too much valuable time could well be wasted in attempting to develop speech and lip-reading skills in school. This could lead to a great deal of frustration and failure, and is likely to result in emotional disturbance. There needs to be an individual prescription for management for each deaf child and this will depend upon assessment. Moreover, if the prescription for any individual child is to be correct, many disciplines need to be involved — not only the audiologist, otologist and the teacher, but the psychologist, the social worker and other disciplines as required.

It is the firm belief of our research team that if assessment and management of deaf children were really multidisciplinary and all the professional staff had an understanding of the psychosocial implications of deafness, they would be better able to counsel and guide parents.

By counselling parents and providing them with realistic guidance and giving them the opportunity to develop effective channels of communication, workers would be able to help parents towards the successful management of their child, thus relieving the worry and resentment experienced by so many of them. Perhaps in some cases the behaviour problems and maladjustment of some of the young people referred to our services might have been prevented if the right sort of help had been given at the right time.

In this project we studied only young people handicapped by deafness alone, all those with additional handicaps having been excluded. However, it is important to remember that in some instances the factors responsible for deafness, such as meningo-encephalitis and maternal rubella in pregnancy, can also result in more widespread brain damage so that additional handicaps, such as epilepsy, motor disorder, cerebral dysrhythmia and intellectual handicaps, are more common than with hearing children. Indeed a very high proportion of the young disturbed deaf patients admitted to our unit have intellectual and other handicaps. In this context it must be appreciated that if the development of verbal language is difficult for deaf children without additional handicaps, then it must be so much more difficult when additional handicaps are present. If a deaf child has an intellectual handicap of a degree to preclude literacy and is denied the use of sign language, the child will remain not only nonoral, not only nonverbal, but a noncommunicating child. To deny any such child communication through sign language is to deny him all communication. Many such children have the potential to acquire sign language at a functional level. One can only conjecture what additional problems of behaviour and adjustment additionally handicapped children must present if they are denied the opportunity to acquire these skills. They also clearly require special educational strategies and their families also must need long-term social work support.

Our study was a retrospective one and dealt with deaf adolescents who left schools some six years ago. In the past few years there has fortunately been a move away from the rigid purely oral approach to communication in many schools and also towards multidisciplinary assessment and management. However, to my knowledge there are few programmes for parents of deaf children providing the counselling and guidance they need 1) to come to a full understanding of their child's problems and 2) to convince them of the vital need for two-way communication involving the whole family with their deaf child.

The following letter illustrates the not uncommon experiences and feelings of the mother of a deaf child:

I am writing to congratulate you upon your excellent report which I have just read with considerable interest and whose recommendations I heartily endorse. My son of 17½ 'can hear loud noises' (through vibration), is a poor lipreader, his speech is not good (sometimes it is better than at others), and he has an I.Q. of 135. We were told to talk as much as possible, speak normally always facing the child and never to use our hands . . . However, we eventually decided that the so-called 'experts' knew too little in practice about very deaf children, and that something more was required. We learned to finger spell, and subsequently tried to find a school which admitted to using signing as a teaching aid — a practically impossible task! Also unfortunate was the fact that Charles soon adopted the view that signing was 'bad'. So, although I have strongly advocated total communication since the advent of the Lewis Report, my worst enemy has been, in fact, my son! He has always insisted that his poor speech and lipreading were the result of my teaching him to finger spell and wanting him to sign.

At last, however, progress has been made. After one week's

holiday with the Breakthrough Trust in Norfolk, Charles has come home and informed me that I have to learn to sign and must use total communication! The fact that I did learn to sign 6 years ago but never became proficient because of lack of use was all forgotten!

In your next report, I suggest you also stress the necessity for a strong (or perhaps 'warped') sense of humour if one wishes to keep sane as the parent of a deaf child/adolescent!

I most sincerely hope that your Project is carefully studied and assimilated by the unconverted, who have been biased for far too long, and have in consequence ruined the futures of too many deaf children.

Some cases of deafness can be cured, some deaf people can be helped to hear by hearing aids, some deaf people can aspire to high academic achievement. However, not all deafness can be cured, not all deafness can be alleviated by an aid to hearing, not all deaf children can even achieve literacy. Moreover, the perpetuation of the myth that all deaf children have residual hearing which can be amplified and so enable them to hear and to speak has minimised the severe communication problems of many deaf children. If that myth can be dispelled perhaps people will come to have a better appreciation of the problems of all deaf people and parents of all deaf children will receive the help they require to understand and fully accept their child.

Our study supports the hypothesis that there is a higher incidence of behaviour and adjustment problems amongst young deaf people. In some cases this may well result from such factors as minimal brain dysfunction but in others it seems that this is the result of adverse factors which could be remedied. It is from his parents in the early formative years that the child first learns the rules of living and yet, as Gregory (1976) demonstrated, parent/child communication is often virtually non-existent. Better parent counselling and more realistic guidance leading to improved parent/child communication must surely play a part in terms of preventive mental health.

In 1963, the late Professor Kallmann wrote:

A straight approach to the prevention of maladjustment is to centre on family life since it is in this context that the most unhappiness and behaviour disorders manifest themselves.

13 SIGN LANGUAGE IN AN UNFAVOURABLE SETTING: A PERSPECTIVE*

William Edmondson

Introduction

Over a period of about six years the author has spent many hours in schools for the deaf making informal observations and videotape records of classroom communication. Statistical analysis, individual child data, observational techniques such as frequency counts of various activities or events, all of these are significant aspects of observational research. However, the most important results of such observations are ideas, the theories and explanations which occur to the worker and which offer some insight into the behaviour observed. This chapter presents, with some illustrations and discussion, a few of the results of the author's observational work (see also Edmondson, 1980). Specifically, the topic addressed here is that of sign language in the classroom.

It is my view that the classroom is an unfavourable setting for sign language and, somewhat paradoxically, that British Sign Language *must* be used in classrooms in schools for the deaf. The resolution of the paradox is suggested by Tervoort and Verberk (1967, cited in Moores 1978, p. 169) who write:

> ... it seems clear that the choice has to be: either well controlled, monitored signing tending towards an adult level, semantically and syntactically, or no signing whatsoever; but no signing that is uncontrolled and left to find its own ways.

The unfavourable setting for sign language is the typical classroom in a school for the deaf, a setting where signing is 'uncontrolled and left to find its own ways'. A consequence of this tolerance of signing is that the language environment of the deaf child is far from satisfactory,

* The author is indebted to the Leverhulme Trust Fund for financial support (grant BB/L1) and to Margaret Deuchar, Susan D. Fischer, Brian M. Foss, Sue Foster, James Kyle, Elizabeth R. Valentine, and Bencie Woll, each of whom has contributed comment and criticism during the preparation of this chapter. The views expressed are, however, the author's, as is all responsibility for any error.

and it is this idea which is explored in this chapter. Another very important consequence is the effect upon British Sign Language itself and this is discussed in the final section of this chapter.

Any discussion of classroom communication and the use of British Sign Language in an educational context must also cover Signed English. In what follows attention will be drawn to the problems posed for the child by Signed English. However, before dealing with the unfavourable nature of the classroom it is necessary to consider one or two points about school life which are important for deaf children. It is also necessary to state that my use of terms such as unsatisfactory language environment, unfavourable setting, tolerance, and so on should not be thought to reflect teachers or their work in a bad light. On the contrary, I am well aware of their hard work and very appreciative of the courage and goodwill shown to me by teachers who agreed to participate in observational work. If critical attention is to be directed anywhere, and teachers participate in this as well, it is to those who are responsible for the perpetuation of inaccurate and derogatory remarks about sign language.

The Setting

For many deaf children the school is the place where language is first learned. Signing, when it is not directly forbidden, is discouraged or frowned upon in most schools. Despite the efforts of teachers and parents, the deaf child's first language is likely to be Sign, learned with and from peers and older children in school. 'Sign' is the term used here for the sign language of school children, and it can be considered a sort of proto-British Sign Language. Peers are particularly important; friendships form amongst classmates although in the playground children associate with others of different ages. The primary schools will not contain children older than about 11-12 years of age who may not be very sophisticated linguistically.

The classroom will probably be the place where a lot of language learning takes place; because the children are grouped by age for much of the day, peer group interaction is especially significant. Children also act as interpreters for each other in the classroom and, furthermore, novel material introduced by the teacher will demand extension of the children's language skills.

The classroom may not, however, contain many children from deaf families. It is commonly assumed that approximately 5 per cent of deaf children have deaf parents. This point is of obvious significance for any discussion of classroom communication. In the USA Jensema and Trybus (1978), using a random sample of 657 hearing-impaired children (from a larger sample of 10,509), found that 39 (9 per cent) had one hearing-impaired parent and 18 (3 per cent) had two hearing-impaired parents. For the UK, Conrad (1979) reports that of the 468 children in his study in both schools for the deaf and partially hearing units, there were 27 with deaf parents – 6 per cent. In classrooms in which I have worked (with predominantly 10-12-year-old children) I have found that the percentage can be higher; small class sizes are not uncommon, and clearly provide opportunities for wide fluctuation caused by sampling. There is also the possibility that hearing families are increasingly seeking to have their deaf children educated in partially hearing units or integrated with hearing children, and this would have the effect of turning the figure quoted above into a likely minimum for any school population today. Nevertheless, the fact remains that one may encounter classrooms where only a small proportion of the children come from deaf families. It is therefore important to consider some of the basic conditions required for language learning.

Language Achievement – Preconditions

This section deals with the preconditions required for successful development of linguistic skills, a process which I prefer to call language achievement as this stresses the essentially creative work put in by a child learning to use any language for the first time, an aspect of this process not conveyed by the term language development. Language acquisition, the other common term, has the potential for evoking notions of physical exchange, of 'picking something up' as if from a shop counter, an article to be supplied and acquired in its entirety.

In order to assess the satisfactoriness or otherwise of any language environment it is necessary to have some conceptualisation of the process of language achievement. Ideally such a conceptualisation should allow one to itemise the essential components of any language environment. Such a list then permits assessment of the encountered environment, the assessment being made on the basis of a list of preconditions – the degree to which these are or are not satisfied.

The conceptualisation of language achievement which I have arrived at in the course of my observational work is a perceptual one based on the notion of perceptual models, or internal models as they are sometimes called (Gregory, 1970). This simple idea is that perception proceeds predictively; internal models are continuously employed against which sensory information is compared. Thus children learn to perceive the world around them by constructing within themselves models of that world. If a growing child is to model successfully any aspect of her surroundings the interaction between her sensory systems and that 'to be modelled' complex of events must conform to certain requirements ` — preconditions must be met. I suggest that language achievement is a perceptual learning process, one which proceeds in precisely the same way as any other. However, the requirements or preconditions for successful language achievement are slightly more complex because the elements to be perceived are the products of other people. In the following paragraphs six independent preconditions which I have identified are described, with a few examples, and these will illustrate the significance of this particular theoretical approach.

The first precondition is concerned with *the amount of linguistic data in the language environment* of the child achieving language. Language achievement is the process of modelling the language(s) encountered and for this to be possible we must ensure that the child is not being asked to proceed on the basis of too little information — we must avoid a dearth of data.

The second precondition is that we must avoid *sensory mismatch* between the child and the language data. An example of such mismatch would be the use of lip-speech with a child who could not see well. Such a sensory mismatch is not avoided by attending to the requirement of the first precondition; the preconditions are independent. It is possible, however, that in some cases a sensory mismatch may also cause a dearth of data. Examples of this are readily found in most classrooms in schools for the deaf. It is usually assumed that the use of amplification devices such as the group aid or the person aid (perhaps operating on the loop system) has the effect of turning the children into hearing children who can and do make use of acoustic linguistic information. The evidence is quite clear, many deaf children may be made aware of sound which is amplified but that does not mean that they can hear *speech* in any useful sense. Sensory mismatch may have another important consequence, it may lead to distortion of the data. The combination of amplified sound and hearing loss is again an example; certain sounds in speech may become indistinct, if not inaudible, with the effect that the deaf child is deprived of some of the information contained in the sounds she 'hears'. In the worst case the 'hearing' may in fact be sensitivity to vibrotactile stimulation of the outer ear.

Before proceeding to the remaining preconditions, it is necessary to draw the reader's attention to the grammatical construction employed in the statement of the preconditions. There is a general sense in which it is easier to appreciate the importance of the preconditions if they are formulated as pitfalls to be avoided. As such the preconditions can be readily interpreted or understood in practical terms. More importantly, however, the apparently straightforward positive statement may not have the same meaning as the 'double negative' form used here, and this difference may be a simple semantic one or it may be based on practical issues. Consider, for example, the first precondition. We are not in a position to require the provision of 'enough data' because we are not in a position to identify that state. It does not matter that we may not know the use to which the data are being put. Furthermore, even if we accept the notion of 'enough data' there may well be problems with variations in individual requirements. On the other hand, a dearth of data can be conceptualised, and examples can be found of children for whom this precondition was not satisfied, children such as Victor (Lane, 1977) or Genie (Curtiss, 1977).

The third precondition relates to the quality of the language environment: *the linguistic data must not be inconsistent.* Once again the amplification of speech for the child with hearing loss offers an example. Suppose that there are three amplification systems available in the classroom and that all are used by the teacher and children for speech communication. Suppose further that with one of these devices a child can discriminate successfully two speech sounds, say 's' and 'sh' as in *sip* and *ship.* Both sounds are heard by the child who distinguishes between them on the basis of auditory sensation. With the second amplification device the child finds that discrimination is possible, but only because she can hear the first sound perhaps much as before, and not the second. The amplification equipment is clearly not the same in the two instances, nor is the basis for the child's successful discrimination. However, there is no inconsistency. The inconsistency would be provided by the third device if it rendered 's' as the sound known to the child as 'sh', and 'sh' as some other speech sound also known to the child. Note that discrimination of the two sounds would still be quite possible on the basis of two distinct auditory sensations. The problem arises when the auditory experience of speech heard via the third amplifier is inconsistent with the other auditory experiences, when it is contradictory and confusing. Such inconsistency might be encountered whenever a child's hearing aid is replaced by an 'improved' model. The requirement that the linguistic data must not be inconsistent is clearly independent of the first two preconditions.

The next precondition, the fourth, concerns the relationship between the language environment and the child's developing model of the language(s) in that environment. The requirement is that *the linguistic data must not be inaccessible* if they are to be of any use to the child. The adult who modifies her language to suit the child makes the language more accessible, and thereby more effective for communication. Inconsistency too may be reduced. Newport *et al.* (1978) refer to 'three special characteristics of Motherese' — brevity, well-formedness and intelligibility. They note that perceptual limitations in the child may influence the structure of Motherese, rather than requirements of syntactic simplicity, and they interpret their finding of low propositional complexity as the effect of a 'gross bias toward brevity'. It nevertheless remains perfectly plausible that from the child's point of view Motherese *is* syntactically simple. It is the child's internal model of Motherese which determines its syntactic simplicity. This view is derived not from its relationship with adult language, but from its relationship with child language.

An example of inaccessible linguistic data, from my own video-tape records, concerns the inability of some deaf children to remember written words and copy them into their notebooks. For these deaf children it appears that such data are inaccessible linguistically whenever they are required to copy written language. The words and sentences are copied two or three letters at a time despite the fact that the children appear to understand the content. Thus it seems that data apparently compatible with a child's internal model may sometimes be inaccessible to that model. The child's model will render some linguistic data inaccessible, a point to which we shall return.

The fifth precondition is that *the child should not be deprived of exposure to adult language*. This means both the simplified language offered to children by an adult and the language an adult uses when communicating with another adult. This precondition is necessary because it is only by means of exposure to the whole gamut of language and communication behaviour produced by an adult, and thus reflective of the adult's model (these data may be examples of discourse management, eye contact patterns, turn-taking, etc.), that the child will grow to achieve her own model as an adult.

Lastly, the sixth precondition for language achievement is that *the child should not not be obliged to 'depend' upon an inadequate language model*. Children who are achieving language naturally make errors — it is only when her hypothesis fails that the child learns a little more about the language with which she is coming to terms. There is a fine balance which exists between parental interpretation of a child's utterance and that child's exploration of her linguistic milieu. This balance is essential if the child is to make progress by abandoning or changing from time to time the faulty elements in her understanding of language. This balance is upset when the child is prematurely encouraged to rely upon, and thus retain for too long, her childish version of language.

Language Achievement — Sign and Signed English

We can now turn to consideration of the extent to which the deaf child can build appropriate models of British Sign Language. Assessment of the language environment will include where necessary reference to Signed English. Using the preconditions set out above as a framework for discussion, we can come to an appreciation of the nature of Sign and demonstrate that Signed English may not be useful to the deaf child.

Clearly the first precondition is not met. Deaf adults are rarely seen in schools for the deaf and the deaf child, especially the younger deaf child, will not be exposed to much that could be called British Sign Language. This dearth of data must surely affect all aspects of Sign: the syntax, the vocabulary and the set of gestural components used for fashioning signs. Faced with the need to communicate the children will invent what they cannot cull from the available data. Children may request signs from adults, but to further fill the need for signs the children will most probably create them. It is to be expected that signs for people, things, events or concepts of importance to children (e.g. the sign for Christmas), will vary from school to school, or even from class to class. Individual differences may also exist, tolerated as idiosyncratic by other children. Mimetic signing may constitute the major creative resource of the child and this too will permit much idiosyncratic signing (Edmondson, 1980).

Assessment of the syntax of Sign in relation to spoken and written languages has been undertaken by Cokely and Gawlik (1974) who consider school Sign, or Childrenese, as pidgin, and by Fischer (1978) who concludes that re-creolisation best describes the linguist's understanding of the child's approach to sign language achievement. It would seem to me (and the difference here is one of emphasis) that the child's view is better described as re-creation of language with eclectic use of all available linguistic data, the corollary being that the subset of syntactic data derived from the hearing community is relatively easily plundered (but see below). There is of course one other source of syntactic data and this is the Sign of other children. Inasmuch as we accept hypothesis-testing we must conclude that signing will be to some extent idiosyncratic at all levels, including syntax. Thus we can sum up by saying that the poor linguistic data available to a deaf child includes the idiosyncratic products from other children in various stages of language achievement, and some components from the hearing world. For each child the dearth of data will be determined at least partly by the home environment, and this variable factor will contribute to the variation between the children.

Moving on to the next precondition — lack of sensory mismatch — there is little to be said that is relevant to sign language. The assumption here is that the children are deaf and the precondition is, in a sense, automatically met because the children select the use of sign language — they would not be expected to select a medium for which they were ill matched.

Inconsistency, the focus of the next precondition, is clearly not avoided. It can arise from the hypothesis-testing of other children who will by definition produce some inconsistent utterances. Additionally, the language models of some of these children will be changing and this will add to the inconsistency (the communication of deaf children is not always successful). The behaviour of adults with whom a child interacts may cause confusion, an important factor being the use of natural gesture (sometimes unnatural gesture, Edmondson, 1980). For example, counting from 1 to 20 in Sign is usually done with the fingers of one hand; the hand configuration sequence chosen for the numbers 1 to 5 determines in part the representation employed for subsequent numbers, 6 to 10, and 11 to 20. Some of the hand configurations employed (and there are several different systems in use in the UK) are counter-intuitive or, at best, not obvious and teachers and parents may use (invent) different idiosyncratic systems for what is a very arbitrary process. The deaf child may have to struggle with several different inconsistent systems and risk communication failure.

The fourth precondition requires that inaccessibility be avoided. This refers to the relationship between a child's existing internal models and the linguistic data available. Two important and related ideas pertinent to any discussion of accessibility are those of rate and simultaneity. Bellugi and Fischer (1972), and more recently Grosjean (1979a, 1979b) have reported on comparisons between spoken and signed languages (American) and one can be in no doubt that the two types of language are organised in fundamentally different ways (see also Klima and Bellugi, 1979).

Rate of production of propositions is not language dependent but rate of articulation is, as is rate and manipulation of pause production. This is a possible source of perceptual difficulty. For example, is comprehension improved by reducing the rate of articulation or by rapid repetition? I have observed in classrooms and in a deaf club, that when signers wish to make something clear or to emphasise it, they usually choose rapid repetition unless they consider the recipient to be inexperienced, when they may alter rate. Sign language is characterised as essentially simultaneous or spatial in organisation, in contrast to speech which is sequential and temporal in its organisation. Thus it appears that experienced signers who modify their rate of signing (or fingerspelling) for inexperienced signers, are using their model of spoken language to control the production of sign language. It thus seems probable that some linguistic element in the environment may be inaccessible because the language models of the children vary in the significance they attribute to the different dimensions available for expression (different attitudes to sign language in the home may contribute to this variation). This could be considered an undesirable influence of the spoken language on sign language.

The point can be reiterated in more general terms so as to reveal its significance for discussion of Signed English. Language models — that is, perceptual models and models of production — appropriate for speech are not appropriate for sign language, and vice versa. Whilst the evidence for influence on Sign from spoken and written language might be construed as counter to this proposition, it must be remembered that deaf children do not achieve or invent Signed English for themselves, despite the incredible emphasis placed upon English at home and in the school. The implication is quite clear: Signed English should not work. It should not work in the sense that the Sign of the deaf community will not be utilised and because the English to be Signed is not fully considered. As far as I know no proponent of Signed English has considered the differences between written and spoken English. To confuse these is to add inconsistency to the problems posed the deaf child by Signed English.

Others too have doubts about the validity of Signed English. Baker (1978a) writes:

To my knowledge, all of the linguists who have studied [these] Manual English systems have concluded two things: (1) that they do not accurately and completely model English . . . and (2) that they can't ever accurately and completely model English . . . Both conclusions are, in part, based on the differences in language structure which stem from modality differences — vocal-auditory versus visual-gestural. (p. 20)

However, the issue of Signed English is a very complex one which involves intricate social factors beyond the scope of this chapter (for an authoritative positive view of Signed English the reader is referred to Bornstein, 1979). It is important to keep in mind that assessment of the effectiveness of Signed English can only be made if a comparable teaching programme, based on sign language in a bilingual context, is also established. It would be astonishing if Signed English was not more effective than oralism in an educational setting, but a bilingual approach should be even more effective.

The two remaining preconditions relate to interactive aspects of communication. The fifth precondition is that which requires that in our linguistic provision for children achieving language we must avoid the lack of adult language. In the usual course of things the adult furnishes information about many aspects of communication behaviour. We should not be distracted by the observations that young children also modify their language for their younger siblings (see Snow, 1979). These very young caretakers are themselves exposed to adult language and communication, even if only occasionally, while very young.

The deaf schoolchild who is achieving sign language is not so well off. The small percentage with deaf parents must be important, but the possibility remains that these children will come to accept some of the Sign in school as a dialect of British Sign Language. Furthermore, being outnumbered in school, these children may in their turn be considered by the majority only to be users of a dialect. For these reasons the small percentage of 'native' signers may not be influential. As an example of what this reduced influence can mean, I would cite a deviant form of the fingerspelled 'e' which is used in one school in which I have worked. The correct form — the manual alphabet appears to be standardised throughout the deaf community — is rejected when offered to some of the children.

It is not difficult to accept that lack of exposure to adult language deprives a child of linguistic data and encourages reliance amongst groups of children on distorted or invented 'data'. There is, however, a more subtle reason for suggesting that such deprivation is important, and it is this: adults constrain the product of a child's invention without restraining the inventiveness. The child thus receives, in effect, comment and criticism on the products of her hypothesis-testing, but without being discouraged from further experimentation. The carefully manipulated, constraining environment requires of the child's interlocutor marvellous interpretative skills, skills concerned with much more than just the content of an utterance (and all this is motivated by the desire for communicative success). Parents are not language teachers, they simply assist the child in her endeavours. The abilities of deaf children to fill this role for each other are surely limited (they are perhaps too willing to interpret), and it is not surprising that language achievement is a drawn-out process. We should note in passing that contrived systems such as Signed English will make it difficult for adults to fulfil their task because these systems are poorly defined and have no status as a natural language used by adults.

The final precondition is that children should not be obliged to *depend* upon inadequate language models. The nature of the inadequacy is not an issue. A child has inadequate language models because she is still a child busy with the process of achieving language, testing hypotheses, acquiring vocabulary and so on. The essential point is that dependence on inadequate models is ultimately a restraining influence on hypothesis-testing and therefore on language achievement. Moreover, tolerance of idiosyncratic language achievement is encouraged.

In the language environment of the deaf child such inappropriate dependence on inadequate models is fostered by the people with whom the child is communicating. Adults expect a lot from the deaf child — they focus on the communicative act and may be less prepared than they would be with a hearing child to act interpretatively — and the child has to learn to interpret a lot, that is, to rely on her inadequate models of language (this is particularly the case with lip-reading) (see Gregory and Mogford, this volume). Her deaf peers at school make similar demands on her because their idiosyncratic communication behaviour also requires that she react interpretatively.

The restraining influence on invention operates in a different way from the constraints applied through interaction with adults. In the latter case the constraints direct the language achievement whereas dependence on inadequate models restrains the inventive process itself; the invention is slowed rather than influenced in its course. The children receive encouragement to interpret, from hearing adults and deaf children alike; to do so requires that they rely heavily on their language models and so achievement slows. The children's idiosyncratic languages are tolerated, even nurtured by these same interpretative skills — up to a point. A consequence of this is that a child's highly idiosyncratic communication behaviour may be tolerated initially but it may become so individual as to be ineffective, the result of unrestrained and undirected inventiveness. Alternatively a child may be restrained so readily that language achievement and communication skills are very slow to develop. It is really not surprising that some deaf children become frustrated and violent, or apathetic and isolated.

In this section I have attempted to show how the six preconditions set out earlier can be used in an assessment of the language environment of the classroom. I have demonstrated that each of these independent preconditions reveals different aspects of the language environment to be unsatisfactory, and furthermore I have indicated why I consider the notion of Signed English to be unsatisfactory from the point of view of language achievement.

It should be noted that it is possible to state the aim of Signed English in terms of the six preconditions — to overcome the problem of sensory mismatch and *thereby* to provide a suitable English Language environment for the deaf child. My contention is that this aim is too simplistic; the complexities of the process of language achievement are being ignored.

The use of British Sign Language plus English as separate languages is advocated, not just because a bilingual environment looks more promising for the children in the classroom, but because the present attitude, tolerance, is plainly not in the best interests of the children and seems to be having an undesirable effect on British Sign Language as well. It is this last point which is the topic of the next, and final, section.

Sign Language — Variation

As we have seen, the sign language environment of the deaf child is one which encourages the development of idiosyncratic language. It is this which I consider to be undesirable.

Language achievement (in a general sense now) is a question of constructing for oneself a model of communication behaviour (or plurality of such models) which is functionally congruent with the models possessed by those with whom one is to communicate. One does not have to arrive at precisely the same model, merely one that produces acceptably few misunderstandings (this latter is worthy of more study). The requirement of functional congruence — how else would one come to the conclusion that one's model development was complete? — applies to all levels of communication: phonological, syntactical, semantic, discourse control, and paralinguistic (including natural gesture). There really are three billion idiolects, we just don't notice this most of the time, because of the high degree of functional congruence.

The alternative view of language achievement requires a defence of fundamental congruence (i.e. the assumption of conformity at the level of competence), and this at once raises several questions. For example, why do conforming competence models produce incongruent performance models? What is the scope of the conformity of the competence, is it just syntactical or does it range over all aspects of communication? If the latter, is the conformity to be sought in the totality of the competence model or do the several components conform separately? I do not subscribe to the view that everyone who uses language ZZZ has the *same* basic understanding or model of that language, and that they fail to make full use of it. If this assumption *is* made then one is forced to impose on language achievement the most fantastic expectations. These are not required if one relaxes the tau(gh)tness of one's notion of language achievement.

Variation in language is to be expected, and variation in sign language is being studied (see, for example, Deuchar, Chapter 6 in this volume). Fischer (1980) deals with variation at several levels, in both sign language and English, and by a different route reaches the same point: users of a language may not share all of the grammar. Fischer's conclusions are important, and they are i) that determination of *the* grammar of (American) Sign Language may be a fruitless enterprise — various elicitation techniques may yield different grammars; ii) that experimental linguists will have to 'become more cautious' because '. . . we can no longer accept one person as a representative sample; rather, we shall have to consider more group data'. Thus we see that variation is in essence predictable, rather than a problem with the data. Functional congruence will vary from society to society, from language to language, and so also will the degree of variation found — some languages may be tolerant of greater variation.

Returning now to our deaf heroine (for the language achievements of the deaf are indeed heroic) I am suggesting that for the deaf child functional congruence — if it is reached at all — is reached at a point which permits a lot of variation. We have seen how this variation arises, how it is encouraged, and how it is tolerated. My concern is that it is too much. I would go so far as to suggest that it is only in sign languages achieved in the unfavourable circumstances outlined here that variation limiting of language development is to be found. And the importance of this is that both the individuals who use the language, and the language itself, may be restricted in clarity of expression.

The suggestion that British Sign Language should be used in schools, therefore, has significance for the language itself. Deaf adults must be available to help the children break out of the cycle of new language, but this may take time. Deaf adults too are very interpretative and tolerant of variation, as would be expected from all of the discussion so far. It is not surprising to discover from a deaf woman that signs offered (i.e. invented) by one of her hearing children are accepted as having the status of an 'adult' sign. The overinterpretative language model is also an adult model, the language itself requires this. Nonetheless, the presence of deaf adults in the classroom (the practical implication of bilingualism in education) will be of enormous help to the children and the teachers. Thus it is to be expected that British Sign Language will develop into something less varied and more 'standard'.

I cannot conclude without mentioning the hearing parents of deaf children or the important pre-school years. My belief is that the parents and children should be encouraged to develop sign language for themselves, under the influence of the deaf community. The period of time involved before the deaf child can be exposed to a lot of 'standard' signing is not too long, and we have to accept that children will do a lot more language learning in school than their hearing counterparts. English will be available in the bilingual school setting, as a second language. The important thing is to establish good communications between the parents and the young child, and the guided co-creation of language (which for the child eventually evolves into the sign language of the deaf community) is likely to be much more bonding as an experience than is Signed English, and ultimately more successful. The disadvantages of such an approach are obvious but it should be noted that for the very young child the guided co-creation of sign language probably comes much closer to meeting the required preconditions than any other alternative.

14 EARLY LANGUAGE DEVELOPMENT IN DEAF CHILDREN

Susan Gregory and Kay Mogford

Introduction

Despite intensive debate for many years about the value of various forms of communication for the deaf, particularly in educating the deaf child, surprisingly little is known of the development of their communication skills. Many of the studies that concern themselves with the early stages of communication, have been concerned with the development of the ability to use manual forms. These have emphasised the normalcy of this development when compared to spoken language acquisition in hearing children (Bellugi and Klima, 1972; Schlesinger and Meadow, 1972; Schlesinger 1978), but their focus of attention has been almost exclusively deaf children of deaf parents, a point we shall return to later.

The vast majority of work on the language of the deaf has been concerned with the spoken and written language of the older deaf child and deaf adult. It is perhaps unfortunate that most of the studies are based on written rather than spoken language. This may make data collection easier, but is likely that the discrepancy between the written and spoken language of the deaf is greater than that for hearing people. Arnold (1978) comments, in his study of the deaf child's written language, that 'it is, however, an unfortunate fact that even the most educated and verbal deaf students experience some difficulty with writing'. However, this does not detract from the overall conclusion of all such research, expressed by Russell, Quigley and Power (1976) in their excellent review of the area, that 'deaf children do, in fact, possess a set of rules which frequently deviate from those of standard English'. This conclusion is reaffirmed by later studies (Leslie and Clarke, 1977; Arnold, 1978; Kyle *et al.*, 1978).

Despite the concordance in the view that the language of the deaf child, once acquired, is deviant in many ways, the assumption implicit in most approaches to developing and fostering language in deaf children, is that normal natural development is possible in the early stages. The implication is that language goes wrong because the input to the child is inadequate, in that the hearing loss limits the amount of linguistic material he can receive. In some ways these approaches are a reaction to the earlier grammar-based systems of educating the deaf child (Fitzgerald, 1926; described by Schmitt, 1966). Even so, they are emphatic in seeing the path to oral competence as involving mimicking the normal process as far as possible in terms of the language the child receives. Groht (1958), Van Uden (1968) and many others present this view, recently expressed by Ling (1978), 'The development of speech in hearing impaired children must follow a similar path', (to that in hearing children).

Tate (1979), in comparing the development of language in deaf and hearing children, writes

It seems that hearing loss results in a reduced exposure to language relative to the amount of exposure enjoyed by young hearing children and that, in most cases, hearing impaired children are developing language along much the same lines as the hearing child, thereby generating their own sentences and making mistakes in the process. (p. 159)

It is this very assumption, that hearing-impaired children can develop language along the same lines as the hearing child, that we wish to question in this chapter. It cannot be simply assumed that the deaf and hearing child set out on the language acquisition path from the same place, and that it is only inadequate input to the deaf child that causes deviant development.

It may seem strange that in a book that is titled *Perspectives on British Sign Language and Deafness* that we should present a paper that concentrates solely on the development of spoken language in deaf children. We make no apology for this. Firstly, because in our sample of eight prelingually deaf children of hearing parents, who were not specially selected in any way, not one of them developed spontaneously, or was taught, any form of sign language, however loosely one uses the term. Also, their use of natural gesture was certainly no more than the use of gesture by hearing children of the same developmental level, and we suspect it may well have been less. This lack of signing and gesture is interesting in view of the findings of Feldman, Goldin-Meadow and Gleitman (1978) in the USA. They followed six deaf children not exposed to manual language who were observed 'to use manual gestures of their own to reveal their thoughts and wishes to others'. Their study reports that these gestures were strung together in ways that showed evidence of a grammar. We have read their paper carefully, but can find no evidence that the gestures they observed, apart from pointing, occurred in the deaf children we studied. The mode of communication of the deaf children in our study was essentially that of spoken language.

The second reason for which we feel it justified to make a detailed consideration of the development of oral communication skills, is that we wish to consider, in general terms, the notion that deaf and hearing children commence their language acquisition from the same position. This assumption is as important to a consideration of the development of sign language, as it is to that of spoken language, a point we will return to later in the discussion.

Eight prelingually deaf children of hearing parents have been studied from when they were fifteen to eighteen months of age, i.e. as soon as possible after diagnosis of their hearing loss, until their fourth birthday. The eight children constitute a representative sample of deaf children who are diagnosed early, in that they were all the children picked up in three Local Authority areas, in one twelve-month period, according to certain criteria. These were, firstly, that the child should have no other overriding handicap, and secondly that the language of the home should be English. The sample consisted of five boys and three girls, all first- or second-born children, from homes of social classes II, III white collar and III manual, with a range of hearing loss from partially hearing to profoundly deaf. Full details of this group are given in the Appendix to this chapter.

The intention was to examine the development of communication skills as thoroughly as possible, and to this end a variety of situations were employed to collect data, involving five contacts with every mother and child in each three-month period. The situations which form the basis for the results to be reported here were as follows:

(a) A free-play situation which was video recorded in the child's own home twice in every three months. The mother and child played together with toys brought by the experimenter. These were a pop-up-cone tree or trigger-jigger, the Galt pop-up men toy, and the Escor roundabout, which consists of two men on horses and two men in chairs riding on a roundabout which can be taken to pieces. These toys were selected to provide opportunities for play throughout the age and ability range under consideration. It is often asked whether behaviour recorded on video can be considered as representative of the behaviour in general. In one sense, of course, it never can be. The very presence of a third person, whether to film, record, observe, or just be there, will change the situation. However, given this, our feeling is that our observations are fair ones. Firstly, because they sampled ten to fifteen minutes of a visit that was rarely shorter than an hour and thus the behaviour on film could be compared with the unrecorded part of the session. Secondly, in making regular visits for thirty months or more we established a relationship with the families, such that it seemed unlikely they felt a need to 'put on a performance' for us. The option of erasing from the tape any session they felt unhappy about, was offered to all families. Not one took this up, although some recordings definitely showed sequences where mother and child were far from their best.

(b) A guided interview with the mother, once every three months, considering all aspects of the child's communication. The interview took about two hours, and as well as questions about words and gestures used and understood by the child, it dealt with communications the mother and child could get over to each other, whatever the means, e.g. How does he let you know he's hungry, bored, cross etc? Can you make him understand that he has to wait for something?

Other questions looked at situations where the child violated the mother's expectations, e.g. Can you remember a time when he's surprised you by telling you something you didn't think he would tell you? Have you ever found it impossible to get him to understand something you felt he should be able to?

As the child reached the stage of about twenty words, it became more difficult for the mother to report on his total vocabulary. For this reason, from this stage on, we used a checklist of 150 words, partly derived from the records of Thatcher (1976) and Gillham (1979) of the first hundred words of hearing children, supplemented with words based on our own experience of deaf children. On the checklist, the words were grouped in categories, so those words that the child used that were not on our list could be recalled by the mother in the context of the other words in that category.

(c) Diaries were kept on each child, and after every visit an account was written up. This included general information about family events, details of any new competences of the child including new words, and a description of any interesting episode during the visit.

In this chapter, the development of oral language in the deaf child will be described based on information from these sources. There are two parts, firstly the rate of acquisition will be considered, and secondly the content of the first hundred words.

The Rate of Acquisition of Language

In considering the rate of acquisition of language we shall look at the emergence of the first hundred words of our deaf children. The problem of deciding what is a word, in those early stages, is well known, and has been discussed from Leopold (1939) onwards. The appearance of the first word* has been recorded as occurring anywhere between nine months and eighteen months and much of this difference is due more to the definition of word than to variation between children. Another problem in this area concerns data source. This can be mother's or father's report, observation by trained observers or film recordings made under specified conditions. In this study a word was taken to be a consistent sound, spontaneously used by the child, with a particular recognisable meaning. The information was from interviews with the mother supplemented by diary accounts and recordings of the child playing.

In order that the results for deaf children could be compared with normal language acquisition, the study by Thatcher (1976) discussed by Gillham (1979), was used for comparison. Thatcher replicated with English infants the work of Nelson (1973) with American infants. Nelson looked at the growth in vocabulary from ten to fifty words of eighteen infants from volunteer mother-baby pairs. Thatcher repeated this, looking at the first hundred words of fourteen mother-baby pairs. The comparison is not ideal, as Thatcher's sample, like Nelson's, is drawn from middle-class homes. In addition, Thatcher's group is based totally on first-born children whose mothers are school teachers. However, as his results are consistent with Nelson's (1973) and other studies of early language acquisition, they may be considered adequate for comparison here. His definition of word was 'a sound used consistently to refer to an event' and the data is based on mother's records and fortnightly visits.

The age at which deaf children spoke their first word, and reached ten, fifty and one hundred words is given in Table 14.1. The deaf children are listed in this, and every, table in order of hearing loss, starting with the least deaf. It will be noticed that only six children of the eight studied are given. The two most profoundly deaf are now four years old and neither has reached the ten word milestone. Thus the discussion of rate of acquisition is based on children with a mild to severe loss, and excludes profoundly deaf children (with a loss greater than 110 decibels, in the better ear, averaged over the speech frequencies).

Table 14.1: Age at One, Ten, Fifty and One Hundred Words for Deaf and Hearing Children

Name*	First word	Ten words	Fifty words	Hundred words
Dominic	10m	19m	22m	30m
Jason	13m	17m	24m	26m
Michael	19m	22m	29m	34m
Paul	15m	22m	28m	33m
Amanda	19m	30m	38m	43m
Heather	18m	26m	34m	36m
Average	16m	23m	29m	34m
Normal Group	11m	12m	19m	20m

* These are changed to preserve confidentiality.

It will be seen that deaf children start to speak later than hearing children; on average their first word appears five months later, at sixteen rather than eleven months. This gap has widened to fourteen months at the one hundred word milestone. The age at which the deaf child reaches every milestone, except the first word, shows a significant correlation with the degree of hearing loss, in that, as might be expected, the children with a greater hearing loss take longer to reach each milestone. (At 10 words rho = 0.87 $p < .01$, 50 words rho = 0.89 $p < .01$, 100 words rho = 0.83 $p < .01$.)

The rate of acquisition of words is shown in Figure 14.1. In the one to ten word stage hearing children learn remarkably quickly and take only one month to acquire ten words, whereas for the deaf children it takes seven months. This difference could partly be accounted for by the difficulty, already mentioned, in deciding what constitutes a word. This is a particular problem in the early stages with normal children, as words seem to exist in embryonic form for several months before they emerge. The normal child's first words are not the beginning of something, but a point on a continuum between making sounds in a conversational way and using words in a totally adult form and manner. Grieve and Hoogenraad (1979) report the early words of

Jacqueline as described to them by her mother: 'at nine months Jacqueline "attempted to make words", at eleven months she "was using some words but not necessarily understanding" and at fourteen months she was "saying her first words". Her commonsense tells this mother that her child is using her first words when she uses them as an adult might, properly with the right meaning; nonetheless, she describes the child's earliest attempts as words too.' Thus the words of a hearing child seem to exist in embryonic form for several months before they can strictly be called words. Once one word fulfils the criteria, others follow quickly and acquisition appears to be relatively rapid.

Figure 14.1: The Rate of Acquisition of Words of Deaf and Hearing Children

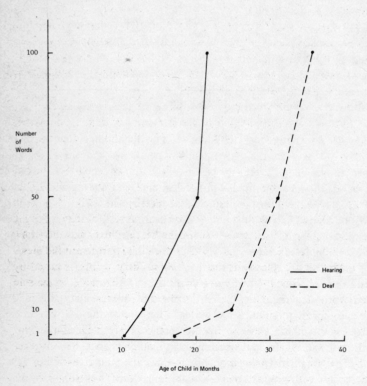

However, if for hearing children this rapid emergence of the first ten words is related to the criteria for a word, and the point at which it should be counted, an interesting point emerges. The problem of

deciding when a word is a word does not occur in these early stages with deaf children. Sounds approximating to words do not exist in the interaction of deaf children with their mothers for several months before the true word is formed. Although they do vocalise, and these vocalisations have functions within the interaction, there is no impression that the vocalisation may be words. The first words of the deaf child are deliberately elicited and trained. When the child chooses to mark something in his or her mother's shared world by a sound, this sound seems to be coaxed and shaped by the mother. Mothers are quite clear about when their deaf child has a word. They mean that the child has used a sound spontaneously in a certain context. The way in which the mother talks of her deaf child's language is interesting. Many of them describe 'working on' a word: 'We're working on "Mummy" at the moment'. A mother of a hearing child would never talk like that. It seemed to us, as outside observers, that the deaf child 'performs' words, and that the saying of a word, in these early stages, is an end in itself, rather than part of a transaction within interaction. Thus clearly in the one to ten word stage, the process of acquisition for deaf and hearing children is different.

In the ten to fifty word stage the hearing children have slowed down in the rate of acquisition, the deaf children have speeded up, and both groups are acquiring new words at the rate of about six or seven a month.

The period from fifty to one hundred words reveals a striking difference between the deaf and hearing groups. The deaf group are increasing their vocabulary more quickly than in the ten to fifty word stage but still at a steady rate of ten words a month. However, for the hearing group there is a massive snowball effect and they gain fifty new words in one month. This rapid gain of vocabulary from around eighteen months, and a vocabulary size of about fifty words, is noted by Nelson (1973), Bloom (1975) and many others. This rapid increase in vocabulary size coincides with the beginnings of two-word utterances at about eighteen months.

For deaf children, too, two-word utterances start at about the fifty-word stage (see Table 14.2), though this is at an average age of thirty months rather than eighteen months. A two-word utterance was defined, in our study, as a combination of two words, where each of the words must also exist on its own, and at least one of the words must exist in another combination. It was not counted if the two words were learnt together as a pair. The age at which two-word combinations emerged correlates with hearing loss, in that the children with the most hearing tended to use two-word combinations earlier (rho = 0.83, p < .05).

Table 14.2: The Two-word Combination Stage for Deaf Children

Name	Age when first used two-word combinations	Number of words when first used two-word combinations
Dominic	24m	60
Jason	21m	39
Michael	30m	57
Paul	28m	50
Amanda	43m	103
Heather	33m	43
Average	30m	59

Thus hearing children and deaf children enter the two-word combination stage at the same vocabulary size. For hearing children this is accompanied by a rapid increase in vocabulary, but the rate of vocabulary growth for deaf children only increases slightly. This is seen as a creative period for hearing children in linguistic development, their language is seen as 'taking off'. The same feeling is not there with deaf children, and there may be consequences for deaf children, that the onset of their syntactical development is not associated with a dramatic increase in vocabulary size. Although we have not carried out a systematic analysis of this stage yet, we know that some two-word utterances that the deaf child evolves, *de novo*, for himself, later become ritualised, and go into the vocabulary as a word pair, used as a single word. A particularly striking example of this was Paul, who at thirty months had formed several two-word combinations, including 'not hot' and 'hot tea'. At thirty-two months he said 'not hot hot tea' to mean cold tea. 'Not hot' functioned as a word meaning 'cold' and 'hot tea' functioned as a word meaning 'tea'. We feel that the two-word utterance stage may be different for deaf children and our next analysis will be of that period.

Vocabulary Content

In this section the context of these hundred-word vocabularies will be considered, using the data from Thatcher as a comparison. Following

Nelson (1973), Thatcher divided the words of hearing children into six categories.

General nominals: words that name a particular class of objects or events, e.g. ball.

Specific nominals: words that name a specific object or event, e.g. Mummy.

Action words: words that describe an action that has taken place or demand that an action takes place, e.g. down.

Modifiers: words that describe an attribute or quality of something, e.g. wet.

Personal-social words: words that are used within social relationships or to describe affective states, e.g. thank you, ouch.

Function words: words that have a solely grammatical function, e.g. for.

(For further details see Nelson, 1973, p.`16-17.)

Nelson classified the words of her children into these groups in terms of the use the child made of the word rather than by any grammatical definition of the word. This procedure was followed by Thatcher and in the present study. Hence 'outside' could be a general nominal if it named a place, an action word if it was used to demand to be taken outside, and a modifier if it described where something was.

The percentage of the vocabulary falling into each category at the fifty and one hundred word stage is given in Table 14.3. For both deaf and hearing children general nominals form the largest group of words, and function words form only a small part of the total.

There are, however, differences in the vocabulary distribution for deaf and hearing children. It will be noticed that at both stages the deaf children have fewer nominals than the hearing children. Taking raw scores of vocabulary, the difference is significant for both the fifty ($\chi^2 = 19.88$, p < .01) and hundred ($\chi^2 = 30.9$, p < .01) word vocabularies, taking into account the whole corpus. Throughout, deaf children have a greater proportion of personal social words and this is significant at the fifty ($\chi^2 = 13.1$, p < .01) and hundred ($\chi^2 = 17.05$, p < .01) word stage. At the fifty-word stage the deaf children have a significantly higher proportion of action words ($\chi^2 = 9.81$, p < .01) and at the hundred-word stage they have a significantly higher proportion of modifiers ($\chi^2 = 29$, p < .01). These results, on first reflection, are surprising. If the language of deaf children tends to be a taught one, and the language of hearing children tends to arise within interactive dialogue, one would expect deaf children to have a relatively higher proportion of nominals, and hearing children to have a relatively higher proportion of personal-social words, rather than the other way round.

Table 14.3: The Percentage of the Vocabulary of Deaf and Hearing Children that Falls into Given Categories

	Vocabulary 50 words		Vocabulary 100 words	
	Deaf	Hearing	Deaf	Hearing
General nominals	46	67	49	61
Specific nominals	14	9	10	9
Action words	21	12	16	18
Modifiers	7	6	16	7
Personal social words	11	4	8	3
Function words	1	2	1	2

The data for hearing children is taken from Thatcher, 1976

An examination of the first twenty words of the deaf children makes the issue clearer. Table 14.4 shows all the words acquired by more than one of the deaf children within their first twenty words. The number of hearing children having each word in their first twenty is also shown. Thus two words used by all six deaf children in their first twenty words are 'No' and 'Thank you', words acquired by less than half the hearing children. The words that occur for more than one deaf child, that do not occur for the hearing group at all, are 'Look', 'Sit down', 'Peep bo', 'Come on', 'Here you are'. Thus while nominals form a high proportion in both groups in the early vocabulary, the deaf group also have a high proportion of words that comment on something that has happened, or is happening ('Thank you', 'All gone', 'Hello', 'Bye bye', 'Good boy/girl') and of words that request and demand something to happen ('No', 'More', 'Look', 'Sit down', 'Peep bo', 'Come on' 'here ya'). Thus the features of the environment that are salient for the deaf child are his own and others' activity, as much as objects within the world. His need is also for words that give him control over the world. It is also clear that many of the words he uses are those that will be used to him, with emphasis, by his mother. The higher level of personal-social words throughout may thus reflect a greater tendency to name features of social relationships, and the higher level of activity words in the fifty-word vocabulary may indicate the higher concern of the deaf child in getting things to happen, and things that do happen.

Table 14.4: The Content of the First Twenty-Word Vocabulary of Deaf Children (The adult form of the word is listed to represent all variation of that word)

	Number of deaf children using word (possible total 6)	Number of hearing children using word (possible total 14)
Thank you	6	5
No	6	5
Daddy	5	12
Mummy	5	13
Dog	5	7
All gone/gone	5	7
Bye-bye	5	6
Cat	4	2
Hello	4	5
Horse	4	6
Sheep	3	2
More	3	2
Car	3	12
Name . . .	3	9
Look	2	0
Clock	2	5
Sit down	2	0
Shoes	2	10
Peep bo	2	0
Good boy/girl	2	1
Come on	2	0
Here you are	2	0
+ 40 words used by one deaf child only		

There seems to be another possible interpretation of these findings. It may be that the deaf child is acquiring a vocabulary appropriate to his developmental level. Thus at ten words he is on average twenty-three months, compared with the average age of twelve months of the hearing child. Hence it is more appropriate for him to acquire words like 'No' and 'Thank you', and he is at a stage of wanting to control and direct his world. This would also explain the higher level of modifiers in the hundred-word vocabulary, where the deaf child is on average thirty-four months, fourteen months older than the average hearing child. Thus colour, size and properties of objects are important to him, and inspection of the vocabularies shows it is a high proportion of colour names in particular which increases the proportion of modifiers. Thatcher (1976) reports that in a final interview with the mothers of the hearing children, when the children have one hundred and twenty to one hundred and thirty words the mothers were reporting an increase in colour, number and size modifiers. These hearing children would still be younger than the deaf group at one hundred words, but it shows how vocabulary content reflects developmental level.

The different developmental level does not seem to be the complete answer, however, as some differences remain throughout. Deaf children do seem to use their language to talk about different things from hearing children. The language that arises through interaction for hearing children seems to be a language of predominantly joint reference to objects, the language that is elicited from deaf children seems to be one concerned with labelling features of social relationships and activity as much as with labelling objects.

Summary and Discussion

So far we have attempted to bring together several different analyses of the early language of deaf children and made comparisons with the early language of hearing children. It has been demonstrated that the deaf do not show the same pattern of development as hearing children, in terms of the rate of acquisition of language, and the content of their early vocabulary.

There seem to be three main hypotheses one could have about early language development in the deaf. Firstly, it could be supposed that the deaf child develops language normally, albeit more slowly. Secondly, one could feel that language development in the deaf is slower, and that there are deviations from normal development, but that these are due to his greater general maturity at each linguistic stage. These differences would then be superficial rather than basic, and would be observed in different interests and emphases at each stage, rather than a totally different pattern of development. The third view would be that the deaf develop language in a way that differs fundamentally from the way in which hearing children do.

The evidence put forward in this paper makes the first view untenable, as the whole pattern of development is different. However, it is interesting to note that both groups do start forming two-word utterances when they reach a vocabulary size of around fifty words. The second hypothesis does seem to account for a minor part of the findings, in particular, the relatively high proportion of modifiers in the hundred-word vocabulary of deaf children, and possibly other variations in the content of the vocabulary at different vocabulary sizes. Overall, however, we believe the results show fundamental differences in the development of deaf children, the main features of which are as follows:

They take longer to get from their first word to a vocabulary of ten words.

The emergence of their first words is qualitatively different.

Their rate of vocabulary growth does not increase dramatically from a vocabulary size of fifty words.

Their early vocabularies contain relatively fewer general nominals and relatively more personal-social words.

Their fifty-word vocabularies contain significantly more action words.

Their hundred-word vocabularies contain significantly more modifiers.

It should be remembered that the findings are based on a sample which has, of necessity, to exclude the profoundly deaf children. If it had been possible, their inclusion could only have served to increase the differences between the two groups. Thus we feel confident in concluding that the deaf child develops language differently from the hearing child.

It is, of course, hardly surprising that the handicap of deafness should effect the development of communication skills. It is clear from the findings of the study that differences between deaf and hearing children are present from the early stages. Recent accounts of language development in hearing children have stressed the continuity of preverbal and verbal behaviour, and thus we should like briefly to consider three aspects of infant development that seem to relate to language development, which may be different for the deaf child.

Turntaking From the very beginning of interaction, mothers and babies have been observed to take turns; that is, while one is active the other will be responsive and vice versa. In observations of babies from two months of age Trevarthen (1974, 1979) has described how the mother's voice seems to have special significance for the infant, and how the child's behaviour changes as the mother begins to talk. The infant, too, takes an active role in the situation, and as he takes the initiative, the mother moderates and subdues her behaviour. Although many aspects of behaviour, facial expression, gesture and eye contact have a role in these exchanges, a major component is the sounds made by mother and child. Schaffer, Collis and Parson (1977) have observed mother-baby interaction with babies of twelve and twenty-four months. They describe the turntaking that takes place in these exchanges, where first one holds the floor and then the other. They find that the one-year-old is as competent as the two-year-old and conclude 'In one year old as much as two year old children vocal exchanges with the mother are "smooth". This smoothness is indicated above all by the ability of the two parties to take vocal turns and avoid overlapping response.'

Joint Reference   Joint reference refers to activity where both mother and baby are attending to the same thing, and often these accounts describe how the focus of attention is 'marked' vocally. Collis and Schaffer (1975) and Collis (1977) have demonstrated that mothers often follow the gaze of their infants; they look to where the infant is looking. This, more often than not, is accompanied by a comment on the joint focus of attention. Newson and Newson (1975) describe how such joint reference is a starting point for 'conversation'. They say, 'Mothers and babies begin to conduct "conversations" concerning objects and events to which both parties are attentive, even though there is as yet no evidence for understanding on the babies' part'. At a later stage the mother will co-ordinate her interaction with the baby's activity, and make aspects of his behaviour particularly significant. Even later, intonational markers are used to impose structure on the child's activity, to create meaning from within it (Shotter and Gregory, 1976). Thus a shift in mothers occurs from matching vocalisation to the child's focus of attention to using vocalisation to focus the child's attention. Bruner (1975) stresses the importance of this development and says 'language is acquired as an instrument for regulating joint activity and joint attention'.

Anticipation Games   Anticipation games are those mother-baby games which are characterised by a build-up of tension, and then release, often accompanied by laughter. There are many such games; 'peek-a-boo', 'round and round the garden', 'this little piggy', 'I'm coming to get you', etc. Bruner (1975), Ratner and Bruner (1978), suggest that such anticipation games provide a structure for communication which models that of the structure of language. Because the game is highly predictable the child can take an active role, and in fact the roles are reversible. Also vocalisations systematically mark features of the game. Such activities are seen as building up cognitive structures which guide the child in decoding the grammatical system.

Thus the preverbal period has elements, many of them relying on the articulatory/auditory channel, which are important in the later development of communication. As Newson (1979) puts it

> ... infants can be involved in complex and sophisticated dialogues of action and expressive gesture long before the emergence of anything which could properly be called speech. Because with their regular care-givers they share a familiar context in which the actions take place, a joint history of well practised interaction rituals within a dialogue format, babies gradually evolve a pre-verbal code of communication which fosters the growth of a whole corpus of shared understandings. Upon this foundation the development of language can subsequently be built. (p. 221)

The picture emerges of the preverbal child knowing about language before he comes to use it for himself. This knowledge may well be missing for the deaf child. Turntaking may be difficult to establish, and in fact a previous analysis of our data has shown that vocal clashes, i.e. those times when both mother and child vocalise together, are significantly more frequent for deaf child-mother pairs, than for hearing child-mother pairs (Charles, 1978; Gregory, Mogford and Bishop, 1978). Joint reference may be more difficult to establish, which may be why hearing children have significantly more nominals in their vocabulary than deaf children. Nominals, i.e. words which 'name', may well arise from a joint focus of attention for mother and child. Although it may not seem obvious that anticipation games are more difficult for deaf children (although these games normally have a vocal component, there seems no reason why the essential nature of the game could not be represented visually and tactilely), we know that mothers of deaf children do not play these games. In the early stages of our research we included a 'play with toys' sessions, in order to see how mothers played such games with their deaf children. We had to abandon it as the mothers were unable to play in this way, although the mothers of hearing children had no problem. Mogford (1979) notes the difficulty mothers of pre-school deaf children have in instituting a climax to games.

Thus in this paper we have shown that from the start there are differences in the way that deaf children of hearing parents develop language, from the way that hearing children of hearing parents develop language. We have placed the origins of the differences in the preverbal period and have briefly and sketchily described aspects of this period which may be contributory to later deviant linguistic development. We have suggested that turntaking routines, joint reference and anticipation games are harder to establish with deaf children, and yet all these are on a continuum with language development for the hearing child. The problem for the deaf child is not simply a deficit in the language he is exposed to, but that early dialogue and communication skills do not develop in the same way as for the hearing child.

In conclusion, we would like to consider briefly some implications of these findings for the use of signing as a mode of communication for deaf children. As has been previously stated, most of the studies of deaf children who use sign language have involved deaf children of deaf parents. If we may speculate, it could be that deaf parents have skills in the prelanguage period of establishing turntaking, joint reference and anticipation games that do not depend on sound. It may thus be that deaf children and deaf parents develop prelanguage communication skills, and that the facility the children show with sign language, is not with sign language *per se*, but because of their early communication skills. A colleague of ours, Gillian Hartley, has made video recordings of deaf mothers with deaf babies. Although analysis is still in a preliminary stage, it seems that there mothers establish communication routines differently from hearing mothers with deaf children. The whole structural organisation of play is different. This is despite the fact that many of these mothers are using oral rather than manual means of communication. More detailed analysis should elucidate this issue further. However, hearing mothers may find some of the same problems with manual communication as with oral communication.

Thus it may be that the problem for the deaf child is not the mode of communication, but the structure of communication itself. Our task is not just to look at the development of language skills, but at the very process by which language emerges.

Appendix: Details of the Deaf Children

Basic Information

Name	Hearing loss A	Hearing loss B	Cause of deafness	Age at diagnosis (months)	Additional handicaps	Social class	Position in family
Dominic	Partially hearing	45	Unknown	10	None	III Manual	1st
Jason	Partially hearing	70	Prematurity	10-12	None	III Manual	2nd Twin
Michael	Moderately deaf	83	Rubella	8	None	II	2nd
Paul	Moderately deaf	97	Unknown	11	None	III White collar	1st
Amanda	Severely deaf	102	Unknown	11	None	II	1st
Heather	Severely deaf	107	Unknown	11	None	III Manual	2nd
Nigel	Profoundly deaf	113	Prematurity	16	Visual defect (treated)	III Manual	1st
Zena	Profoundly deaf	not available	Rubella	6	Visual defect (treated)	III White collar	2nd

Intellectual and Language Assessment

Name	Developmental Assessment	Merrill Palmer A	Merrill Palmer B	Reynell Comprehension	Reynell Expressive
Dominic	Average	5.1	5.9	3.4	2.10
Jason	Above average	4.8	5.0	3.3	3.9
Michael	Average	Above average at 2.11		2.7	2.8
Paul	Average	4.7	5.1	2.9	2.8
Amanda	Average	3.6	4.1	1.3	1.8
Heather	Above average	4.8	5.3	2.9	2.7
Nigel	Below average	3.4	3.11	0.11	0.11
Zena	Below average	3.2	3.9	No score	No score

Notes

Hearing loss A is a functional assessment of hearing loss made at eighteen months based on that used by Gregory (1976). Briefly:

Profoundly deaf: little or no response to sound, no response to human voice
Severely deaf: response to voice but limited to situations when child is attending
Moderately deaf: response to voice in favourable situations
Partially hearing: near to normal responses though hearing loss constitutes a handicap

Hearing loss B is based on the average hearing loss in the better ear over the speech frequencies.

The developmental assessment is based on an assessment made by us, using a range of items from several developmental tests.

The Merrill Palmer and Reynell tests were administered by us within three months of the child's fourth birthday. The assessments are given as the age level attained by the child in years and months.

Merrill Palmer A is the Merrill Palmer result obtained when no allowances were made in the scoring for the fact the child was deaf, i.e. all the language items that the child did not pass were scored as failures.

Merrill Palmer B is the Merrill Palmer result obtained when allowance is made for the child being deaf, i.e. all the language items before the child's basal level, that the child did not pass, were scored as ommissions.

Acknowledgement

This research is supported by an MRC Project Grant G975/782.

APPENDIX: BRITISH SIGN LANGUAGE TRANSCRIPTION AND NOTATION

A number of conventions regarding the transcription and notation of BSL examples have been obeyed and characters in the Linguistic Aspects section should be read in conjunction with this appendix.

Glosses: English glosses of signs are in upper-case letters. A gloss represents an approximate translation of a sign or compound sign into English and should not be regarded as a direct equivalent, e.g. PARENTS. Where one sign can only be translated by more than one English word, these are linked by hyphens, e.g. DON'T−LIKE.

Fingerspelling: Use of the manual alphabet or signs deriving from it are represented by lower-case letters separated by dots, e.g. p·a·t, f·f.

English Examples: Where an example does not represent a gloss of a sign, normal orthography and inverted commas are used e.g. 'Is it bigger than a breadbox?', 'Half-past eleven'.

Translation: Translations are given in normal orthography below sign glosses.

Notation: The notation used is based on that developed at Bristol University for computer analysis of sign. The notation is derived from that developed by W. Stokoe (1960) but modified for the particular structures found in BSL. The system recognises four elements in signs: the *Tab* (T) − place of articulation; the *Dez* (D) − the hand-shape; the *Sig* (S) − the movement made; and the *Ori* (O) − the orientation of the hands in making the sign. This system is shared with the American notation systems, but it differs in its approach to the problems involved in notating the relationship between two hands in neutral space, contact between the two hands and signs derived from the BSL two-handed manual alphabet.

238

Hands Used	*Notation Formula*	
1) One hand	$T\,D\,{}^{\circ}_1\,{}^{\circ}_2{}^{S}$	– T = Tab D = Dez S = Sig O = Ori S = $(S_1 \ldots S_4)$
2) Two hands: both active	$T\,D\,D\,{}^{\circ}_1\,{}^{\circ}_2{}^{S}$	– S and ${}^{\circ}_1\,{}^{\circ}_2$ apply to both Dez – dominant hand described: non-dominant assumed to be mirror image
3) Two hands: one active	$T\,D\,{}^{\circ}_1\,{}^{\circ}_2{}^{S}D\,{}^{\circ}_1\,{}^{\circ}_2{}^{S}$	– S and ${}^{\circ}_1\,{}^{\circ}_2$ of both hands described: non-dominant hand first

The dominant hand is assumed to be the right hand unless specified to the contrary.

Tab gives the location of the sign in terms of its proximity to a specified part of the body.

Secondary Tab refers to that specific part of one hand in contact with or proximate to the other hand.

Dez refers to the handshape and is described using the symbols of the American one-handed fingerspelled alphabet.

Sig symbols give movement and relationship of the hands (at present 4 have been found to be maximally necessary). Movement within a sign is perceived as consecutive or simultaneous: vertically aligned Sigs are used to indicate simultaneity.

Ori_1 gives the palm direction (wrist direction if palm direction is in doubt).

Ori_2 gives the finger direction (established by opening the hand flat and notating the direction of the straightened fingers).

When signs are derived from fingerspelled words, they are notated with lower case letters representing two-handed manual alphabet configurations, separated by raised dots.

Examples of notated signs follow. A complete list of symbols may be found in the table at the end of this appendix.

One-hand Sign

1. WOMAN Ꝫ G ⊥ ᴧ ˣ˙

The right hand is held against the cheek (T= Ꝫ) , with the index finger extended from the fist (D= G), palm faces left (O_1= ⦗) and the extended finger points up (O_2= ᴧ); the movement of the sign simultaneously touches and moves leftwards on the cheek; this is repeated (S= ⦂ᐟ).

Two-hand Sign:
    both active

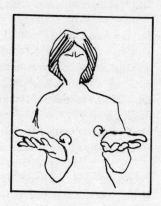

2. WHERE Ᏼ ᴧ Ᏼ ᴧ ⊥ ᶻ

Both hands are held in front of the body (T= ⧈) , both hands are opened, fingers spread and slightly bent (D= Ᏼ Ᏼ), with palms up (O_1= ᴧ) and fingers pointing away from the body (O_2= ⊥) , both hands move side to side   (S= ƻ) . As the hands are the same and without contact, it is assumed that the left hand is a mirror image, and therefore the side to side movement is reciprocal — first both hands towards each other, then both hands away from each other. Where two hands are in contact, or approximate to each other in neutral space, a secondary Tab (t) is used. The neutral space is considered the primary Tab, and the distinctive part of the hand is considered the secondary Tab. This is placed immediately before the primary Tab on the upper notation line. Secondary Tab may be notated for both hands if they are not mirror images.

3. FULL ⊔Ė˅ ⊓Ė ˷ ‹ ⌃ ˣ

   Two-hand Sign:
   one active

The active hand is opened straight, with fingers together (D = Ė) . The primary Tab is the non-active hand, which has the same hand-shape (T = Ė). There are two secondary Tabs: the palm of the left hand (t= ⊔) and the back of the right hand (t= ⊓); the palm of the Tab faces down (O₁= ˷) ; the palm of the Dez faces down, fingers left (O₁ = ˷, O₂ = ‹) and the right hand moves up and touches the primary Tab (S= ⌃ ˣ).

The description above provide only a brief and incomplete introduction to BSL notation. Readers should consult Kyle, Woll and Carter (1979), Brennan, Colville & Lawson (in press) and Carter and Maddix (1980) for further information.

TAB (Location)

⊠	Neutral Space in front of Body	*Trunk*

◻	Whole Face
⌂	Top of Head
⌒	Forehead, Brow
⊔	Eyes
⊔	Nose
⌴	Lower Face, Chin
▱	Lips
)	Ear
ᴣ	Cheek, Side of Face
π	Neck

[]	Area between Shoulder and Hips
[ı	Upper left quadrant of Trunk
ı]	Upper right quadrant of Trunk
]ı	Lower left quadrant of Trunk
ı]	Lower right quadrant of Trunk

Arm

∿	Shoulder and Arm above Elbow
◞	Elbow
◞	Forearm
ꟼ	Wrist
ᴛ	Back of Wrist

When the location of a sign is the non-dominant hand, its handshape (see Dez) is coded as primary Tab.

SECONDARY TABS

FINGERTIPS

a   thumb

e   index finger

i   middle finger

o   ring finger

u   little finger

BASE OF FINGERS

a   base of thumb

e   base of index
    finger

i   base of middle
    finger

o   base of ring
    finger

u   base of little
    finger

BETWEEN FINGERS

1   Thumb/Index

2   Index/Middle

3   Middle/Ring

4   Ring/Little

GROUPS OF FINGERS

tips of one or
more fingers

length of one or
more fingers

EDGES OF HAND

ｱ   thumb edge (from
    base of thumb to
    tip of index finger)

ﾞ   little finger edge

SURFACES OF HAND

u   palm

n   back of hand

WRIST

palm side

back of hand side

ELBOW

DEZ (HANDSHAPE)

A		F		O		Y	
Ä		Ḟ		Ô		T	
Â		G		R		ö	
B		Ĝ		V		A	
Ḃ		H		V̇		3	
Ė		Ḣ		W		4	
Ê		Ĥ		Ẇ		5	
C		I		X		"5	
E		L		Ẋ		7	
Ë		L'		Ẍ		8	

245

SIG (Movement)

🗅 No Movement

ᴋ Touch

✛ Cross another Articulator

▪ Repeat

Movement of Hand(s) Relative to Body

⌃ Up

⌄ Down

ᴎ Up and Down

‹ Left

› Right

ᴢ Side to Side

ᴛ Towards Body

⊥ Away from Body

ᴤ To and Fro

Movement of Wrist(s)

ᴅ Supinate

ᴅ Pronate

ᴌ Twist

ᴉ Nod

Movement of Finger(s)

☐ Opening Hand

#️ Closing Hand

ᴢ Flicker

ᴤ Circular

ᴍ Crumble

Movement of Hands Relative to each other

ᴈᴄ Approach

ᴍ Interlock

☯ Enter

÷ Separate

ᴌᴉ Interchange

᷍ Alternate

ORI (Orientation)

⟫	Right	⌄	Down
⟨	Left	⊤	To Body
⌃	Up	⊥	Away from Body

MANUAL ALPHABET

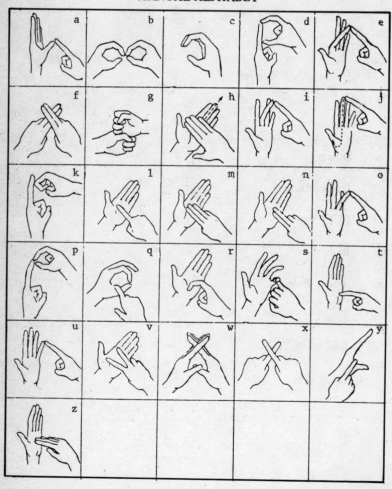

BIBLIOGRAPHY

Ahlgren, I. (1977) Early linguistic cognitive development in deaf and severely hard of hearing children. Paper presented at the First National Symposium on Sign Language Research and Teaching, Chicago

Anthony, D. (1971) *Seeing Essential English*. Anaheim, California: Educational Services Division, Anaheim Union High School District

Arnold, P. (1978) The Deaf Child's Written English — Can we measure its quality? *The Teacher of the Deaf*, Vol. II, No. 6

Baddeley, A.D.B. (1966) Short term memory for word sequences as a function of acoustic, semantic and formal similarity. *Quart. J. Exp. Psychol.*, 18, 362-5

Baddeley, A.D.B. (1979) Working Memory and Reading, in P.A. Kolers, M. Wrolstad and H. Bouma (eds.) *The Processing of Visible Language*, New York: Plenum Press

Baker, C. (1977) Special Field Examination. American Sign Language. Unpublished

Baker, C. (1978a) How does 'Sim-Com' fit into a Bilingual Approach to Education? Paper presented at the second National Symposium on Sign Language Research and Teaching, San Diego, USA, October 1978

Baker, C. (1978b) Regulators and Turn-Taking in A.S.L. Discourse. In Friedman, L. (ed.), *On the Other Hand*. New York: Academic Press

Bakker, D.J. (1972) *Temporal order in disturbed reading*. Rotterdam: Rotterdam University Press

Barik, H.C. (1972) *Simultaneous Interpretation: Temporal and Quantitative Data*. Chapel Hill, NC: The L.L. Thurston Laboratory, University of North Carolina

Barik, H.C. (1973) *Simultaneous Interpretation: Qualitative and Linguistic Data*. Chapel Hill: The L.L. Thurston Laboratory, University of North Carolina

Basilier, T. (1964) Surdophrenia. *Acta Psychiatrica Scandinavica, supplementum* 180, Vol. 40, pp. 362-74

Bates, E., Camioni, L. and Volterra, V. (1975) The acquisition of performance prior to speech *Merrill Palmer Quarterly*, 21, 205-26

Batkin, S., Groth, H., Watson, J.R. and Ansberry, M. (1970) The Effects of auditory deprivation in the development of auditory sensitivity in albino rats. *EEG Cl. Neurophysiol.*, 28, 351-9

Battison, R. (1974) Phonological Deletion in American Sign Language. *Sign Language Studies*, 5, 1-19

Beggs, W.D.A. and Breslaw, P.I. (1980) Reading, clumsiness and the deaf child. Unpublished

Beggs, W.D.A., Breslaw, P.I. and Wilkinson, H.P. (1980) Eye-movements and reading achievement in deaf children. Paper to the *XXIInd International Congress of Psychology*, Leipzig, East Germany

Beggs, W.D.A. and Foreman, D.L. (1980) Sound Localisation and Early Binaural Experience in the Deaf. *British Journal of Audiology*, 14, 41-8

Bellugi, U. (1977) The signs of language. Paper presented at the First National Symposium on Sign Language Research and Teaching, Chicago

Bellugi, U. and Fischer, S. (1972) A comparison of sign language and spoken language. *Cognition*, 1, 173-200

Bellugi, U. and Klima, E.S. (1972) The roots of language in the sign talk of the deaf. *Psychology Today*, 6, 61-76

Bellugi, U., Klima, E.S. and Siple, P. (1974) Remembering in Signs, *Cognition*, 3, 93-125

Bench, J. (1979) Auditory Deprivation — an intrinsic or an extrinsic problem? *British Journal of Audiology*, 13, 51-2

Berger, K.W. (1970) Vowel confusions in speechreading. *Ohio Journal of Speech and Hearing*, 5, 123-8

Berger, K.W. (1972) *Speechreading, Principles and Methods*. National Educational Press

Bergman, B. and Ahlgren, I. (eds) (1980) *Proceedings of the First International Symposium on Sign Language Research*, Stockholm

Blank, M. (1965) Use of the deaf in language studies. *Psychological Bulletin*, 63, 442-4

Bloom, L. (1975) *One Word at a Time*. The Hague: Mouton

Bornstein, H., Hamilton, L.B., Saulnier, K.L., Roy, H.L. (1975) *The Signed English Dictionary for Preschool and Elementary Levels*. Washington DC: Gallaudet College Press

Bradford, L.J. and Hardy, W.G. (eds) (1979) *Hearing and Hearing Impairment*. New York: Grune & Stratton

Brasel, K.E. and Quigley, S.P. (1977) Influence of certain language and communication environments in early childhood on the development of language in deaf individuals. *Journal of Speech and Hearing Research*, 20, 95-107

Brennan, M. (1976) Can deaf children acquire language? *Supplement to the British Deaf News*, February 1976

Brennan, M. (1977) The practical benefits of linguistic research. Paper presented at the B.D.A. Triennial Congress in Eastbourne, June 1977

Brennan, M. (1978) *Communication*. In *Deaf Education*, Strathclyde Regional Council

Brennan, M., Colville, M. and Lawson, L. (1980) *Words in Hand*. Moray House College, Edinburgh

Brill, R.G. (1969) The superior IQ's of deaf children of deaf parents. *The California Palms*, 15, 1-4

Brooks, N. (1964) *Language and language learning: theory and practice* (2nd ed.). New York: Harcourt, Brace and World

Brown, R. (1977) Why are signed languages easier to learn than spoken languages? Paper presented at the First National Symposium on Sign Language Research and Teaching, Chicago

Brown, R. and Bellugi, U. (1964) Three processes in the child's acquisition of syntax. *Harvard Education Review*, 34, 133-51

Bruce, D. and Cofer, C.N. (1965) A comparison of recognition and recall in S.T.M. In *The Proceedings of the 73rd Annual Convention of the American Psychological Association*, pp. 81-2. Cited in J.A. Adams, *Human Memory*. New York: McGraw Hill, 1967

Bruhn, M.E. (1942) Methods of teaching lip reading: a symposium. Lip reading as living language. *Volta Review*, 44, 636-38

Bruhn, M.E. (1949) *Mueller-Walle Method of Lipreading*. Washington, DC: Volta Bureau

Bruner, J.S. (1964) The course of cognitive growth. *American Psychologist*, 19, 1-15

Bruner, J.S. (1975) The ontogenesis of speech acts. *Journal of Child Language*, 2

Bullowa, M. (ed.) (1979) *Before Speech: The Beginnings of Inter-Personal Communication*. Cambridge University Press

Burchett, J.H. (1950) *Lip Reading*. London: National Institute for the Deaf

Butt, D. and Chreist, F.M. (1968) A speechreading test for young children. *Volta Review*, 70, 225-35.

Carter, M. (1980) Noun Phrase Modification in BSL. Bristol University: Centre for the Study of Language and Communication

Carter, M. and Maddix, F. (1980) The Notation of BSL. Unpublished paper

Carter, M. and Woll, B. (1980) Aspects of BSL Structure. Paper presented LAGB meeting, September

Chall, J. (1967) *Learning to Read: The Great Debate*. New York: McGraw-Hill

Charles, J. (1978) A comparison of mothers' speech to deaf and hearing children of two different ages. Unpublished Dissertation. Department of Psychology, University of Nottingham

Charrow, V.R. (1975) A psycholinguistic analysis of 'deaf English'. *Sign Language Studies*, 7, 139-50

Charrow, V.R. and Fletcher, J.D. (1974) English as the second language of deaf children. *Developmental Psychology*, 10 (4), 436-70

Chomsky, N. (1965) *Aspects of the Theory of Syntax*. Cambridge, Mass: M.I.T. Press

Clegg, D.G. (1953) *Pattern for the Listening Eye*. London: National Institute for the Deaf

Clouser, R.A. (1976) The effects of vowel consonant ratio and sentence length on lipreading ability. *American Annals of the Deaf*, 121, 513-18

Cokely, D.R. and Gawlik, R. (1974) Childrenese as Pidgin. *Sign Language Studies*, No. 5, pp. 72-81

Collis, G.M. (1977) *Visual Co-orientation in Maternal Speech*, in Schaffer, H.R. (ed.)

Collis, G.M. and Schaffer, H.R. (1975) Synchronisation of Visual Attention in Mother Infant Pairs. *J. Child. Psychology and Psychiatry*, 16

Colville, M. (1980) The Importance of Positioning and Direct Directionality. *Readings for Sign Language Instructors*. Carlisle: British Deaf Association

Conference of Executives of American Schools for the Deaf (1976) Forty-eighth Meeting, Rochester, New York

Conrad, R. (1964) Acoustic confusions in immediate memory, *British Journal of Psychology*, 55, 75-84

Conrad, R. (1971) The effect of vocalizing on comprehension in the profoundly deaf. *British Journal of Psychology*, Vol. 62 (2), pp. 147-50

Conrad, R. (1976) Towards a Definition of Oral Success. Paper given at the RNID/NCTD Education Meeting, Harrogate, 1976

Conrad, R. (1977a) Lipreading by deaf and hearing children. *British Journal of Educational Psychology*, 47, 60-65

Conrad, R. (1977b) The Reading Ability of Deaf School Leavers. *British Journal of Educational Psychology*, 47, pp. 138-48

Conrad, R. (1979) *The deaf school child: Language and cognitive function*. London: Harper & Row

Craig, W.N. and Collins, J.L. (1970) Analysis of communicative interaction in classes for deaf children. *American Annals of the Deaf*, Vol. 115, No. 2

Croneberg, C. (1978) 'The Linguistic Community', in *A Dictionary of American Sign Language*. Stokoe, Casterline and Croneberg, Linstok Press, Silver Springs, USA

Crystal, D. (1969) *Prosodic Systems and Intonation in English*. Cambridge University Press, Cambridge

Curtiss, S. (1977) *Genie: a psycholinguistic study of a modern day 'wild child'*. New York: Academic Press

Dalgleish, B. and Mohay, H. (1979) Early holophrastic communication without a mature language model: Gesture types at 20 to 26 months. *Sign Language Studies*, 23, 161-6

Davison, F.M. (1977) *The written language of deaf children*. Unpublished manuscript, Department of Linguistic Science, University of Reading

Dawson, E.H. (1979a) *Cognitive functioning of prelingually deaf children*. Unpublished Ph.D. thesis, University of Durham

Dawson, E.H. (1979b) Are the deaf really a homogenous population? *Teacher of the Deaf*, 3, 188-93

Denes, P.B. and Pinson, E.N. (1963) *The Speech Chain*. Murray Hill, New Jersey: Bell Telephone Laboratories

Denmark, J.C. and Eldridge, R.W. (1969) Psychiatric Services for the Deaf. *The Lancet*, 2 August, pp. 259-62

Denmark, J.C., Rodda, M., Abel, R.A., Skelton, U., Eldridge, R.W., Warren, F. and Gordon, A. (1979) *A Word in Deaf Ears. A Study of Communication and Behaviour in a Sample of 75 Deaf Adolescents*. London: Royal National Institute for the Deaf

Denmark, J.C. and Warren, F. (1972). A Psychiatric Unit for the Deaf. *British Journal of Psychiatry*, Vol. 120, No. 557, April

Denton, D.M. (1970) Remarks in support of a system of total communication for deaf children. Communication symposium, Maryland School for the Deaf, Frederick

Deuchar, M. (1977) Sign Language Diglossia in a British Deaf Community. *Sign Language Studies* 17, 347-56

Deuchar, M. (1978) *Diglossia in British Sign Language*. Unpublished Ph.D. dissertation, Stanford University

Dodd, B. and Hermelin, B. (1977) Phonological coding by the prelingually deaf. *Perception and Psychophysics*, 21, 413-17

Dornic, S., Hagdahl, R. and Hanson, G. (1973) *Visual Search and Short Term Memory in the Deaf*. Reports from the Institute of Applied Psychology, No. 38, University of Stockholm

Edmondson, W.H. (1980) Acquisition of sign language in an unfavourable setting, in B. Bergman and I. Ahlgren (eds.)

Edwards, D. (1978) Social Relations and Early Language, in A. Lock (ed.)

Eisen, N.H. (1962) Some effects of early sensory deprivation on later behaviour. *J. Abnorm. and Soc. Psychol.*, 65, 338-42

Erber, N.P. (1971) Auditory and audiovisual reception of words in low-frequency noise by children with normal hearing and by children with impaired hearing. *Journal of Speech and Hearing Research*, 14, 496-512

Evans, L. (1965) Psychological factors related to lipreading. *Teacher of the Deaf*, 63, 131-7

Feldman, H., Goldin-Meadow, S. and Gleitman, L. (1978) Beyond Herodotus: The creation of language by linguistically deprived deaf children, in A. Lock (ed.)

Ferguson, C.A. (1959) Diglossia, *Word*, 15, 325-40

Fischer, S.D. (1973) Two processes of reduplication in the American sign language. *Foundations of Language*, Vol. 9, 469-80

Fischer, S.D. (1978) Sign Language and Creoles. Chapter 13 of *Understanding language through sign language research*. Edited by P. Siple. Academic Press

Fischer, S.D. (1980) The Issue of Variation: Some Consequences for Sign Language Research Methodology, in B. Bergman and I. Ahlgren (eds.)

Fisher, M.T. (1968) *Improve Your Lipreading*. Washington, DC: Volta Bureau

Fletcher, P. and Garman, M (eds.) (1979) *Language Acquisition: Studies in First Language Development*. Cambridge University Press

French, P. and MacLure, M. (1979) Getting the right answer and getting the answer right. *Research in Education*, 22, 1-23

Friedman, L. (ed.) (1978) *On the Other Hand*. New York: Academic Press

Frishberg, N. (1977) A linguist looks at sign language teaching. Paper presented at First National Symposium on Sign Language Research and Teaching, Chicago

Fry, D.B. (1964) The reception of speech. Chapter 4 in Whetnall, E. and Fry, D.B., *The Deaf Child*. Heinemann Medical Books

Furth, H.G. (1966) *Thinking without language*. London: Collier, Macmillan

Furth, H.G. (1973) *Deafness and hearing: a psychosocial approach*. Belmont, California: Wadsworth Publishing Company

Fusfeld, I.S. (1955) The academic program of schools for the deaf. *Volta Review*, 57, 63-70

Fusfeld, I.S. (1958) How the deaf communicate — written language. *American Annals of the Deaf*, 103, 255-63

Gemmill, J.E. and John, J.E.J. (1977) A study of samples of spontaneous spoken language from hearing-impaired children. *Teacher of the Deaf*, 1 (6), 193-201

Gerver, D. (1972) *Simultaneous and Consecutive Interpretation and Human Information Processing*. London: Social Science Research Council Report, HR 566/1

Gerver, D. and Sinaiko, H.W. (eds.) (1978) *Language Interpretation and Communication*. New York: Plenum Press

Gillham, B. (1979) *The First Words Language Programme*. London: George Allen & Unwin

Goldin-Meadow, S. and Feldman, H. (1975) The creation of a communication system: A study of deaf children of hearing parents. *Sign Language Studies*, 8, 225-36

Green, W.B. and Shepherd, D.C. (1975) The Semantic Structure of deaf children. *J. Communic. Disorders*, 8, 357

Greenberg, J.H. (1966) Language Universals, in T.A. Sebeok (ed.) *Current Trends in Linguistics*, The Hague: Mouton

Gregory, R.L. (1970) On how so little information controls so much behaviour. *Ergonomics*, 13 (1), 25-35

Gregory, R.L. and Wallace, J.G. (1963) *Recovery from early blindness*. Experimental Psychological Society Monograph No. 2. Cambridge: Heffer

Gregory, S. (1976) *The Deaf Child and his Family*. London: George Allen & Unwin

Gregory, S. Mogford, K. and Bishop, J. (1979) Mothers' speech to young hearing impaired children. *The Teacher of the Deaf*, 3

Grieve, R. and Hoogenraad, R. (1979) First Words in Language Acquisition, in Fletcher and Garman (eds.)

Groht, M. (1958) *Natural Language for Deaf Children*. Alexander Graham Bell Association for the Deaf. Washington, DC

Grosjean, F. (1979a) A study of timing in a manual and spoken language: American Sign Language and English. *Journal of Psycholinguistic Research*, 8, 379-405

Grosjean, F. (1979b) The Production of Sign Language: Psycholinguistic perspectives. *Sign Language Studies*, No. 25, 317-29

Grove, C., O'Sullivan, F.D. and Rodda, M. (1979) Communication and language in severely deaf adolescents. *British Journal of Psychology*, 70, 531-40

Gustason, G., Pfetzing, D. and Zawolkow, E. (1972) *Signing Exact English*. Rossmoore, California: Modern Signs Press

Halliday, M.A.K. (1975) *Learning How to Mean*. London: Edward Arnold

Heider, F. and Heider, G.M. (1940) A comparison of sentence structure of deaf and hearing children. *Psychological Monographs*, 52 (1), whole no. 232, 42-103

Herriott, P. (1970) *An Introduction to the Psychology of Language*. London: Methven

Hockett, C.F. (1955) *A Course in Modern Linguistics*. New York: Macmillan

Howarth, C.I. and Wood, D.J. (1977) A research programme on the intellectual development of deaf children. *Teacher of the Deaf*, 1 (1), 5-12

Howarth, S.P., Wood, D.J., Griffiths, A.J. and Howarth, C.I. (1980) A Comparative Study of Reading Lessons of Deaf and Hearing Primary School Children. Submitted for publication

Ingram, R.M. (1977) *Principles and procedures of teaching sign language*. Carlisle: British Deaf Assocation

Ives, L.A. (1976) A Screening Survey of 2060 hearing impaired children in the Midlands and North of England. *British Deaf News*, 10, Supplement 1

Ivimey, C.P. (1976) The written syntax of an English deaf child: an exploration in method. *British Journal of Disorders of Communication*, 11 (2), 103-20

Ivimey, G.P. (1977) The perception of speech: an information-processing approach, part 3 — lip-reading and the deaf. *Teacher of the Deaf*, 1 (3), 90-100

James, W. (1901) *The Principles of Psychology vol 1*. London: Macmillan

Jensema, C.J. and Trybus, R.J. (1978) *Communication Patterns and Educational Achievement of Hearing Impaired Students*. Series T2, Office of Demographic Studies, Gallaudet College, Washington, DC

Johnson, E. (1948) Ability of pupils in a school for the deaf to understand various means of communication. *American Annals of the Deaf*, 93, 194-213, 258-314

Jordan, I.K., Gustason, G. and Rosen, R. (1979) An update of communication trends at programs for the deaf. *American Annals of the Deaf*, 124, 350-7

Jorm, A.F. (1979) Cognitive and neurological basis of developmental dyslexia. *Cognition*, 7, 19-33

Kallmann, F.J. (1963) *The Psychiatric Problems of Deaf Children and Adolescents*, London: National Deaf Children's Society

Karchmer, M.A. Trybus, R.J. and Paquin, M.M. (1978) Early manual communication, parental status, and the academic achievement of deaf students. Paper presented at American Education Research Association Annual Meeting, Toronto, Ontario, Canada

Kavanagh, J.F. and Cutting, J.E. (eds.) (1975) *The Role of Speech in Language*, Cambridge, Mass: MIT Press

Kegl, J. (1979) Further Breaking-down the A.S.L. Verb. Paper presented at NATO Symposium on Sign Language. Copenhagen

Klima, E.S. and Bellugi, U. (1979) *The Signs of Language*. Cambridge,

Mass: Harvard University Press

Kyle, J.G. (1977) Raven's Progressive Matrices — 30 years later. *Bulletin of the British Psychological Society*, 30, 406-7

Kyle, J.G. (1978) The Study of auditory deprivation from birth. *British Journal of Audiology*, 12, 37-9

Kyle, J.G. (1980a) Auditory Deprivation from Birth — Clarification of some issues. *British Journal of Audiology*, 14, 34-6

Kyle, J.G. (1980b) *Sign Language and Internal Representation*, in B. Bergman and I. Ahlgren (eds.)

Kyle, J.G. (1980c) Measuring the Intelligence of Deaf Children. *Bulletin of Brit. Psychol. Soc.*, 33, 54-7

Kyle, J.G., Conrad, R., McKenzie, M.G., Morris, A.J.M. and Weiskrantz, B.C. (1978) Language Abilities in Deaf School Leavers. *The Teacher of the Deaf 2*, No. 2

Kyle, J.G., Woll, B. and Carter, M. (1979) *Coding British Sign Language*. University of Bristol School of Education Research Unit

Labov, W. (1972a) *Language in the Inner City: studies in Black English Vernacular*. Philadelphia: University of Pennsylvania Press

Labov, W. (1972b) *Sociolinguistic Patterns*. Philadelphia: University of Pennsylvania Press

Labov, W. (1972c) Some principles of linguistic methodology. *Language in Society*, 1, 97-120

Lane, H. (1977) *The Wild Boy of Aveyron*. London: Allen and Unwin

Leopold, W. (1939) *Speech Development of a Bilingual Child: A Linguist's Record. Vol I, Vocabulary Growth in the First Two Years*. Evanston: Northwest University Press

Leslie, P.T. and Clarke, B.R. (1977) A Study of Selected Syntactic Structures in the Language of Young Deaf Children. *The Teacher of the Deaf 1*, No. 4

Liddell, S. (1978) Non-Manual Signs and Relative Clauses in A.S.L., in Siple, P. (ed.) *Understanding Language through Sign Language Research*. New York: Academic Press

Ling, D. (1978) Forward Trends — Towards Order in Teaching Verbal Skills. *The Teacher of the Deaf 2*, No. 4

Llewellyn-Jones, P., Kyle, J.G. and Woll, B. (1979) Sign Language Communication. Paper presented at International Conference on Social Psychology of Language, Bristol

Lock, A. (ed.) (1978) *Action, Gesture and Symbol: the emergence of language*. London: Academic Press

Locke, J. and Locke, V. (1971) Deaf children's phonetic, visual and dactylic coding in a grapheme or call task, *Journal of Experimental Psychology 89*, 142

Lowell, E.L. (1957) *A Film Test of Lipreading*. Research Paper II. Los Angeles: John Tracy Clinic

MacGinitie, W.H. (1964) Ability of deaf children to use different word classes. *Journal of Speech and Hearing Research*, 7, 141-50

McDougall, R. (1904) Recognition and recall. *Journal of Philosophy*, 11, 229-33

McIntire, M. (1976) Untitled report in *Signs of our Times, No. 43*.

Washington, DC: Gallaudet College Linguistics Research Laboratory

McNeill, D. (1966) Developmental psycholinguistics, in *The genesis of language: a psycholinguistic approach*. F. Smith and G.A. Miller (eds.). Cambridge, Mass: MIT Press, pp. 15-84

McNeill, D. (1970) *The acquisition of language: the study of developmental psycholinguistics*. New York: Harper & Row

Maestas Y Moores, J. (1980) Early Linguistic Environment: Interactions of Deaf Parents with their Infants. *Sign Language Studies*, 26, 1-13

Markides, A. (1977) Rehabilitation of People with Acquired Deafness in Adulthood. *British Journal of Audiology*, Supplement No. 1

Markowicz, H. (1977) *American Sign Language: Fact and Fancy*. Washington, DC: Gallaudet College Public Service Programs

Markowicz, H. (1979) Sign Languages and the Maintenance of the Deaf Community. Paper presented at the NATO Symposium on Sign Language Research, Copenhagen

Markowicz, H. and Woodward, J.C. (1975) Language and the Maintenance of Ethnic Boundaries in the Deaf Community. Paper presented at the Conference on Culture and Communication, Philadelphia

Marmor, G.S. and Petitto, L. (1979) Simultaneous communication in the classroom; how well is English grammar represented? *Sign Language Studies*, 23, 99-136

Mead, M. (1964) Vicissitudes of the study of the total communication process, in T.A. Sebeok (ed.), *Approaches to Semiotics*. The Hague: Mouton

Meadow, K.P. (1968) Early manual communication in relation to the deaf child's intellectual, social and communicative functioning. *American Annals of the Deaf*, 113, 29-41

Meadow, K.P. (1976) Personality and social development of deaf persons, in B. Bolton (ed.), *Psychology of Deafness for Rehabilitation Counsellors*. Baltimore: Univ. Park Press

Menyuk, P. (1971) *The acquisition and development of language*. Englewood Cliffs, NJ: Prentice-Hall

Milan International Congress on Education of the Deaf (1880) *Report of the Proceedings*. London: W.H. Allen

Miller, G.A. (1956) The Magical Number Seven, plus or minus two: Some limits on our capacity for processing information. *Psychology Review*, 63, 81-97

Mogford, K. (1979) *Interaction and Communication between handicapped children and their parents: A Study of Remedial Play*. Unpublished Ph.D. thesis, University of Nottingham

Montgomery, G.W.G. and Lines, A. (1976) Comparison of several single and combined methods of communicating with deaf children. Paper presented at Seminar on Visual Communication held at Northern Counties School for the Deaf, Newcastle upon Tyne

Moores, D.F. (1970) An investigation of the psycholinguistic functioning of deaf adolescents. *Exceptional Children*, 36, 645-52

Moores, D.F. (1974) Non-vocal systems of verbal behaviour, Chapter 15, in *Language perspectives — acquisition, retardation and inter-*

vention. R.L. Schiefelbusch and L.L. Lloyd (eds.). London: Macmillan

Moores, D.F. (1978) *Educating the Deaf: Psychology, Principles, and Practices*. Boston: Houghton Mifflin

Morris, D.M. (1944) Quoted in O'Neill, J.J. and Oyer, J.H. (1961). *Visual Communication for the Hard of Hearing*. Englewood Cliffs: Prentice-Hall

Morton, J. (1978) *Perception to Memory*. Unit 14, Cognitive Psychology. Milton Keynes: Open University Press

Moser, B. (1978) Simultaneous Interpretation: A hypothetical model, in Gerver, D. and Sinaiko, H.W. (eds.)

Moulton, R.D. and Beasley, D.S. (1975) Verbal coding strategies used by hearing-impaired individuals. *J. Speech and Hearing Res.*, 18, 559-70

Murphy, H.J. (1978) Research in Sign Language Interpreting at California State University, Northridge, in Gerver, D. and Sinaiko, H.W. (eds.)

Myklebust, H.R. (1964) *The psychology of deafness: sensory deprivation, learning and adjustment*. (2nd ed.). New York: Grune and Stratton

Nash, J.E. (1975) Cues or signs: a case study in language acquisition. *Sign Language Studies*, 8, 79-91

Nelson, J. (1979) The growth of shared understanding between infant and caregiver, in Bullowa, N. (ed.)

Nelson, K. (1973) *Structure and Strategy in Learning to Talk*. Monograph 38, Society for Research in Child Development

Neville, H.J. and Bellugi, U. (1978) Patterns of cerebral specialisation in congenitally deaf adults; a preliminary report, in P. Siple, *Understanding Language through Sign Language Research*. New York: Academic Press

Newport, E.L. and Bellugi, U. (1978) Linguistic expression of category levels in a visual gestural language, in E. Rosch and B.B. Lloyd, *Cognition and Categorization*. New Jersey: Lawrence Erlbaum

Newport, E.L., Gleitman, H.R., and Gleitman, L.R. (1978) Mother, I'd rather do it myself: some effects and non-effects of maternal speech style, in *Talking to Children: Language Input and Acquisition*. Snow, C.E. and Ferguson, C.A. (eds.), Chapter 5. Cambridge University Press

Newson, J. and E. (1975) Intersubjectivity and the Transmission of Culture: on the social origins of symbolic functioning. *Bulletin of the British Psychological Society*, 28

O'Connor, N. and Hermelin, B. (1973) Short term memory for the order of pictures and syllables by deaf and hearing children. *Neuropsychologia*, 11, 437-42

Odom, P.B. and Blanton, R.L. (1967) Phrase-learning in deaf and hearing subjects. *Journal of Speech and Hearing Research*, 10, 600-5

Odom, P.B. and Blanton, R.L. (1970) Implicit and explicit grammatical factors and reading achievement in the deaf. *Journal of Reading Behaviour*, 2 (1), 47-55

Oleron, P. (1977) *Language and Mental Development*. New Jersey: Lawrence Erlbaum

O'Neill, J. (1954) Contributions of the visual components of oral symbols to speech comprehension. *Journal of Speech and Hearing Disorders*, 19, 429-39

Perry, F.R. (1968) The psycholinguistic abilities of deaf children – an exploratory investigation. *Australian Teacher of the Deaf*, 9 (3), 153-60

Pintner, R. and Patterson, D.G. (1921) Learning tasks with Deaf Children. *Psychol. Monographs*, 132, 29

Pit Corder, S. (1973) *Introducing applied linguistics*. Harmondsworth: Penguin Educational

Postman, L. and Rau, L. (1957) *Retention as a function of the method of presentation*. Berkeley: University of California Publication in Psychology. Cited in J.A. Adams, *Human Memory*. New York: McGraw Hill, 1967

Pressnell, L.M. (1973) Hearing-impaired children's comprehension and production of syntax in oral language. *Journal of Speech and Hearing Research*, 16, 12-21

Quigley, S. (1969) *The Influence of Fingerspelling on the Development of Language, Communication, and Educational Achievement in Deaf Children*. Urbana: University of Illinois, Institute for Research on Exceptional Children

Quigley, S.P. (1979) Environment and Communication in the Language Development of Deaf Children, in L.J. Bradford and W.G. Hardy (eds.)

Quigley, S.P., Montanelli, D.S. and Wilbur, R.B. (1976a) Some aspects of the verb system in the language of deaf students. *Journal of Speech and Hearing Research*, 19 (3), 536-50

Quigley, S.P., Wilbur, R.B., Power, D.J., Montanelli, D.S. and Steinkamp, M.W. (1976b) *Syntactic Structures in the Language of Deaf Children*. Urbana, Illinois: Institute for Child Behavior and Development

Rainer, J.D. and Altshuler, K.Z. (1968) *Psychiatry and the Deaf*: being the report of the workshop for Psychiatrists on Extending Mental Health Services to the Deaf, New York, 1967. Social and Rehabilitation Service, Department of Health, Education and Welfare, Washington, DC

Ratner, N. and Bruner, J.S. (1978) Games, Social Exchange and the Acquisition of Language. *Journal of Child Language*, 5

Remvig, J. (1969) Three Clinical Studies of Deaf-Mutism and Psychiatry. Copenhagen: Munksgard

Ries, P.W. and Voneiff, P. (1974) Demographic profile of hearing-impaired students. *PRWAD Deafness Annual*, IV, 17-42

Rodda, M. (1970) *The Hearing Impaired School Leaver*. London, University of London Press

Rosch, E. (1973) On the internal structure of perceptual and semantic categories, in J. Moore (ed.), *Cognitive Development and the Acquisition of Language*. New York: Academic Press

Rosch, E., Mervis, C.B., Gray, W., Johnson, D. and Boyes-Braem, P. (1976) Basic concepts in natural categories. *Cognitive Psychology*, 8, 382-439

Ross, P., Pergament, L. and Anisfeld, M. (1979) Cerebral lateralization of deaf and hearing individuals for linguistic comparison judgements. *Brain and Language*, 8, 69-80

Ruben, R.J. and Rapin, I. (1980) Theoretical Issues in the Development of Audition, in L.T. Taft and M. Lewis (eds.), *Symposium in Developmental Disabilities in the Preschool Child*. New York: Spectrum

Russell, W.K., Quigley, S.P. and Power, D.J. (1976) *Linguistics and Deaf Children: Transformational Syntax and its Applications?* Washington, DC: Alexander Graham Bell Association for the Deaf

Sankoff, D. (ed.) (1978) *Linguistic Variation*. New York: Academic Press

Sapir, E. (1921) *Language*. New York: Harcourt, Brace & World

Sarachan-Deily, A.B. and Love, R.J. (1974) Underlying grammatical rule structure in the deaf. *Journal of Speech and Hearing Research*, 17 (4), 689-98

Savage, G.A. (1978) Handwriting of the deaf and hard of hearing. *Canad. Soc. Forens. Sci. J.*, 11, 1-14

Savage, R.D., Evans, L. and Savage, J.K. (1981) *Psychology and Communication in Deaf Children*. North Ryde, New South Wales: Harcourt Brace Jovanovich

Schaffer, H.R. (ed.) (1977) *Studies in Mother Infant Interaction*. Academic Press: London

Schaffer, H.R., Collis, G.M. and Parson, G. (1977) Vocal Interchange and Visual Regard in Verbal and Pre-Verbal Children, in Schaffer (ed.)

Schein, J.D. and Delk, M.T. (1974) *The Deaf Population of the United States*. Silver Spring, Md., National Association of the Deaf

Schildroth, A.M. (unpublished, no date) The relationship of non-verbal intelligence test scores to selected characteristics of hearing-impaired students. Office of Demographic Studies, Gallaudet College, Washington, DC

Schlesinger, H.S. (1978) The Acquisition of Signed and Spoken Language, in Liben, L.S. (ed.)., *Deaf Children: Developmental Perspectives*. New York: Academic Press

Schlesinger, H.S. and Meadow, K. (1972) *Sound and Sign, Childhood Deafness and Mental Health*. Berkeley: University of California Press

Schmitt, P. (1966) Language Instruction for the Deaf. *Volta Review*, 68

Scott, W.R. (1870) *The Deaf and Dumb*. London: Bell and Daldy

Seleskovitch, D. (1978) *Interpreting for International Conferences*. Washington, DC: Pen and Booth

Shannon, C.E. (1948) A mathematical theory of communication. *Bell System Technical Journal*, 27, 379-423, 623-56

Shother, J. and Gregory, S. (1976) On First Gaining the Idea of Oneself as a Person, in *Life Sentences*, R. Harre (ed.). London: John Wiley & Sons

Siegel, S. (1956) *Nonparametric Statistics for the Behavioral Sciences*. New York: McGraw-Hill

Simmons, A.A. (1959) Factors related to lipreading. *Journal of Speech and Hearing Research*, 2, 340-52

Simmons, H.A. (1962) A comparison of the type-token ratio of spoken and written language of deaf and hearing children. *Volta Review*, 64, 417-21

Siple, P. (ed.) (1978) *Understanding Language through Sign Language Research*. New York: Academic Press

Siple, P., Fischer, S.D. and Bellugi, U. (1977) Memory for nonsemantic attributes of ASL signs and English words. *J. Verb. Learning Verbal Behaviour*, 14, 561-74

Skinner, M.W. (1978) The hearing of speech during language acquisition. *Otolaryng. Clin. of N. America*, 11, 631-50

Smith, F. (1978) *Understanding reading: a psycholinguistic analysis of reading and learning to read*. Holt Saunders

Snow, C.E. (1979) Conversations with Children, in Fletcher and Garman (eds.)

Snow, C.E. and Ferguson, C.A. (eds.) (1977) *Talking to Children Language Input and acquisition*. Cambridge: Cambridge University Press

Sorensen, R.K. and Hansen, B. (1976) *The Sign Language of Deaf Children*. Copenhagen: Døves Centre for Total Kommunikation

Stein, B.E. and Schuckman, H. (1973) Effects of sensory restriction upon the responses to cortical stimulation in rats. *J. Comp. Physiol. Psychol.*, 63, 182-7

Stevenson, E.A. (1964) *A study of the Educational Achievements of Deaf Children of Deaf Parents*. Berkeley: California School for the Deaf

Stokoe, W.C. (1960) Sign Language Structure: An Outline of the Visual Communication Systems of the American Deaf. *Studies in Linguistics: Occasional Papers 8*

Stokoe, W. C. (1969) Sign Language diglossia. *Studies in Linguistics*, 21, 27-41

Stokoe, W.C. (1975) The use of sign language in teaching English. *American Annals of the Deaf*, 120, 417-21

Stokoe, W.C. (1978) *Sign Language Structure: The First Linguistic Analysis of American Sign Language*. Silver Spring, Maryland: Linstok Press

Stokoe, W.C., Casterline, D. and Croneberg, C. (1965) *A Dictionary of American Sign Language on Linguistic Principles*. Silver Spring, Maryland: Linstok Press

Stout, G.F. (1899) *A Manual of Psychology*. London: Univ. Correspondence Coll. Press

Stuckless, E.R. and Birch, J.W. (1966a) The influence of early manual communication on the linguistic development of deaf children. *American Annals of the Deaf*, 111, 452-60

Stuckless, E.R. and Birch, J.W. (1966b) The influence of early manual communication on the linguistic development of deaf children, II. *American Annals of the Deaf*, 111, 499-504

Taafe, G. and Wong, W. (1957) *Studies of Variables in lip reading stimulus materials*. Research Paper III. Los Angeles: John Tracey Clinic

Tate, M. (1979) Comparative Study of Language Development in Hearing Impaired Children and Normally Hearing Infants. *The Teacher of the Deaf*, 33, No. 5

Tervoort, B.T. (1975) Bilingual interference between acoustic and visual communication, in *The Proceedings of the International Congress on Education of the Deaf*. Tokyo, 25-28 August, 319-22

Tervoort, B.T. and Verberk, A.J. (1967) *Analysis of communicative structure patterns in deaf children*. Groningen, Netherlands: Z.W.O. Onderzock, NR

Tervoort, B.T. and Verberk, A.J. (1975) *Developmental features of visual communication*. North Holland Linguistic Series, Vol. 21. North Holland, 1975

Thatcher, J. (1976) *An analysis of the structure, function and content of the vocabularies of babies: The First Hundred Words*. Unpublished M.A. Dissertation. University of Nottingham

Thompson, W.H. (1936) An analysis of errors in written composition by deaf children. *American Annals of the Deaf*, 81, 95-9

Trevarthen, C. (1974) Conversations with a two month old. *New Scientist*, 62

Trevarthen, C. (1979) Communication and Co-operation in early infancy: a description of primary intersubjectivity, in M. Bullowa (ed.)

Trudgill, P. (1974a) *The Social Differentiation of English in Norwich*. Cambridge University Press

Trudgill, P. (1974b) *Sociolinguistics: An Introduction*. Harmondsworth: Penguin Books

Tylor, E.B. (1878) *Researches into the Early History of Mankind*. London: Murray

Ulijn, J. (1977) An integrated model for first and second language comprehension and some experimental evidence about the contrastive analysis hypothesis. *International J. Language Learning and Educational Technology*, 187-199

Valtin, R. (1979) Dyslexia: deficit in reading or deficit in research. *Reading Research Quarterly*, 14, 201-23

Van Uden, A.A. (1968) *A world of language for deaf children. Part 1 Basic Principles*. St Michielsgestel, Netherlands: Institute for the Deaf

Vernon, Mc C. (1967) Relationship of Language to the thinking process. *Archives of Gen. Psychiatry*, 16, 325-33

Vernon, Mc C. and Koh, S.D. (1970) Early manual communication and deaf children's achievement. *American Annals of the Deaf*, 115, 529-36

Vernon, Mc C. and Koh, S.D. (1971) Effects of oral preschool compared to early manual communication on education and communication in deaf children. *American Annals of the Deaf*, 116, 569-74

Vernon Mc C. and Mindel, E.D. (1971) Psychological and psychiatric aspects of profound hearing loss, in Rose, D.E. (ed.), *Audiological Assessment*. Englewood Cliffs: Prentice-Hall

Wakelin, M.F. (1972) *English Dialects*. London: Athlone Press

Walter, J. (1955) A study of the written sentence construction of a group of profoundly deaf children. *American Annals of the Deaf*, 100, 335-52

Walter, J. (1959) Some further observations on the written sentence construction of profoundly deaf children. *American Annals of the Deaf*, 104, 282-5

Wampler, D. (1971) *Linguistics of Visual English: Morpheme List One, An Introduction to the Spacial Symbol System*. Santa Rosa, California

Wells, U.G. (1979) Variation in Child Language, in Fletcher and Garman (eds.)

Wilbur, R.B. (1976) The Linguistics of Manual language and Manual systems, in L. Lloyd (ed.), *Communication Assessment and Intervention Strategies*. Baltimore: University Park Press

Wilbur, R.B. (1977) An explanation of deaf children's difficulty with certain syntactic structures of English. *Volta Review*, 79, (2) 85-92

Wilbur, R.B. (1979) *American Sign Language and Sign Systems*. Baltimore: University Park Press

Wilbur, R.B. and Jones, M.L. (1974) Some aspects of the bilingualism/bimodal acquisition of Sign and English by three hearing children of deaf parents, in R. Fox and A. Bruck (eds.), *Proceedings of the Tenth Regional Meeting, Chicago Linguistic Society*, Chicago: Chicago Linguistic Society

Wollman, D.C. and Hickmott, J. (1976) Language development for deaf pupils. *Dialogue* (Schools Council), No. 23, 6-7

Wood, D.J., McMahon, L. and Cranstoun, Y. (1980) *Working with Under-Fives*. London: McIntyre

Wood, D.J., Wood, H.A., Griffiths, A.J., Howarth, S.P. and Howarth, C.I. (1980) The Structure of Conversations with 6-10 year old deaf children. Unpublished

Wood, H.A. and Wood, D.J. (1980) An experimental study of teaching techniques with the young deaf child. *Paper to the XXIInd International Congress of Psychology*, Leipzig, East Germany

Wood, K.S. and Blakely, R.W. (1953) The Association of lipreading and the ability to understand distorted speech. *Western Speech*, 17, 259-61

Woodward, J.C. (1973) Some Characteristics of Pidgin Sign English. *Sign Language Studies*, 3, 39-46

Woodward, J.C. (1975) How you Gonna get to Heaven if you Can't Talk with Jesus: The Educational Establishment versus the Deaf Community. Paper presented at the annual meeting of the Society for Applied Anthropology. Amsterdam

Woodward, J.C. (1976) Black Southern Signing. *Language in Society*, 5, 211-18

Woodward, J.C. (1978) Some Sociolinguistic Problems in the Implementation of Bilingual Education for Deaf Students. Paper presented at the Second National Symposium on Sign Language Research and Teaching. San Diego

Woodward, J.C. and De Santis, S. (1977) Negative incorporation in French and American sign language. *Language in Society*, 6, 379-88

Woodward, M.F. and Barber, C.G. (1960) Phoneme perception in lip-reading. *Journal of Speech and Hearing Research*, 3, 213-22

Woodward, M.F. and Lowell, E.E. (1964) *A Linguistic Approach to the Education of Aurally-handicapped Children*. United States Department of Health, Education and Welfare, project 907

Zubeck, J.P. (1969) *Sensory Deprivation: 15 years of research*. New York: Appleton-Century Crofts

CONTRIBUTORS

Mary Brennan   Moray House College of Education, Edinburgh
Martin Colville   Moray House College of Education, Edinburgh
R. Conrad   MRC Applied Psychology Unit, Oxford
Elisabeth Dawson   Psychology Department, Southampton University
John Denmark   Whittingham Hospital, Preston, Lancashire
Margaret Deuchar   School of European Studies, University of Sussex, Brighton
William Edmondson   Department of Psychology, Bedford College, London
Lionel Evans   Department of Education, Newcastle University
Susan Gregory   Psychology Department, Nottingham University
James Kyle   School of Education, Bristol University
Lilian Lawson   Moray House College of Education, Edinburgh
Peter Llewellyn-Jones   School of Education, University of Bristol
Kay Mogford   Psychology Department, Nottingham University
Bencie Woll   School of Education, University of Bristol
David Wood   Psychology Department, Nottingham University

INDEX